PILGRIM IN LOVE

PILGRIM IN LOVE

An Introduction to Dante
and
His Spirituality

James Collins

A Campion Book

Loyola University Press
Chicago
1984

© 1984 James Collins

Printed in the United States of America

Book design by Carol Tornatore

Library of Congress Cataloging in Publication Data

Collins, James Daniel.
  Pilgrim in love.

  Bibliography: p. 285
    1. Dante Alighieri, 1265-1321. Divina commedia.
  2. Dante Alighieri, 1265-1321—Religion and ethics.
  3. Spirituality in literature.   I. Title.
PQ4416.C58   1984   851'.1   83-25163
ISBN 0-8294-0453-8

To Sister Mary Lillian of the Congregation of the Sisters of the Holy Family of Nazareth: a gentle, courteous lady who spread peace and love on earth, and went to gaze on "the Love Who moves the sun and the other stars."

CONTENTS

FOREWORD

In the current retrieval of the rich and pluralistic tradition of Catholic spirituality, art, and theology, it is shocking that so little theological attention has been accorded to Dante. As James Collins's judicious use of contemporary Dante scholarship in this illuminating study makes clear, Dante scholars themselves remain a remarkably creative and fascinating group. It is surely not the fault of these experts in the intricacies of medieval thought and life if the rest of us—the non-specialists and especially the theologians—remain ignorant. It is our fault and ours alone.

That fault, however, can be healed. For with a *caritas* which Dante himself would have applauded, James Collins, an expert in and, just as important, a lover of Dante's vision, has produced a text to allow us all to re-enter that classic pilgrimage. It is, I believe, just the right moment for such a study. For Catholic theology today is now, in ever widening circles, engaged in new and liberating rediscoveries of its own classics. And among those classics, there is none like Dante. Here we find—especially in the breathtaking vision of *The Divine Comedy*—the entire world of Catholic medieval life, spirituality, thought and art brought together into a whole which can transform every willing reader.

We all always knew that Dante was one of our greatest classics. Yet many of us have hesitated to plunge alone into that luxuriant forest without some guide. In James Collins's work we may find that guide. For as the reader of this disclosive work will soon discover, James Collins knows contemporary theology and spirituality, he knows Dante scholarship and, above all, he knows Dante. His choice of Dante's vision of pilgrimage and love as his leit-motif strikes me as exactly the right choice.

For when we are guided through *The Divine Comedy* with this choice of leitmotifs we find we are at the heart of the matter: a journey, a vision, a healing, a transforming, a home. Through Collin's generous commentary we are led to re-enter the classic text of Dante himself. And through Dante we can rediscover that envisionment of all reality which *caritas*—and *caritas* alone—discloses. For reality itself is present in Dante: reality in all its ambiguous actuality and pluralistic power disclosed and transformed through the gift of divine love. To sense that gift is to enter the same kind of journey which Dante risked. And to enter with Dante is to begin anew with all the spiritual, theological, and artistic resources of his medieval world: with the Scriptures and the ancient classics, with Dominic and Francis, with Thomas, Bonaventure, Joachim, and all the rest.

Collins shows us that to risk entering that world with Dante as our guide is ineluctably to undertake a journey which cannot but become a spiritual pilgrimage. Every true classic forces the reader, often against her or his will, to undertake an unexpected journey. Dante forces every true reader to undergo a journey in this world now recognized as a rite of initiation into a spiritual pilgrimage. It is not possible to remain a mere tourist-reader with Dante. It is necessary to become a pilgrim.

We may seem an unlikely lot of pilgrims—we late twentieth century Catholics. But we are no more unlikely and no less needy than Dante's own curious contemporaries crowding the stanzas of his great poem. Yet we too need some guide to aid us: in James Collins's work we may find that guide. Dante's work, like theology itself, is too important to be left to the specialists alone. Thanks to James Collins, who is a specialist, the rest of us can re-enter and experience anew one of the greatest classics of our heritage, a vision of reality where theological concepts yield to their source in the classic metaphors and symbols of the Catholic faith, where our everyday journey is disclosed for what it is in truth—a spiritual pilgrimage, where the vision of *caritas*—of pure, unbounded love—becomes as palpable and realistic as the earthiness and beauty of Italy itself. Dante's is a classic, believable vision and, as James Collins makes clear, that vision can become ours if we would risk an exposure of our tragic-comic lives to *The Divine Comedy.*

David Tracy

The University of Chicago

PREFACE

During the past three decades of the twentieth century, we have witnessed, or perhaps experienced personally, many profound changes in religious thought and practices. Trends in theology and spirituality have radically transformed our ways of approaching God, the world, and ourselves. In the sixties, for instance, the writings of Pierre Teilhard de Chardin helped to reshape our vision of the material universe by rediscovering for us the divine presence within the evolving processes of creation. Teilhard de Chardin and others led us to a greater appreciation of the sacredness of matter, the immanence of God, and a deeper concern for the real potentials and problems of this world; and by so doing they helped to generate a "worldly" spirituality, which has already expressed itself in social and political reforms of enormous proportions.

Whereas in the sixties we looked at the world outside ourselves, in the seventies we looked within ourselves. This was a decade of introversion, a rediscovery of our human potential and a keener awareness of the human person as a transcendent being, whose full meaning and center can be found only beyond—in God. Interest in a deeper spirituality and prayer erupted into what might be called a spiritual explosion. The charismatic movement, as well as organized Bible study and prayer groups, spread with amazing rapidity and continues to attract enthusiasts.

This surge of interest in spirituality should be attributed first of all, I believe, to the hidden activity of the Holy Spirit. His inspiring words found in the Scriptures have been the focal point of this remarkable renewal among Christians of all denominations. As a result, there has been a return to the traditional "masters of the spiritual life," the long-neglected mystics of the Christian tradition. In short, there has been a rediscovery of the "Christian classics": the Bible, "the classic" *par excellence*, and the many other works written by spiritual men and women throughout the twenty centuries of the Church's life on earth.

Among the many periods of Christian spirituality being rediscovered today, one of the richest is undoubtedly the medieval period. Thomas Merton, as well as other modern masters of the spiritual life, has introduced many Christians to the wealth of medieval spirituality. As a result, relatively unknown medieval treasures, such as the writings of Julian of Norwich, have become sources of spiritual inspiration and growth for many Christians today.

One of the most outstanding medieval treasures extant is, without doubt, Dante's *Divine Comedy*; indeed, it is a classic of Christian literature, a work whose enduring beauty, depth, and relevance continue to fascinate readers. The vast differences between our modern world and the world of the thirteenth and fourteenth centuries are not quite so radical as we might assume. The historian Barbara Tuchman in her book *A Distant Mirror* has brilliantly painted a picture of that medieval world, and she helps us to realize how much it resembles the time in which we live. The profound intellectual, religious, social, and political upheavals of that era—with all their hope and optimism as well as their fear and pessimism—are indeed a "distant mirror" of our present darkness and turmoil and also of our present brightness and confidence.

Dante, perhaps more than any other writer, provides us with a portrait of the medieval soul. He is a mirror of the virtues and vices of that era. As a layman he was actively involved in the political and social movements of his medieval world. As a scholar he was well informed of the intellectual and scientific achievements of antiquity, as well as the contributions of his own age. As a Christian he was inspired and nourished by the Scriptures and the writing of the theologians and mystics of the Christian tradition. He was a man with an insatiable thirst for knowledge and an unquenchable desire for peace and justice in this world. He was a Christian who believed, hoped, and loved with the intensity of a saint. One might say today that he was "a secular saint," although he would certainly have preferred classification among sinners.

Dante's life and writings not only hold the interest of the professional historian, theologian, or literary critic but they also attract with particular urgency those who share the same Christian faith, hope, and love that sustained him in his own troubled and often frustrated life. He is a Christian for all seasons, whose vision enlightens our own experiences today. It is a vision of a universe where God is the center and source, and the human person is the struggling pilgrim, unsettled and incomplete.

The pilgrim's world is held together by a God Who is Love, a God Who is constantly drawing the human pilgrim to his transcendent home.

This vision, or spirituality, is the main subject of this book. I have written it after many years of studying and teaching Dante. It represents the fruit not only of studying and teaching but also of personal reflection and experience. My own faith, hope, and love have been enlivened and deepened by my contact with Dante's works, especially by his *Comedy*. I wish to share these reflections with the general reader who may not possess a degree in theology, history, or literature. Such credentials are not necessary, since Dante purposely wrote in the vernacular language in order to be understood by any Christian.

For the most part I have avoided technical language or questions of interpretation which might interest only the professional scholar. At times, however, I have had to delve into some unavoidable topics which require either a historical or theological explanation. This has been done to help the reader on his way to a better understanding of Dante. Some knowledge of the customs, the thought patterns, and the theology and literature of the Middle Ages, is certainly indispensable for an adequate appreciation of his life and spiritual message.

This book begins with a brief summary of Dante's life and times, and then explores his writings, which reveal his inner development and spiritual growth. The main focus of this book is on Dante's masterpiece, *The Divine Comedy*, and in many respects it is a commentary on the *Comedy*. It is not, however, an exhaustive commentary on every one of the hundred cantos of the work. Rather, I have focused on two themes of Dante's life and spirituality: Pilgrimage and love. These themes keep reappearing throughout the *Comedy* and taken together really constitute the one leitmotiv which I believe is at the very heart of Dante's spirituality.

The reader will want to refer to a good English translation of Dante's *Divine Comedy* in order to follow more closely the drama of Dante's spiritual journey. There are many such published translations available: some in prose; others in poetry. Among the poetic renditions are those by Dorothy Sayers and John Ciardi. Charles Singleton's prose translation is very literal, often sacrificing literary grace to the precise rendering of Dante's words and meaning. The passages which I quote from Dante's works are for the most part my own translations, although I have leaned heavily on Singleton's translations. There is, of course, no adequate substitute for the original poetry of Dante's *Comedy*; but most American readers with little or no knowledge of Italian can, nonetheless, appreciate Dante by reading any of the good translations available today. In my own translations I have attempted to be as faithful as possible to Dante's words and meaning. The depth and beauty of his thoughts, I trust, have not been betrayed, in spite of the ancient adage that "every translator is a traitor."

I am deeply indebted to the many scholars who have written commentaries and studies on Dante's life and work. A complete bibliography would be impossible to compile, but I have indicated in the bibliography at the end of the book some of the works that I have consulted. They are listed according to the chapters of the book and may thus serve the reader who wishes to pursue in depth a particular area. I have purposely avoided footnotes in order to make the book both less cumbersome and less scholarly for the general reader, who may be a beginner in the study of Dante.

My indebtedness and gratitude should also be expressed to Monsignor Giovanni Fallani, at the Lateran University in Rome, the teacher who introduced me to Dante. He, together with my Italian classmates, Antonio Rosato and Antonio Santantoni, communicated to me a *passione* for Dante and his works that has ever since remained with me. Two present colleagues at Holy Family College, where I presently teach a course on Dante, have also contributed to this present work by their support and encouragement. They are Angelo Randazzo and John Scioli. Their historical and literary expertise have helped me to clarify many aspects of the book. To them and to the Sisters of the Holy Family, I owe special thanks and appreciation.

DANTE ALIGHIERI:

A Biographical Sketch

Dante deservedly won the highest titles for so
many and such excellent studies, and while he
lived some always called him poet; others, philosopher; and many, theologian. . . . Studies in
general, and speculative studies in particular,
to which our Dante completely applied himself, usually demand solitude, distance from
care, and tranquility of mind. Instead of this
retirement and quiet, Dante almost from the
beginning of his life down to the day of his
death had a violent and insufferable passion of
love, a wife, domestic and public cares, exile,
poverty, not to mention those more particular
cares which these necessarily involve.

from *The Life of Dante*,
by Boccaccio

Boccaccio, the first biographer of Dante, wrote these
words sometime between 1358 and 1363, close to forty
years after Dante's death. They were not intended to be
a summary of Dante's life, but only a list of Dante's bur-
dens and cares.

Some of Boccaccio's other comments that deal with Dante's marital life and his extramarital affairs have shocked pious admirers of Dante; but Boccaccio did not set out to write the life of a saint. Even though Dante scholars through the centuries have argued about Dante's virtues and vices, especially about his amorous inclinations, none of them has yet been so zealous as to present him as a candidate for canonization. And even though scholars judge Boccaccio's biography to be somewhat romanticized, they accept as historical truth its basic outline of Dante's life, written, as it was, by a fellow Florentine who personally knew many of Dante's relatives and friends.

It is noteworthy that the first observation Boccaccio makes after his praise of Dante's scholarly pursuits is of Dante's "passion of love." Throughout his biography he considers Dante's "amorous sighs" to be defects and obstacles that, nevertheless, did not prevent Dante from producing works of genius. But what seems to be the truth is that this "passion of love" was the very source of inspiration for Dante's greatest works. We know this from Dante's own words. His exile, also considered by Boccaccio to be an impediment to Dante's career as a writer, proved to be the occasion, if not one of the principal causes, for Dante's perception of the Christian's life as a kind of exile and pilgrimage toward his true home. These two themes of "love" and "pilgrimage" seem to be the dominant and deciding factors in Dante's own life and works. I perceive them as the two fundamental human experiences that shaped Dante's spirit.

Dante's spirituality is the main theme of this book; but before exploring his "inner" life, it is necessary to be acquainted with some of the known facts of his "outward" life. Obviously, a person's spiritual life develops in the context of the time and culture to which he belongs, with all the influence of family, friends, and teachers.

A biography of Dante is a formidable task since so little reliable information is available to us today about the man himself. Besides the early biography of Dante by Boccaccio, many attempts have been made over the centuries to write a life of Dante. There have been endless disputes among the historians over certain aspects of Dante's life, but such academic questions we prefer to leave to others, contenting ourselves at this time with the few facts that are definitely known about Dante. What follows is, therefore, a very brief, general summary of Dante's life. It serves merely to introduce the general reader to the person of Dante Alighieri, his time and his works. Sources for more detailed information can be found in the bibliography at the end of the book.

◆

Dante Alighieri was born in Florence in 1265 to a family that we might describe as "upper middle class." From certain legal documents of the time we know that Dante and his family were "well-to-do," but often had large debts—a situation common today to our own middle class. The infant Dante was baptized at Easter in the beautiful baptistry of St. John (*bel San Giovanni*, he called it) which still stands in all its splendor facing the Cathedral of Florence. Years later—in 1300, to be exact—he was to describe his second baptism or rebirth as happening at Easter. His *Divine Comedy* is mainly the description of a new Easter experience, or conversion, in midlife.

Both of Dante's parents died when he was quite young: his mother when he was only six and his father when he was about twelve. Dante has left nothing in writing about them, although in his writings he often reveals that he knew by experience the tenderness of a mother's love. His father remarried, but we know nothing about Dante's stepmother. The loss of his parents at such a young age may shed some light on the way he relates to Virgil and Beatrice in his *Comedy*: Virgil in many respects fulfills the paternal role, and Beatrice, the maternal role. Virgil, especially at the beginning of the *Comedy*, is addressed as father, and Beatrice throughout the work often acts as mother to Dante. We might also mention the "dear, benign, paternal image" of Brunetto Latini, a Florentine statesman and scholar who greatly influenced Dante. Dante revered him as teacher and father; and no reader of the *Comedy* can forget the pathos of their meeting in Hell, nor can any commentator fully explain why Dante places him there with the sodomites.

Of Dante's childhood and early education we know few particulars, but we can acquire some idea of his education from what we know generally of the education of boys in thirteenth-century Florence. Boccaccio sums it up simply with the words "the liberal arts." That general term would include the *trivium* (Grammar, Logic, Rhetoric) and the *quadrivium* (Arithmetic, Music, Geometry, and Astrology). Grammar was mainly the study of Latin, especially the classics of Latin literature. Apparently Dante developed a deep love and admiration for the Latin poets, and in particular for Virgil, whose *Aeneid* fascinated him. Other poets, such as Horace, Ovid, and Statius, were also well known to Dante. Direct or indirect quotations from all of these poets can be found throughout Dante's works.

The religious education of thirteenth-century Florentine children seems to have had as its chief goals learning the stories of the Old and New Testaments in a versified form as well as learning the Psalms. Learning through poetry and stories was at that time the chief pedagogical method. Among the "textbooks" were "bestiaries," which contained descriptions of real or imaginary animals, usually interpreted as symbols of Christ, virtues, or vices. Even the profound theology of St. Augustine was learned by children in simplified verses which could be easily memorized. All of these formative studies—the Bible, symbolic stories, Augustinian theology—left a lasting impression on the sensitive Dante, who later in life was to express his own religious experiences in the language and images learned as a child. The beautiful Latin hymns of the Church's liturgy must have delighted him as a child. He often alludes to them in the *Comedy*. In Bruni's biography of Dante (*circa* 1404), we learn that Dante loved music, especially singing, and also that he could draw very well. In Dante's writings there is evidence of both: from the quality of the poetry it is apparent that he was sensitive to music; and from his descriptions of colors and shapes it is equally apparent that he had the keen eye of an artist.

Only one specific childhood experience is recorded by Dante in his writings: his meeting with Beatrice at the age of nine. He describes this in his *Vita Nuova*. This encounter with Beatrice was "love at first sight"; later in Dante's life Beatrice became the dominant passion of love and even the incarnation of God's love. Although many Dante scholars have denied the historical reality of Beatrice, most commentators today agree that she was, in fact, the nine-year-old Beatrice Portinari, described by Boccaccio as the charming daughter of Folco Portinari, a neighbor of the Alighieri family.

A portrait of the poet Dante as a young man is difficult to paint, but we do know the kind of company he kept, and this gives us a trustworthy clue to his life-style.

Dante's close friends were the poets, artists, and musicians of Florence, a lively group whom we might describe as "bohemian": a medieval version of later groups of artists who brought fame to the "Left Bank" in Paris and "the Village" in New York City. Dante mentions in his writings such friends as the poets Guido Cavalcante, Dino Frescobaldi, and Labo Gianni; the artist Giotto, one of the most famous Florentine painters; and the musician Casella.

One of the main subjects of the poetry at that time was "love," the "courtly love" celebrated in song by the medieval troubadours. Dante was very much a part of this poetic movement which had originated in southern France (*La Provence*), was developed in Sicily under the patronage of Frederick II, and had become extremely popular in Dante's region, Tuscany. This poetic style with its stress on the theme of love was known in Italy as the *dolce stil nuovo*, the "sweet new style." Its passionate celebration of human love, its adoration of a particular "lady," its romantic sighs and pathos, must have fascinated Dante in this period of his life.

Young men in thirteenth-century Florence as well as in the other Italian "city-states" were usually expected to become soldiers because of the constant battles between "Guelf cities" and "Ghibelline cities" or between factions within the cities themselves. Although Dante in his works describes in detail battles between Florence and her Tuscan neighbors, Arezzo and Pisa, we cannot be absolutely sure that he actually fought in those battles.

We would be wrong, however, to think that Dante was a total recluse since we know that he enjoyed the conviviality of his fellow poets: the camaraderie of drinking, singing, joking, and the romantic adventures of young Florentines. What some critics have called the "scandalous exchange" of poems between him and his friend Forese Donati is evidence that Dante was not above expressing a somewhat crude and vulgar sense of humor. His relationship with Forese has led some modern, as well as early, commentators to conclude that there was a homosexual relationship between the two poets, a type of liaison not uncommon among the literati of medieval Florence; however, there is no substantial evidence to affirm or deny this.

At about the age of twenty-five, shortly after Beatrice's death, Dante seems to have plunged himself into a consuming study of philosophy and theology. The early biographers tell us that he studied in Bologna, Paris, and even Oxford; whether or not Dante studied formally in these cities is debated by historians. Dante himself writes that he frequented the schools of philosophy and theology of "the religious." We do know that the Dominican and Franciscan friars had schools in Florence in Dante's time. Perhaps Dante acquired much of his philosophical and theological knowledge by attending lectures in his native Florence at the monasteries of *Santa Maria Novella* (the Dominican house) and *Santa Croce* (the Franciscan house). It is very likely that he heard lectures from the Franciscan "spirituals," those friars who followed a strict interpretation of St. Francis's role of poverty. The Franciscan "spirituals" were in turn very much influenced by the writings of Joachim of Fiore, a visionary whose zeal for Church reform and a new age of the Holy Spirit no doubt found a sympathetic ear in Dante. Dante's own prophetic zeal for reform of the Church must have been kindled by the lectures of Pier Giovanni Olivi, a Franciscan spiritual who promoted Joachim's visions and ideas in Florence. In this same period Dante must have become acquainted with the soaring mysticism of St. Bonaventure, one of the most famous Franciscan teachers of theology at Paris.

It is also probable that Dante heard the lectures of Fra Remigio Gerolami, a Dominican scholar who had been a student of St. Thomas Aquinas's in Paris. Dante's works show a profound knowledge of St. Thomas as well as of Aristotle, whose philosophy Thomas had courageously promoted and used in the service of theology.

One of the most mysterious facets of Dante's life is his marriage with Gemma Donati, which took place about the year 1290. It appears that it was prearranged while Dante's father was still living. That was not an unusual practice. In any case, Dante never mentions Gemma in his writings. One would conclude from Boccaccio's biography that she was a nagging shrew. We have no evidence for that. We do know that there were at least three children from that marriage: two sons, Pietro and Jacopo, and a daughter, Antonia, who later became a religious sister with the name Beatrice. There is evidence that Dante's children rejoined him during his exile and were with him in Ravenna toward the end of his life.

Dante's career as a statesman is a testimony to his profound sense of duty and service to his community. This was a very strong conviction of Dante's. It was also the cause of his many woes. In 1296 he was among the "council of a hundred men," an elected body in Florence, somewhat similar to our city council today. In 1300 he was elected one of the six priors of Florence, a two-month office according to Florentine law: an indication of the instability and oscillation of Florentine politics. The year 1300 turned out to be a disastrous year politically for both Dante and Florence.

Italy for some time had been divided into two warring factions, the Guelfs and the Ghibellines. In a sense the Guelfs can be thought of as the rising middle class of that period. Members of this group were becoming more and more independent of the nobility through their own industriousness and prosperity. Florence was itself a Guelf city-state, flourishing economically and culturally with its own monetary unit, the *florin*, which was to the Europe of Dante's time something like what the American dollar is to the international money market today.

The Guelfs, the *nouveaux riches* of that time, tended to support the papacy in the power struggle between empire and Church in medieval Europe. The Ghibellines, the "old money," were the supporters of the established nobility, whose titles and privileges could be traced to the Holy Roman Emperor. The constant strife between the two political parties is really the story of medieval Italy in particular and of medieval Europe in general.

Dante, being a loyal Florentine, was at first a Guelf, but he later declared himself "a party to himself," since he was no slave to partisan politics. He had his own political principles, which eventually led to his permanent exile from Florence. The events leading up to his exile are quite complicated. In Dante's time the Florentine Guelfs were divided into two factions, the Whites and the Blacks. The Blacks supported the reigning Pope Boniface VIII even to the point of enlisting his military aid in settling local disputes. Pope Boniface VIII was only too happy to supply troops, since the wealth and political power of Florence were dear to his greedy heart.

Dante was a White Guelf and in the council advised against papal use of troops in settling differences. The pope's mission, according to Dante's philosophy, was not to exercise political and military power. In order to attain peace the priors banished certain Black and White Guelfs. The pope then intervened to restore the power of the Blacks. Charles of Valois, the brother of King Philip the

Fair of France, was the pope's instrument of vindication. It was a disastrous event for the Whites: their property was burned and their leaders were fined and banished. Dante and other priors were unjustly accused of political corruption and opposition to the pope. Since Dante refused to pay the unjust fine and admit guilt to the unfounded charges, he was sent into exile and sentenced to death by burning if he should ever return to Florence.

Dante never returned to his native city, which he loved so much. His exile, which lasted twenty-one years, must have been a heartrending experience for him. Separation from family and friends, wandering from city to city in search of support and employment, must have been a long, painful experience. This sad, depressing period of his life is best described in his own words at the beginning of his work *Convivio*, or *The Banquet*:

> From the time when it pleased the citizens of Florence . . . to cast me out from her sweet bosom (in which I had been born and nourished even to the summit of my life, and in which, at good peace with them, I desire with all my heart to repose my weary soul and to end the time allotted to me), through almost all the regions to which our language extends I have gone a pilgrim, almost a beggar, displaying against my will the wound of fortune, which often is imputed unjustly to the discredit of him who is wounded. Truly I have been a bark without sail and rudder, carried to different ports and bays and shores by that dry wind which painful poverty breathes forth, and I have appeared vile in the eyes of many who, perhaps through some report, had imagined me in other form; and not only has my person been lowered in their sight, but every work of mine, whether done or yet to be done, has been held in less esteem.

Dante expressed again the bitterness and anguish of his exile in a moving passage of the *Comedy*, where he meets his great-great grandfather, Cacciaguida, in Paradise. Cacciaguida predicts the sufferings of his offspring in these pathetic words:

> You will leave everything loved most dearly; and this is the arrow that the bow of exile shoots first. You will learn how salty the bread tastes in others' houses, and how hard is the going up and down of others' stairs. And what will weigh heaviest upon you will be the evil and senseless company into which you will fall in this valley, a company which, ungrateful, mad, and impious, will turn against you.

> (*Paradise* XVII: 52-65)

What was left for Dante? Nothing and everything. His political career in Florence was finished; his family life was destroyed. Yet his exile with all its hardships proved to be a time of prodigious creativity. He produced several works of lasting literary importance, but above all he created his masterpiece, the *Comedy*, during this "tragic" period of his life.

One of the main difficulties of this exile was, of course, the basic struggle to survive. Dante needed the basics of life, food and shelter, in order to be able to live and to write. Fortunately, during these many years of wandering through Italy, several wealthy patrons of the arts offered hospitality and financial support to Dante. It is impossible to trace his steps and name all the persons, places, and times; but we can mention at least two of these patrons and their cities: Can Grande della Scala in Verona and Guido Novello da Polenta in Ravenna. Besides being the poet and scholar in residence at the courts of these patrons he would often perform diplomatic missions for them.

Throughout these years Dante never gave up his vision and dream of a peaceful world guided by two rulers, each of whom received his authority directly from God Himself. The two rulers, emperor and pope, had different but yet complementary missions. The two missions corresponded to two basic goals of the human being: to live a peaceful, happy existence in this world and to enjoy eternal happiness in the afterlife. The monarch and the pope respectively were appointed by Divine Will to guide humans in their pursuit of these two goals.

This amalgamation of political and religious philosophies might seem like a utopia to us today, but it was a firm conviction of Dante's, an idea for which he sacrificed the comfort and security of his family, career, and native city. For the time he lived in, Dante was quite bold and revolutionary in his insistence on *two* "divine" purposes of human existence: an earthly happiness and an eternal one, which should be under the guidance of two separate representatives of divine rule. His idea brought him political failure; but after many centuries of struggle and controversy, his "heretical" idea of separation of Church and State is one that is widely endorsed.

We twentieth-century Americans, who have inherited the political ideals of our founding fathers, have no difficulty in accepting the "pursuit of happiness" in this world as a valid goal of human existence; but in medieval Europe the one eternal goal of heaven usually reduced earthly existence to a "vale of tears," to be tolerated at best on one's way to the true homeland. The life of the majority of the population in Europe was sheer drudgery, interrupted occasionally by religious feasts.

Although most of us today would reject the idea of monarchy in favor of democracy as a system of government, no one can deny that the world has always desired and still yearns for a just, universally recognized authority which could keep peace and settle disputes among individual nations. Our modern United Nations is a concrete expression of that innate desire for peace on earth. In many ways it is a modern incarnation of Dante's idea and unfortunately just as ineffective and utopian as Dante's idealistic monarchy. Dante's conviction of the need for universal rule and authority sprang from his realistic awareness of the dark side of humanity, what theologians call "original sin": that tendency of human nature to surrender to evil. This tainted human nature can always slip into devastating vices, such as pride, greed, and other "capital sins," which render harmony and happiness impossible in this world. Dante was a realist, not a naïve dreamer, as one might suppose. Although his proposed form of government might differ from ours we can still support his basic affirmations.

Dante developed his political theories in a work called *De Monarchia*, a treatise in Latin in which he systematically presented his vision with philosophical and theological arguments. In many respects the work was a direct reply to Boniface VIII's famous Bull *Unam Sanctam*, which asserted universal rule over every creature on earth. Since the ideas in *De Monarchia* contradicted the papal claims of divinely given jurisdiction in temporal and spiritual matters, it was publicly condemned to be burned by a papal legate soon after Dante's death. That was the fate of "heretical" teaching in the fourteenth century and the fate of heretics as well. The papal legate tried in vain to subject Dante's bones to the same public disgrace.

For many years Dante anxiously expected to have his dream of the ideal emperor fulfilled in the person of Henry VII of Luxemburg. Henry even had the support of Clement V, who succeeded to the papacy in 1305, but the Guelfs would not accept him despite the papal support and the coronation ceremony in Rome. The pope, now residing in Avignon in southern France, was practically a puppet of the French monarchy. Clement therefore supported Henry only out of fear of complete domination by the French kings. Dante vigorously campaigned for Henry but was bitterly disappointed when his own Florence would not accept Henry as Emperor. Henry died in 1313 from a malarial fever contracted in Rome. Dante had hailed him in messianic terms as the savior of Italy and of the world, but the resistance of the Guelfs prevailed and Henry's untimely death turned Dante's hopes into disillusion and bitterness. In his vision of Paradise Dante saw a special throne prepared for Henry.

An equally profound disappointment for Dante was the state of the papacy in his time. Dante never questioned the papacy as a divinely appointed institution for the spiritual guidance of humanity. On the contrary, he upheld the papacy and tenaciously defended it with theological and philosophical proofs. He was outraged, however, by the corruption, especially the simony, of the popes and had no qualms about locating them among the damned in Hell. Pope Nicholas III (1277-1280) and Boniface VIII (1294-1303) are specifically mentioned in *Hell*. Clement V was also a target of Dante's righteous indignation. Dante fearlessly exposed their greed, their arrogant, selfish abuse of spiritual power, their lust for domination— all betrayals of their sacred office as spiritual guides for humanity and vicars of Christ Himself. Dante shared the hopes of the spiritual Franciscans and other groups of reformers who prayed that a good pope would restore the papacy to its proper function. Such hopes were eventually focused on a humble hermit who became Pope Celestine V in 1294 but resigned after only five months in office. Dante seems to have shared the current belief of the spiritual Franciscans that Celestine's abdication was brought about by the crafty Boniface VIII, who succeeded Celestine.

Although Dante's dual dream of a just emperor and a good pope never materialized in his lifetime, he nonetheless maintained his vision and hope. Hope was a characteristic virtue of Dante. After Clement V's death in Avignon he pleaded with the Italian cardinals to bring the papacy back to Rome, the rightful place for the successor of St. Peter. Such zeal for the common good of the Church was matched only by St. Catherine of Siena, who in 1376 was successful in persuading the pope to return from Avignon. It took the powerful persuasion and the ardent prayer of this saintly woman to put an end to the "Babylonian Captivity" of the papacy.

Dante's last years were spent in Ravenna as a guest of Guido da Polenta. There he continued to write his *Comedy* and finished it shortly before his death. He contracted malarial fever while returning from an unsuccessful diplomatic mission to Venice. Tradition tells us that his daughter and two sons joined him in Ravenna and thus he was comforted by their presence in his last years. He had remained close to the Franciscan friars both spiritually and physically, and was buried in their chapel in 1321 at the age of 56. It seems significant that he died on September 14, the feast of the Exaltation of the Holy Cross. His life had been a heavy burden like the cross, but it led to the glory and exaltation of Paradise. According to tradition Dante on his deathbed composed his own epitaph in Latin verses which briefly describe his life's work as a poet "who sang of the realms of Hell, Purgatory and Heaven as well as the rights of the monarchy." The closing words of the epitaph dwell on the bitter experience of the exile but also reveal his undying hope for a better fate in heaven:

> But a happier lot summoned the poet to a better dwelling place in the stars; and here I am enclosed, Dante, exiled from my shores, whom Florence bore, the mother, who so little did love him.

Those final verses express his sense of being a pilgrim all his life in search of perfect love. They echo the final words of his *Comedy*, which describe the ultimate experience of the pilgrim's attainment of God in Paradise, where "my desire and will were turned like a wheel that is evenly moved by the Love which moves the sun and the other stars."

Dante's passionate love of God and his zeal to promote God's will on earth led him *per aspera ad astra*, the ancient Latin proverb meaning "through the rough roads to the stars." Dante felt and wrote with the art and passion of a poet; he failed with the ordinary weakness of any human being; he preached with the fire of a reformer and prophet; but he believed, hoped, and loved with the ardor of a mystic. In order to penetrate more deeply into his inner life—his spirituality—it is necessary to examine in detail his principal works: *La Vita Nuova* (*The New Life*), *Il Convivio* (*The Banquet*), and *La Commedia* (usually known as *The Divine Comedy*). These three works are often presented as a trilogy that represents Dante's own spiritual development. Of the three works we shall concentrate on *The Divine Comedy*, since that is the work of his mature years, the masterpiece which sums up all his wisdom and experience.

Part One

THE NEW LIFE

D ante describes his encounter with Beatrice in a charming book called *La Vita Nuova*, (*The New Life*), a title which might be translated as "the young life," referring to the stage of life following adolescence. According to Dante, adolescence lasted until a person's twenty-fifth year; followed by "youth," which extended from the twenty-fifth year to the forty-fifth. Most scholars date the *Vita Nuova* shortly after 1290, the year of Beatrice's death, when Dante was, in fact, twenty-five years old. Thus the book describes the beginning of his "youth," the new stage in his life; and it also narrates the result of his meeting with Beatrice. Dante's newness was the transformation of his whole being through his love for Beatrice.

We should not expect to find in *La Vita Nuova* a detailed autobiography of Dante as a young man. It is not a modern "journal of the soul" in which a person keeps a close account of his personal experiences and spiritual development, although this work has much in common with this type of writing. Dante in his *Vita Nuova* employs a literary genre current in his time and popular with the poets of courtly love. In fact he addresses the work to a close friend and fellow poet, Guido Cavalcanti, and seeks Guido's response to the concept of love expressed in the book. Such a literary convention was common among the poets of the "sweet new style," the literary trend which both Dante and Guido followed.

In medieval Italy the "sweet new style" (*dolce stil nuovo*) was a popular poetic movement whose roots can be traced to the love poetry of the troubadours in southern France (Provence). The Provençal poets were imitated at the court of Frederick II in Sicily and the movement then spread to the Italian mainland, especially to Tuscany. The Provençal troubadours celebrated love as their main theme. This love was usually focused on the lady of the court, the master's wife, whose identity was kept secret. The lady was idealized in the poet's imagination as a distant, unattainable dream. The poet's passionate love for her and the praise of love itself were the constant topics of troubadour poetry. Often the poets would address their verses to their fellow poets, engaging in a kind of exchange and friendly competition on the subject of love. The poets thus belonged to a clique, often known as the "faithful ones of love"—faithful to their mistresses, but above all faithful to their intense vision of love itself.

Dante as a young poet was enthusiastically captivated by this popular literary movement which had signaled a breakthrough in European literature. It was a break with the traditional style in classical Latin and an experiment in a new style in the vernacular, from which the Romance languages of Western Europe evolved and thrived. The new style was like the bright burst of spring with all its freshness and delicate beauty. The theme of love gave the impetus to countless outpourings of youthful passion and enthusiasm. St. Francis of Assisi apparently had also been under the spell of this movement and celebrated his spiritual love in terms of courtly love. St. Bernard in France, Hildegarde of Bingen in Germany and Mechtilde of Magdeburg, also in Germany, were among the many Christian mystics from the twelfth century to the fourteenth century who also expressed their love affair with Christ or with Mary in the language and style of the troubadour poets.

Despite the similarity of language and style, however, the Christian mystics and the poets of courtly love were worlds apart in their conceptions of love. For the poets, love was not only a romantic passion but also a noble virtue that inspired acts of heroism for the benefit of the beloved. It inspired full commitment and fidelity to "the lady," but because it was centered on a human being, a mere creature, it was a love with limitations and ambiguity in the view of the mystics and theologians of the Church. According to the mystics and theologians, who were deeply influenced by the writings of St. Augustine, such a love was stunted and myopic: it stopped at the creature and did not reach out to the Creator. It was mere *amor* (human love) and not *charitas* (the supernatural gift of divine love). *Amor* in the Latin tradition, like *eros* in the Greek tradition, was love which embraced another human being because of the enjoyment and fulfillment that the beloved one and the very experience of love gave. Such a love was oriented only to another creature with no reference to the Creator. Often it was self-centered.

This human love was not condemned by the Church as heresy nor was the whole tradition of courtly love condemned. When any churchmen censured the "illicit" aspect of such love, they did so because the beloved was usually the wife of another man, which rendered the relationship adulterous. But for the most part the courtly love tradition was not harassed by the Church, perhaps because of the vague language of the poets and also because the tradition was usually artificial—a literary convention and a fantasy that most often remained something on paper and in the imaginations of the poets. It was rarely acted out in real life. Besides, it was a celebration of human love: a natural phenomenon. The Church was too busy in those centuries combatting Catharism, the heretical movement that denied the value of human love and consequently debased sexuality and marriage. Contrary to many popular misconceptions, the Church normally defended the basic goodness of human love and sexuality, but only within the context of marriage.

On the other hand, the theologians and mystics spoke of another kind of love, a higher love: *charitas* (the Latin translation of the New Testament Greek word *agape*). This distinctively Christian love was identified with God Himself, but was also given by God to humans so that they might love God above all else and their fellow creatures in a way subordinate to their primary love for God. St. Augustine in his writings had developed this New Testament concept of charity and contrasted it with the worldly or self-centered love which sought enjoyment of self and of other creatures for their own sake. Such "bad love" was often identified with the sin of lust in Augustine's theology. Needless to say, in the minds of the medieval theologians and mystics the romantic love celebrated by the troubadours dangerously approached this bad love of the Augustinian tradition. Because of that conflict and ambiguity many of the troubadours repented of their infatuation with courtly love and ended their days in a monastery making reparation for the aberrations of their ill-spent youth. Much medieval literature about courtly love between knights and ladies shows signs of such repentance by the introduction of the "pure love" theme. For example, the pure figure of Galahad and the search for the Holy Grail are introduced into the legend about Lancelot and Guinevere's adulterous love. This conflict between courtly love and divine love remained unresolved and the tension was discerned in European literature as well as in everyday life. It was the well-known tension between the sacred and the profane.

Dante, however, resolved this tension in his *Vita Nuova* and this work deserves to be recognized as a milestone and a masterpiece in all of European literature on the themes of human and divine love. Twentieth-century interpreters Charles Williams and Charles Singleton have recognized the genius of Dante on this topic, and their work has been confirmed by Dorothy Sayers and, most recently, by Rosemary Haughton.

Interpretation of Dante's work, especially his *Vita Nuova*, has a long and varied history. Without entering into a scholarly digression on the topic, it might be helpful to mention at least one *misinterpretation* of his work, which occurred in the sixteenth century after the publication of the first edition of *Vita Nuova*. In this edition many of Dante's original words were either changed or deleted altogether. These words referred to Beatrice either as being "glorious" or being Dante's "blessedness" or his "salvation." Such terms, according to the shocked theologians of that time, were meant to be reserved only for God or for Christ. To describe a woman in those terms was blasphemy and idolatry, tantamount to the creature-worship of the troubadours. Obviously the theologians had missed the point. They not only misunderstood Dante's poetic language but also the basic theological notion of analogy. Dante was quite aware that Beatrice was not Christ or God, but by analogy she was.

Dante was a master at analogy. Throughout the *Vita Nuova* he expressed himself in analogical terms through the use of symbolic numbers, symbolic colors, and poetic images. For example, Beatrice first appeared to Dante when she was nine years old and Dante also was nine. She was clothed in crimson, the color which symbolized love; and she brought to Dante's mind the words of Homer: "she seemed not the daughter of a mortal man, but of God." At that moment Dante felt dominated by love and his spirit told him his "blessedness" had appeared to him. It was nine years later at the ninth hour of the day that Beatrice once again appeared to him and greeted him. The number nine occurred at other significant moments in his relationship with Beatrice, and in *Vita Nuova* Dante explains in rather overt terms the hidden meaning of the number nine:

> This number was her very self; by similitude I mean and understand it thus: the number three is the root of nine because multiplied by itself it makes nine, even as we see clearly that three times three make nine. Therefore if three is the sole factor of nine and the sole factor of miracles is three, namely the Father, Son and Holy Spirit, Who are three and one, this lady was accompanied by the number nine to

give to understand that she was a nine, that is,
a miracle whose root is the wonderful Trinity
alone.

(*Vita Nuova,* **XXX**)

This brings us to the very meaning of Beatrice, a subject which has caused endless disputes among the interpreters of Dante for centuries. The key to interpretation
is precisely the idea of analogy. Analogy means likeness
or similitude, not identity. By similitude, as Dante wrote,
Beatrice was "a nine," an image of God. An image is real
resemblance which shares in the essence of the reality,
but such a participation in the reality does not mean
perfect identification with that reality. The terms "image" and "reality" were often used by the Church Fathers
and theologians to express this similarity as well as this
difference.

Such language was based on the Scriptures, especially
the Wisdom literature of the Old Testament where Wisdom is described as an image of God. Wisdom was often
personified as a woman or a cocreator with God. All of
creation was a work of God and His Wisdom. St. Paul in
the New Testament applied the terms "Wisdom" and
"image" to Christ, the perfect image of the invisible God.
The same concept can be found in the writings of St.
John. Christ is the visible Word, or Wisdom, of God the
Father. This is the language of the mystery of the Incarnation: Christ is the incarnation of God. He is visible, really
"in the flesh." He is the sacrament or visible manifestation of the hidden, divine reality. The Greeks used the
term *mysterion* to express this invisible reality made
visible in Him. In brief, He is true God in visible, human
form.

Such an incarnational theology is at the very core of Dante's conception of Beatrice. She is of course a woman, a human being, a creature; but she images forth, as Christ does, the hidden reality of God. She makes present or "fleshes out" the unseen Godhead; she is a God-bearing image.

Herein lies the meaning of Beatrice for Dante. She mediates God to Dante. Although she is a creature, there is something divine about her. That "something divine" is a share in the very essence of God. God *is* love in the fullest sense of charity, or agape, as St. John described God in his first letter. Beatrice is a human manifestation—a "miracle", as Dante describes her—of God as love. She is both lovable and she loves. But can she, a mere creature, be loved for herself, for her own inherent worth, individuality and beauty? Does the human and particular element have to be destroyed, absorbed or subordinated to God? Dante resolved this dilemma of either/or (either creature or Creator, in Augustinian terms); but he retained a certain tension and ambiguity, which he believed would always exist.

He resolved the dilemma by simply loving Beatrice, the real flesh and blood woman who lived in Florence and smiled at him and spoke to him. Dante recognized the earthly reality of Beatrice and eventually came to realize that she was a temporal manifestation of God's love for him, an eternal love which did not end with Beatrice's death. The death of the beloved Beatrice became for Dante a crisis and turning point in his life. The memory of her (and the *Vita Nuova* is essentially a book about that memory) became not the cause for empty grief and depression but rather, after much suffering, the beginning of a new life of more intense love for the beloved one who had passed to the eternal life with God.

We might say that the analogy with Christ's death gives us the radical clue to understanding Dante's relationship to Beatrice. Dante notes that Beatrice died at the ninth hour of the day, the same hour as Christ's death on the cross. Once again the symbolic number nine serves to signify the hidden meaning of the event. The disciples of Christ learned after His death that He had risen to a new life and had returned to the Father. His new, glorious life was different, but His presence among them was just as real as before. The memory of Jesus' death and resurrection was kept alive by realizing His glorious presence through His abiding Spirit, His sacraments (especially the Eucharist) and His presence in each human person. We know that Jesus identifies Himself with all human beings, members of His body. All of these different but similar presences of Christ mediated the glorious Christ to His disciples then and they continue now to mediate Him to us.

Beatrice was therefore a sacrament of divine love for Dante. That in no way obscured her human reality or reduced her to a symbol. She was an allegorical figure—that is true—but the allegory employed by Dante was the "allegory of the theologians," as Charles Singleton has so clearly observed. Such a use of allegory, common in the Scriptures and to the Fathers of the Church, means that the historical person or event, such as the Exodus event in the Old Testament, is real but at the same time a symbol of the unseen reality: God's eternal love for His people, which continues to show itself in other and even more wonderful ways in the course of history and will finally manifest itself fully in eternity.

The eternal reality is far greater than any of its earthly images or symbols, but those images *were* and *are* real, to be valued and cherished for their own sakes as well as for their function of leading us to the unseen reality, the Absolute. All creatures are thus "relative", that is, related to their Creator, Who shares His qualities of goodness and beauty with them. This is the affirmative way of looking at creation: the whole visible universe is a sacrament of God and this sacramental quality draws us to love the universe for its own sake and ultimately to love God. The either/or dichotomy is thus a false dilemma and a misinterpretation of the Christian mystics, Dante included. Authentic Christian mysticism does not shun or devalue the natural goodness of the physical world, but rejoices in all of God's creatures, the lovable handiwork of the lovable Creator. For the true Christian, then, it is not a question of loving either/or; but rather of loving *both* the creature *and* the Creator. Only the Creator, however, remains the perfect object of love and the perfect lover.

Dante was, in my opinion, an authentic Christian mystic and he expressed his embryonic mystical insights in his *Vita Nuova* and later in a much more developed way in his *Divine Comedy*. He was echoing in these works the fundamental, radical thrust of Christ Himself, Who so loved the world that He embraced it with exuberance and affirmed its worth and lovableness in God's eyes. Jesus went so far as to identify every human creature with Himself: ". . . what you do to the least of my brethren is what you do to Me" (Matt 25:40). St. John echoed Jesus' words by teaching that to love or hate one's visible brother or sister was to love or hate the invisible God. Dante was simply echoing this radical attitude toward the human person when he wrote of Beatrice as his "blessedness" and his "salvation." It was neither blasphemy nor idolatry: it was the Gospel. Beatrice was Christ for him, just as other human persons should be Christ for us today. Beatrice was the human "other" who partially completed Dante's quest for love, happiness, and joy. But she was not *The Other*; she was not God. She reflected and mediated God's love to Dante; but she passed on into God's glory where she continuously faced God and praised Him and led Dante to that divine face and to that praise.

Dante made all this quite clear in the closing paragraphs of his *Vita Nuova*:

> After this sonnet there appeared to me a wonderful vision in which I saw things which made me determine to speak no more of this beloved one [Beatrice] until such time as I could treat of her more worthily. And to attain to this I study all I can, as she truly knows. Thus if it be the pleasure of Him, by Whom all things live, that my life continue for some few years, I hope to write of her what has never been written of any woman.
>
> And then may it please Him, Who is lord of courtesy, that my soul may go see the glory of its lady, that is, the blessed Beatrice, who gloriously gazes on the face of Him Who is blessed through all ages.

We recognize the terminology of courtly love poetry in this passage, such as "the lady" and "courtesy," but we clearly see the distinction between the blessed lady, Beatrice, and the Blessed One, Who bestows blessedness on Beatrice. Dante does not confuse the two: only God is the ultimate source of our happiness. Only He is Lord, but it has pleased Him to draw us to Himself through His creatures, through the beauty of His created universe, and through the love of a woman. The troubadours had stopped short at the woman, but Dante's woman led him to God.

The woman Beatrice was glorious because she reflected God's glory. She was blessed because she shared God's blessedness. She was lovable because she reflected God's love. Yet she was a *real* channel of these divine graces to her one-time fellow pilgrim. She had arrived at the goal of the pilgrimage, but Dante was still on the way. He wrote the *Vita Nuova* as the *homo viator*, man journeying toward his goal.

The theme of pilgrimage is thus an important aspect of the *Vita Nuova*. Dante is still the pilgrim on the way to the face-to-face vision of God, but along the way God has given him a grace—a miracle—who is Beatrice. The name Beatrice literally means "one who makes blessed or happy." Beatrice, the creature, is a created grace, a mediator that eventually leads Dante to the perfect blessedness of the truly "beatific" vision of God. This is precisely the major difference between the *Vita Nuova* and the *Comedy*. In the *Vita Nuova* Dante comes to know and love God only through His creatures; that is, by analogy. In the Paradise of the *Comedy* he will see God face-to-face.

A pilgrim naturally suffers a certain sadness, restlessness, and nostalgia. Dante was well aware of this even before his exile. In a passage of *Vita Nuova* he reflects on this sadness of pilgrims who are far from their homes and loved ones as they travel toward the sacred goal of their pilgrimage. Dante had encountered a group of pilgrims passing through Florence on their way to Rome to behold the miraculous veil of Veronica, on which was impressed the image of Jesus' face. Dante, who was then deep in grief over Beatrice's death, reflects that his lady now looks on that "most beautiful face in glory." He takes the occasion to compose a sonnet to the pilgrims, inviting them to weep with him over the loss of Beatrice.

They who were removed from their homeland and friends could sympathize with him. Dante later in his *Divine Comedy* would develop this theme of pilgrimage, but the *Comedy* is not essentially a journey toward Beatrice. She is not the final goal. She acts as a guide, one of several guides, toward Paradise, which Dante calls "that Rome where Christ is Roman."

The pilgrim thus suffers from a double grief: the loss of beloved human persons and also the absence from his true homeland. The Italians call this *nostalgia*, a word that is best translated into English as "homesickness." The Christian pilgrim has this yearning after the yet unknown but partially revealed Beloved One and Lover, the Lord Himself. This double nostalgia is really the theme of the *Vita Nuova*, a theme which Dante develops in the *Comedy*. In a real sense the *Vita Nuova* is a miniature sketch, or outline, of the *opus magnum*. Like a seed it is planted in the mind and heart of Dante, and after many hardships and sufferings it finally blossoms into the white rose of Paradise.

The journey to Paradise is thus the return to one's true homeland. We are attracted there by an innate desire for God, which has been implanted in us by God Himself at the moment of our creation. This desire is a kind of intuition which we sometimes have unconsciously in our dreams and consciously in those "high" moments of life when we experience the joy of beauty and goodness. In the last analysis this desire is really the inner dynamic of love, which is an irresistible attraction to the Good and the Beautiful and is not satisfied until perfect Goodness and Beauty are fully possessed and enjoyed.

This same intuition is found in the works of Plato, who described our basic human desire (eros) for perfect beauty, goodness, and truth. The earthly manifestations of these eternal ideas are but shadows of the realities as yet unseen. When we encounter the shadows here on earth, we experience remembrance (*anamnesis*) of those eternal realities which the pre-existent soul enjoyed before its incarnation. Plato's intuitions, modified somewhat by a rejection of his belief in pre-existence and re-incarnation of souls, exercised a profound influence on Christian writers such as the author of the Letter to the Hebrews, the Greek and Latin Fathers of the Church, and the whole medieval tradition. St. Augustine in particular was the vehicle of Platonic ideas for Western Europe, even though he accommodated Plato's thought in many ways to Christian faith.

Dante, who was an heir to these Augustinian and Platonic influences, recognized the truth of their intuitions on the nature of love. But they were not abstract truths for him. He experienced them in his own life, reflected on them and wrote of them in the moving poetry and prose of his *Vita Nuova*. His book of memory describes his own development from love for Beatrice (in the sense of *amor*, or eros) to Christian love (*charitas*, or agape) for Beatrice and for God. The two kinds of love were real for Dante: two inseparable attractions which he deeply felt in his pilgrim heart. They inspired his whole life and his writing. But the two loves flowed from one source: God, Who alone is perfect Love, drawing us to Himself by means of His incarnate expression of love, Christ, as well as by Christ's human sisters and brothers. The circle of love would become complete only when Dante, intitially moved by love for Beatrice, would return to love's source, God Himself. In Dante's mind human creatures never lose their value and importance in this process of their return to God. Beatrice, lost from sight for awhile, will be found again in the glory of God, where Dante will find not only her but also himself.

For Dante, the human person is complete and whole only when he or she is reunited with the beloved human "other" and with the divine "Other." Thus the journey to God is really the journey by which we find ourselves: with the other and in the Other. That journey begins here and now. It is the "new" life which we begin by faith, hope, and love. It will be complete only when the pilgrimage of love reaches its goal of union.

THE
BANQUET

The death of Beatrice was for Dante an experience that not only caused much sorrow and pain, but it was also an occasion for deepening his love for her and for God. He accepted it and interpreted it in the spirit of his strong Christian faith. He recorded that acceptance in his memory book, *La Vita Nuova*, where his lively faith, hope, and love were obviously a solid support and inspiration through that painful experience.

Soon, however, many preoccupations, problems, and personal tragedies began to cloud that clear vision of faith. Dante's involvement in public life ended in a disaster that affected every aspect of his life. It brought financial ruin as well as the total uprooting from his family, friends, and the city he loved so deeply. It was a complete collapse of all that was dear to him. His reputation as a man of integrity was ruined. Rumors were also spreading that his romantic nature as a poet of love had led him into disreputable love affairs. In brief, his public image was of a man in disgrace: a corrupt politician, a romantic dreamer, a second-rate literary figure, and worst of all, a moral reprobate.

According to many Dante scholars, *Il Convivio* is Dante's response to such accusations and insinuations. It is his self-defense, his *Apologia Pro Vita Sua*. In it he tries to show that he is a serious man, a man of reason and virtue, and not just another poet of courtly love as his love poems and his *Vita Nuova* may have led the public to conclude. In the *Convivio* Dante very ambitiously proposes to write an encyclopedia of learning: a veritable feast—*Convivio* means "banquet," or "feast,"—of knowledge. Such an undertaking obviously betrays an underlying pride, of which Dante later repented. In the *Convivio* Dante is the pedantic scholar, aloof, and high above the "common herd" to whom he deigns to dispense some of his esoteric wisdom. If this were the only work which Dante left us, we would probably dismiss him as a condescending, intellectual snob, who, suffering from hurt pride, was desperately attempting to compensate for his apparent failures, disappointments, and low public image. He goes so far as to admit that he wrote this work "out of fear of infamy." Infamy then meant simply "the lack of fame."

However, the *Convivio* clearly represents a stage in his life when he legitimately desired to rehabilitate his reputation and establish his identity as a serious scholar and a man of virtue. It is important to notice that in the *Convivio* Dante does not repudiate his *Vita Nuova*. In fact he clearly states at the beginning that in the *Vita Nuova* his thoughts on love were "fervid and impassioned," but that in the *Convivio* the treatment of the same theme would be "temperate and virile." He attributes this change in style to the different stage in his life: he is no longer a youth, but a mature man now. The theme of love, however, is the constant. The passionate approach of youth gives way to the more "reasonable" approach of manhood. This rational approach to love and to life in general dominated Dante during this period of his life. He changed radically his allegiance: from his lady, Beatrice, to a new lady, Philosophy.

Philosophy, which etymologically means love of wisdom, was for Dante the human intellect's pure love of divine wisdom. In Dante's view this wisdom exists primarily in God, the Cause of all things; but it also exists secondarily in the human intellect, which has received from God its appetite for understanding and contemplating universal truth, activities which lead to human happiness. Dante's passionate quest for truth reminds us of the ideal of the Renaissance, and in many ways Dante was a precursor of that renewed pursuit of universal truth. Dante's main guide in this pursuit was Aristotle, although many other Greek and Latin philosophers as well as Christian theologians were guides in this search. Aristotle, however, was *the* philosopher according to Dante. He quoted Aristotle's works more than any other source, except the Bible. Dante subscribed to Aristotle's theory that the perfection of the human soul was the contemplation of truth. This "action" of contemplation is the ultimate fulfillment of human reason: its very raison d'etre, its happiness and goal. According to Aristotle, whose teacher was Plato, the human soul is driven by a spiritual movement, called love (*eros*), toward what it perceives as pleasant and good. The human soul not only contemplates truth, the "good of the soul", but also its own action of contemplating the truth. This love of its own action of contemplation is almost like a spiritual narcissism: a fascination with one's own beauty and perfection. Some authors refer to this stage of Dante's development as his cult of reason, for he was indeed in love with human reason and philosophy.

This love of philosophy helped to fill the void left in Dante's soul by the loss of his beloved lady, Beatrice. After the manner of the philosopher Boethius in his famous work, *The Consolation of Philosophy*, Dante found his own consolation in this love for his new lady. In the *Convivio* Dante bestows on "Lady Philosophy" many of the epithets he had given to Beatrice in the *Vita Nuova*. In his words, philosophy is "truly a lady full of sweetness, adorned with honor, wondrous in wisdom, glorious in liberty." He even states "that the lady of whom I became enamored after the first love was the most beautiful and honorable daughter of the Emperor of the Universe to whom Pythagoras gave the name Philosophy."

Such high praises of philosophy could give the impression that Dante considered philosophy to be superior to religious faith. But Dante was careful to indicate that this divine philosophy, which proceeds from God Himself, is only an aid to faith: it is a kind of miracle which helps us to believe in the miracles of Christ, which are the principal foundation of our faith. Dante thus subordinates the role of reason and philosophy to faith, but in one passage it appears that even faith, hope, and charity are only aids in attaining to the supreme goal of "philosophizing":

> Therefore, since through her [philosophy] one sees by reason and deduction much of those things, which without her appear a marvel, so through her it is believed that any miracle may have reason for a higher intellect, and

in consequence may be true. Hence our rightful faith has its origin, from which comes the
hope for the foreseen desire, and through that
is born the operation of charity. By these three
virtues one mounts up to philosophize in that
heavenly Athens where the Stoics, Peripatetics,
and Epicureans, by the art of the Eternal Truth,
concordantly agree in one will.

(*Convivio*, III, xiv)

These three main schools of classical philosophy
reappear in the last treatise of the *Convivio* where Dante
enters the arena of the celebrated medieval debate concerning which life-style is superior: the active life or the
contemplative life. In his own life he seems to have been
torn between the active pursuit of moral virtue and the
philosophical contemplation of truth. In a remarkable
passage of that treatise he employs the typically medieval
method of allegorical interpretation of the Scriptures. Today we might smile condescendingly at such a curious
way of extracting meaning from Scripture, but Dante's
thesis is quite clear: the contemplative life is far superior
to the active, even though contemplation does not bring
man perfect happiness in this life. The entire passage is
worth quoting:

The mind of man—that is, will and intellect—has a double use, practical and speculative. The speculative is the more delightful: it
consists, not in working for oneself, but in con-
sidering the works of God and Nature. Both the
practical and the speculative form our beatitude and highest happiness. And by much discipline and culture the human mind, even if not
naturally predisposed to this, can attain to it.
The speculative use of mind cannot be brought
to perfection in this world: it consists in seeing

God, Who is the highest intelligible being, and this cannot be done except in so far as the intellect considers Him and contemplates Him in His effects.

The fact that we crave this beatitude as the supreme one, and not the other (i.e., the active life), is taught to us by the Gospel of Mark. Mark says that Mary Magdalene, Mary the mother of James, and Mary Salome went to find the Savior in the tomb and did not find Him; but found a young man clad in white who said to them: "You look for the Savior and I tell you that He is not here: fear not, but go and tell His disciples and Peter that He will precede them into Galilee, and there you will see Him, as He told you."

By those three women may be understood the three schools—the Epicureans, Stoics and Peripatetics—who go to the tomb, namely the present world which is a receptacle for corruptible things, and ask for the Savior, that is, beatitude, and find Him not. But they find a young man in white garments, who was an angel of God. Matthew wrote: "The angel of God descended from heaven, and turned the stone over and was seated on it. His aspect was like lightning and his garments like snow." This angel is this nobility of ours, which comes from God, which speaks in our reason and says to each of these schools—that is, to any one who goes seeking for beatitude in the active life—that it is not there. But let him go and tell it to the disciples and Peter—that is, to those who seek the Savior and are astray as was Peter who had denied Him—that he will precede them into Galilee. This means that beatitude will precede them in Galilee, i.e., in speculation.

Galilee means "whiteness" and whiteness is a color full of light beyond any other. In the same way contemplation is fuller of spiritual light than any other thing that is here below. The angel says "He will precede" and not "He will be along with you" to indicate that God always precedes our contemplation, that we can never reach Him, Who is our supreme beatitude. He also says, "There you will see Him, as He told you," meaning that there you will taste of His sweetness, namely felicity, as is here promised to you, i.e., as you are capable of having it.

And thus it appears that our beatitude, i.e., our felicity, we can first find imperfect in the active life (the operations of the moral virtues) and then almost perfect in the operations of the intellectual virtues. These two operations are paths, quick and most direct, which lead to the supreme beatitude, which here cannot be had.

(*Convivio*, IV, xxii)

This passage reinforces the impression that Dante was, in this phase of his life, the confirmed intellectual, confident in the mind's nobility and its highest calling: contemplation. The will and moral virtues are relegated to a secondary place, although Dante is well aware that they play a complementary role in attaining happiness. The attainment, however, is still beyond this life. Dante's pilgrim soul, his mind in love with the ultimate truth, realizes that not even the most developed contemplation can reach its object of love in this present life.

In the tradition of Aristotle Dante defines love in the third treatise of his *Convivio* as "the spiritual union of the soul and the loved thing, to which union the soul in virtue of its own nature runs swiftly or slowly, according as it is free or impeded." Dante, however, knew Aristotle mainly through his Christian interpreter, St. Thomas

Aquinas, and always related Aristotle's philosophy to his Christian faith. As a result, the ultimate object of this insatiable love is God alone: the human soul "naturally desires and wills to be united to God," as Dante writes. This transcendent dimension of love is merely stated, but not developed in Dante's *Convivio*. Dante does develop it in his *Divine Comedy* where the main focus is the mystics' love of a personal God. Aristotle's impersonal, intellectual approach to love is a far cry from the passionate, ecstatic approach of the mystics in love with the personal God Who is Love.

At this stage Dante is apparently captivated by the soul's own power and ability to know and to love. This captivation, however, did not last long and even in the *Convivio* Dante perceived that this insatiable love could not be satisfied with any object of love in this world. The following passage reveals this restless movement of the soul:

> And like a pilgrim who is travelling on a road where he has never been before, who believes that every house which he sees from afar is the inn, and finding that it is not, directs his belief to another, so from house to house until he comes to the inn. Even so our soul, as soon as it enters upon the new and never-yet-made journey of life, directs its eyes toward the goal of its supreme good, and whatever it sees that appears to have some good in it, it thinks to be *it*. And because its knowledge is at first imperfect, through no experience or instruction, little goods appear great to it. It is the way we see little children intensely longing for an apple, and then going on further, longing for a little bird, and then further on longing for fine clothes, and then a horse, and then a mistress. . . . This happens because in none of these things does

he find what he is ever searching for. . . . But in truth we may lose this way in error.

(*Convivio*, IV, xii)

This passage is particularly important because it reveals Dante's pilgrim soul and his conception of love as the spiritual force always driving him toward some goal which will completely satisfy all human desires. No doubt the Platonic theme of eros is the basic idea of Aristotle, Thomas, the Christian mystics, and Dante himself, the spiritual heir of them all. Dante by immersing himself in the study of philosophy and theology in this period of his life came to realize that human reason and intellectual knowledge could not be the final goal of the quest.

This is probably the reason why Dante never completed the *Convivio*. While writing it he most likely realized that he was taking the wrong road, that he was undertaking a foolish journey: a "mad flight" like Ulysses' journey, which he later described in the *Comedy*. The figure of Ulysses in Canto XXVII of *Hell* is probably an autobiographical sketch of this stage of his life: the restless wanderer, equipped only with a "small boat" and a few fellow travelers. The small boat of Ulysses is the metaphor for the limited resource of human reason. The outcome of Ulysses' journey is tragedy, since the transcendent goal cannot be reached by such inadequate means. But just as there is something heroic and monumental about Ulysses' voyage beyond the pillars of Hercules, so there is something admirable and praiseworthy about Dante's ambitious project to master all knowledge. It heralded the dawn of the great Italian Renaissance.

The sheer *bravura* of Dante's attempt demands our attention and admiration, even if the attempt did not reach completion. It is the same quest for knowledge, the same eros, which compels modern scientists to keep exploring the unknown potentials of energy and the mysteries of our cosmos. Dante was always an avid defender of this God-given nobility in man: the capacity to discover and enjoy the truth. His *Convivio* is a monumental salute to this human nobility, this "miracle" of human intelligence.

It would be an incomplete picture of Dante in this period of his life if we saw him only as a scholar consumed by a desire to know and to expose his acquired knowledge. He was also consumed by a desire to restore peace and justice to the world. Dante became actively involved in the most explosive political issues of his day. The political chaos and incessant wars, caused by the greed of secular and ecclesiastical leaders, were in Dante's mind an evil frustration and a contradiction to God's plan for humanity's happiness and joy in this world. He courageously committed himself to the cause of peace and justice. By public service and incessant writing he became a true prophet and apostle of peace throughout his life, even when he met with failure after failure. A passage from the *Convivio* reveals this major concern of his life:

> Since the mind of man does not rest content with a limited possession of land, but always desires to acquire more land, as we see by experience, disagreements and wars arise between kingdom and kingdom. These things are the tribulations of cities, and through cities of neighborhoods, and through neighborhoods of families, and through families of individuals, and thus the attainment of joy is hindered. Therefore, in order to do away with these wars and their causes, it is necessary that the whole earth should be a monarchy, i.e., a single princedom, and should have a single prince, who pos

sessing all things and having nothing left to desire, may keep the kings confined within the borders of their kingdoms so that peace may reign between them.

In this peace the cities may have rest; in this rest neighborhoods may love each other; in this love households may satisfy all their needs. And when these are satisfied, man may attain joy, which is the purpose for which man was born.

(Convivio, IV, iv)

Dante's ideal of universal peace, love, and joy was of course not realized then, nor has it been realized during the more than six-hundred years since his death. He failed and was defeated in the battle, but his motives were pure and his efforts were not in vain. To quote T. S. Eliot's incisive words:

Whatever we inherit from the fortunate
We have taken from the defeated
What they had to leave us—a symbol:
A symbol perfected in death.
And all shall be well and
All manner of thing shall be well
By the purification of the motive
In the ground of our beseeching.

(Little Gidding)

This brief survey of the middle years of Dante's life, based on his *Convivio*, has revealed to us not only a man of intense intellectual curiosity, a scholar confident in his own talent and gifts, a true lover of wisdom, justice, and peace but also a man who perceives the limitations of his own resources. Dante came to admit the futility of a merely philosophical approach to life. But a brighter vision begins to loom on the horizon. It is the face of

Beatrice, vague and almost forgotten by now. His life begins to take a new course—a journey to her, a return to the beginning.

After so many digressions and exploratory experiences, Dante returns to his initial vision. The much-quoted verses of T. S. Eliot come to mind:

> We shall not cease from exploration
> And the end of all our exploring
> Will be to arrive where we started
> And know the place for the first time.

> (*Little Gidding*)

Dante has learned that the quest to know, to understand, and to contemplate leads into a blind alley. He now perceives that true vision in this life can be found not by seeing the truth perfectly but by changing one's will, one's affections, one's object of love. Dante tells the story of his change in his *Comedy*.

THE DIVINE COMEDY:

An Introduction

S ome of the reasons people write books are: pleasure, financial profit, fame, and commitment to
a cause. Dante's motivation for his *Convivio*
was apparently a desire for fame as well as an
"apology" for his life and works up to that point. His purpose in writing the *Comedy*, however, was quite different. He explicitly states in his letter to his patron Can
Grande della Scala that his purpose was "to remove those
living in this life from the state of misery and lead them
to the state of felicity." He specifically mentions in that
same letter that "the branch of philosophy which regu-
lates the work in its whole and in its parts is morals,
or ethics, because the whole was undertaken not for

speculation but for practical results." Such terms as "felicity" and "morals" may strike our modern taste as quaint and antiquated. Dante's stated intention of "moralizing" might even turn us away from even starting the *Comedy*. The modern world of the late twentieth century has been disillusioned by the moralists and has apparently lost faith in traditional morality. Classical and Christian morality seem as outmoded as the medieval cathedrals and castles: impressive, but incomprehensible relics of the past.

If we are to understand the *Comedy* we must first of all realize that Dante is writing for "those living in this life": his contemporaries, his fellow pilgrims. Thus the many allusions to contemporary medieval persons, places, and customs will be foreign to our modern culture. However, this should not be an insurmountable obstacle, exasperating as it may be at times for those who are not informed on the topic of history, especially medieval history.

The "morality" and "felicity" which Dante speaks of could easily be translated into more modern terms, but the choice of terms changes so rapidly today. The trendy "buzz words" of the late twentieth century change from year to year. In the last thirty years such words as "value system," "personal fulfillment," "self-actualization," "wholeness," and so on have succeeded one another on the hit parade of pop psychology. Some even say that psychology has replaced morality. But the reality of the human person remains the same today as in Dante's time. The same basic needs and desires, choices, dreams, hopes, and fears are deep within the human heart as such. And Dante speaks to the human heart. He might use the term "mind" or "soul" or "will," but all these terms pertain to the human person, whose faculties and dimensions are multifaceted.

Dante is addressing his fellow human beings as such;
but, more specifically, he is addressing his fellow Christian pilgrims. Giovanni Papini in his brilliant book *Dante
Vivo* contends that in order to fully understand the *Comedy* one must be a Catholic, an artist, and a Florentine.
I would agree with the first prerequisite but only with
some reservation. I would include all Christians who share
basically in the life of Christ. Of course, being Catholic,
especially one raised in the pre-Vatican II era, would be
helpful to an appreciation of the cultural backdrop of the
Comedy.

All of us, then, especially those who share Dante's
Christian faith and have experienced some of the joys
and sorrows of this life, can identify with Dante's story
because it is *our* story. Dante discovers that he is lost and
tries to find himself. He sets out on a journey and invites
us, the readers, to join him in this quest for self, which
will simultaneously be a quest for God.

It is important at the outset to notice that Dante
plays a dual role in this journey: narrator and pilgrim. As
narrator of the journey he often adopts a pedagogical
stance. He calmly teaches us some very important truths;
but at times with all the fire of a Hebrew prophet, he
lashes out against the injustice and corruption of his society and Church. At other times he speaks as an inspired
writer, commissioned to communicate a heavenly message to the earth.

As pilgrim, however, he is one of us: lost, incomplete, broken, in need of direction. Sinful, fearful, ignorant, and weak, he is, however, aware that deep down in
the secret chambers of his heart he is being drawn by
some unknown force: a love for what is beautiful and
good and true. But that is not all. This mysterious force
turns out to be God Himself, the Lover Who is drawing
us all back to Himself. It is God Who is reaching out to

us (or should I say, into us?) who, like Dante, are lost in the "dark wood" of ignorance, confusion, and sin. The Lover beckons us to find our true selves and Him through a journey of change and conversion. We find ourselves only when we find Him; and we find our wholeness, completion, happiness, fulfillment (whatever we might call it) only when the spokes of the wheel of our being are united to the center that is God. St. Augustine said it all: "Our hearts are restless until they rest in Thee."

The restless heart of the Christian pilgrim is thus the main prerequisite for making the journey with Dante. If we are satisfied with our present condition, if we are very comfortable with the present state of our soul or the state of the world and the Church, then we are not ready for the journey. If we are not in touch with the dark side of our personality: the uncontrollable passions, the sins, the guilt, and frustrations (all of which Dante sums up as "misery"), then we will not understand Dante's "dark wood" or his journey through Hell. If we do not have a desire to be free of all that, to change and become whole, sane, and "holy" then we will not comprehend Dante's ascent of the mountain, his journey through Purgatory. If we do not sense a longing for that "something beyond," the ultimate joy and unending ecstasy (what Dante calls "felicity"), then we will not appreciate the soaring movement into the white rose of Paradise, to the Omega Point, the Center of the universe.

Thus we have to be alert, aware, and "in touch with" all the facets of our complex inner selves. Dante candidly shares his innermost feelings and perceptions, his awareness of his own sins and aberrations, his experience of conversion, and his inexpressible joy in finding God in his life. Dante shares his story with us in the *Comedy*. It is the most autobiographical of all his works. He invites us to embark with him on a journey which will at times be most painful since it will mean brutal self-honesty and will require a willingness to change, but the ultimate goal will be the inner peace and joy which our hearts have always desired. That is what Dante means when he states that his purpose is to "remove us from misery to felicity." It is a movement or transition from one state to another. It is a complete transformation of the inner self: a spiritual movement, or journey, of the soul to its very center where we encounter God.

The metaphor of a journey is thus the dominant image of the *Comedy*, its basic model and paradigm. Without entering into all the subtle distinctions of the literary critics we will refer to this metaphor as an allegory, since an allegory is basically an expanded metaphor. Allegory is the use of an image or anything perceptible by the senses to represent "something else": an idea, an emotional state, a spiritual experience, or any reality, usually one not perceived directly by the senses.

One of the most important keys to understanding Dante's work is to realize that Dante is communicating his personal experience, his spiritual journey, through the medium of an allegory. The literal journey through the three realms of Hell, Purgatory, and Paradise is an allegory of his own inner process of growth and transformation. The literal journey, of course, is a fiction, the invention of an ingenious poet and storyteller who is indirectly sharing with us an experience which cannot be directly communicated because of its uniqueness and mysterious richness.

The modern reader might ask why Dante's literal journey takes him to "places" outside our everyday experience in this world. He goes beyond our space and time into the unknown worlds of eternity. These other worlds of Hell, Purgatory, and Paradise are not so familiar to the modern reader as they were to the medieval reader. The specter of imminent death, which was raised by frequent epidemics and wars, lurked in all the corners of daily life in medieval Europe. Accompanying the thought of death was the reflection on one's eternal fate. The two were inseparably linked: one's mortal life was viewed in the light of eternity. One's eternal fate was believed to be determined by the state of one's soul at death. The famous "four last things," death, judgment, Heaven, and Hell, were ubiquitous: portrayed on the exterior and interior walls of the churches, heard in the sermons, sung in the hymns, analyzed in the universities. The "other world" was almost as visible and palpable as the grass of the fields and the flowers of the gardens.

The horrible punishments of Hell, the purifying process of Purgatory, and the delights of Paradise were familiar images in medieval culture. They reflected the Church's teaching on the "eternal verities" and were accepted as true. Dante is not concerned with promoting or defending the Church's teaching. He takes it for granted. As a poet he borrows the familiar landscapes of Hell, Purgatory, and Paradise described in art and sermons, and he creatively adapts them for his own story. He uses those traditional images as a medium through which he expresses the inner landscape of his own spiritual life. He tells us what is happening within him by means of images and metaphors already familiar to his readers. That is why he so infrequently pauses in the *Comedy* to explain a metaphor. For the general public those strange, unknown places were known through faith and the Church's teaching, liturgy, and art.

A frequent misunderstanding of the *Comedy* is to view Dante as the supreme judge of humanity who decides the destinies of the many individuals he meets in the three realms. Dante's main concern does not lie there, although in *Hell* he seems to take sweet revenge on some of his personal enemies. His basic purpose is to describe the states of the human soul. In his letter to Can Grande he explicitly states that the subject of the whole work is: "Man, as by good or ill deserts, in the exercise of his freedom of choice, becomes liable to rewarding or punishing Justice."

Hell, then, is an allegory of the soul caught in the sin it has willingly chosen. Purgatory pictures the soul's struggle to be free of the bonds of sin, to become beautiful and whole again in the image of God, as it was created. Paradise is the image of the soul's foretaste even in this life of the joy and ecstasy which union with God gives. Hell is thus a prison of misery in which a person can confine himself in *this* life; Purgatory is the process of freedom and conversion, the *present* pilgrimage toward wholeness; Paradise is the enjoyment *now* of God's love.

Dante, then, is describing the "eternal now." Our present choices bring us into the realms of Hell, Purgatory, or Paradise. Our own wills determine what our inner experiences will be: misery, conversion, or delight. For this reason the realm of Purgatory corresponds most closely to the present state of the Christian soul in this world: freed from the misery of sin, but yet not completely free. The soul is still on its way, moving in time, changing and progressing, always hopeful of attaining the ultimate joy of its true home.

This theme of a journey and a return to one's "homeland" was familiar to Dante from his early childhood acquaintance with the epic poems of classical literature and also from his continued interest in the classics.

In Greek and Latin literary and philosophical circles the journey of Ulysses in Homer's *Odyssey* was usually interpreted as an allegory of the soul's progress through

LORETTE WILMOT LIBRARY
NAZARETH COLLEGE

many perils and its eventual return to its homeland. The Neoplatonists were especially fond of this interpretation. The same was true of Virgil's *Aeneid*. The allegorical interpretation of Aeneas's journey was a favorite theme for the Neoplatonists of the Middle Ages. Aeneas's descent to the netherworld and his successful journey to Italy to become the founder of the Roman Empire was for medieval allegorists an example of the Christian soul's journey to God.

Dante, an ardent admirer of Virgil, adopts the hero of the *Aeneid* as the model of his own soul which descends to the netherworld, journeys through many purifying experiences, but at last reaches its glorious destination. The same basic pattern can be found in the *Aeneid* and in the *Comedy*: descent, conversion, and ascent. It is no surprise that Dante's first guide for the journey is Virgil himself.

When Virgil first encounters Dante in the opening scene of the *Comedy* and proposes to him the journey through the underworld, Dante protests that he is not Aeneas, the hero of Virgil's epic poem. But he also protests that he is not St. Paul, who, according to Christian tradition, also traveled to the netherworld. That tradition came from the popular apocryphal book in the Middle Ages, *The Vision of Paul*. St. Paul, however, had described in his second letter to the Corinthians a journey to the highest heaven. In Paradise he had seen and heard things "that human lips may not speak" (II Cor. 12:2-4). Paul's journey to the other world became in Christian tradition, especially in the works of Augustine and Thomas Aquinas, the model of the soul's itinerary to the beatific vision of God.

But even more important than Paul's experience is the experience of Christ Himself. Christ's passage from death to life is really the central pattern of Dante's *Comedy*. Christ's suffering, death, descent into Hell, and His resurrection and ascension to the Father's glory is the basic paradigm for the Christian pilgrim. Dante models his own experience of spiritual death, descent into Hell, and ascent to Paradise on the central event of Christian history: the death and resurrection of Jesus. He establishes many parallels with Christ's death and resurrection. For example, Dante wrote the *Comedy* in 1300, when he was in his thirty-fifth year, the exact age, according to Dante, of Christ when He died. The biblical "seventy years" was considered the average age of a man: Dante thus began his journey exactly "mid-way" through his life's course, as he states in the opening verse of the *Comedy*. The day of Dante's entrance into Hell is Good Friday, the day of Christ's death.

Dante's ascent of the mountain of Purgatory began on Easter morning, the day of Christ's rising to new life. Dante enjoys the eternal Paschal feast of Paradise during the Easter season. This correspondence with Christ's death, descent, and glorious resurrection is quite obvious. Although Dante never mentions Christ by name in *Hell* (out of reverence for the sacred name in such an evil place), he often refers to Christ's triumphant descent there as "the Mighty One" who delivered the first human couple as well as the Hebrew men and women who were waiting there for His coming. In *Hell* Dante sometimes refers to the cracks in the rocks, caused by the earthquake at Christ's death on the cross. The cosmic dimension of that event reached down into the darkest regions at the center of the earth.

At the very bottom of the pit of Hell, where Satan reigns, Dante hears the only "song" sung in Hell: it is a perverse parody of *Vexilla Regis* (The Banners of the

King), a Christian hymn sung in the Holy Week liturgy
to celebrate the triumph of Christ's cross. The words
sung in Hell are somewhat different: after *Regis* is added
the word *Inferni*, thus transforming the hymn honoring
Christ the King into a mockery of the king of Hell, Satan.
Christ's act of love on the Cross is subtly contrasted with
Satan's eternal hatred of mankind. The "banners" of the
infernal king are hideous, bat-like wings which Satan
uses to generate a freezing wind as he forever devours
Judas Iscariot, Brutus, and Cassius in his three mouths.
The parody of divine love is perfect. The banner of the
Cross, Christ's life-giving sacrifice of love, has its coun-
terpart: the evil of death by eternal torment.

Dante frequently alludes to the death of Christ
throughout the *Comedy*. At the summit of Mount Purgatory in the earthly paradise, the wood of the cross causes
the bare, dead tree in the garden to burst forth into blossoms and grow into the tree of life again. In the heavenly
Paradise the cross is still prominent. There Dante describes his vision of the glorious triumph of Christ's
cross, but he admits that he can find no example to express its splendor. Toward the end of his journey in Paradise he describes the throngs of the blessed as forming a
white rose, which is the beautiful bride whom Christ espoused by his own blood.

Perhaps T. S. Eliot in his final line of *Little Gidding*,
"And the fire and the rose are one," had this scene in
mind. The fire of Christ's love "ignites" the rose of Paradise: His ardent love brings the rose into being. The blood
of Christ shed on the Cross expressed His love for humanity, His bride. This love is at the very heart of the
Comedy. Christ's descending love, expressed in His own
pilgrimage through death to life, is for Dante the ultimate reason that a Christian's pilgrimage to Paradise is

possible at all. The Lord out of love for us went before us in death and resurrection. He not only experienced the suffering and anguish of the journey, but earned for us entrance to the homeland. He broke through the walls and barriers and introduced us, His bride, into the ineffable joys of the wedding feast in Paradise.

In his dedicatory letter to Can Grande della Scala, Dante explains in detail this underlying allegory of the journey in the *Comedy*. In clear terms he defines allegory and focuses the reader's attention on its meaning and on the meanings of his great work. The following passage from that letter is an indispensable introduction to the whole *Comedy*:

> The meaning of this work is not simple, but rather can be said to be of several meanings, for there is one meaning that is derived from the letter and another that is derived from the things indicated by the letter. The first is called *literal*, but the second *allegorical* or *mystical*. That this method of expounding may be more clearly set forth, we can consider it in these lines: "When Israel went out of Egypt, the house of Jacob from a people of strange language, Judah was His sanctuary and Israel His dominion."
>
> If we consider the *letter* alone, the departure of the children of Israel from Egypt in the time of Moses is signified; if the *allegory*, our redemption accomplished in Christ is signified; if the *moral meaning*, the conversion of the soul from the sorrow and misery of sin to a state of grace is signified; if the *anagogical*, the departure of the sanctified soul from the slavery of this corruption to the liberty of everlasting glory is signified. And although these mystical meanings are called by various names,

they can in general all be said to be allegorical,
since they differ from the literal or historical.

This passage tells us what Dante means by allegory
and serves as the key that unlocks for us the hidden
meaning of the entire work. After the manner of the medieval interpreters of Scripture (who imitated the method
of the Scripture writers themselves and the Fathers of the
Church), Dante distinguishes two basic meanings in the
Scriptures: the literal (or historical) and the allegorical (or
mystical). Thus the *Comedy* must be read with "double
vision": an eye on the literal and an inner eye (the spiritual sense) on the deeper meaning. The second meaning
in turn has several aspects or stages: *our* redemption accomplished by Christ, *our* conversion from sin to grace,
and *our* passage from slavery to eternal freedom and glory.

The allegorical meaning then is centered on our salvation, but that salvation is primarily an action performed
by Christ. The example which Dante gives of the historical meaning is the clue to the whole pattern of salvation:
an Exodus, or journey, from slavery to freedom. The Exodus of the Jews from Egypt is the fundamental historical
event or act of God which becomes the basic model of all
God's salvific actions on our behalf. Christ's death and
resurrection was understood in the New Testament as
the new and eternal Exodus or Passover from death to
life, from this world to the Father's glory. Thus the "Paschal Mystery" is the central theological and mystical
theme which gives coherence to the entire *Comedy*. The
Christian pilgrim's immersion into Baptism (a spiritual
imitation of Christ's death and resurrection) is the beginning of the new life of grace: an on-going process and
journey which reaches fulfillment in eternal glory.

This type of allegory, which Professor Singleton calls
the "allegory of the theologians," is firmly rooted in the

historical. The history of the Exodus and the historical event of Christ's death and resurrection are the concrete examples. This kind of allegory differs radically from the "allegory of the poets." Dante was well aware of the distinction, since he alluded to it in *The Banquet* (*Convivio*) where he cites Ovid's description of Orpheus who tamed wild beasts with his lute-playing. Orpheus allegorically means the wise man who softens and moves the cruel, irrational hearts of those who live neither for science nor for art. Thus Orpheus, the *fictional* character in Ovid's poetry, represents "something else."

In the "allegory of the theologians" (which includes Scriptural writers and interpreters) the characters and events of Scripture are *real* and *historical*, but they also represent "something else." Singleton very succinctly simplifies the distinction: the poets use allegory in the sense of "this *for* that," whereas the theologians mean "this *and* that." We are once again in the world of analogy. The concrete and the particular are appreciated and taken seriously as real and historical, but the inner eye of faith penetrates into another meaning placed there by God, the Creator, the Writer of the Scriptures.

As we have observed earlier, this is the incarnational or sacramental interpretation of reality. Dante was a realist, but a realist in the Christian sense of grasping the full reality of persons and events. That full reality includes the hidden meaning and intention of God Himself. The *Comedy* is about this real world, a world interpreted and enlightened by Christian faith. Throughout the *Comedy* the main characters and events are real in this sense. Dante is a real person on a real journey. Virgil is a real, historical person. Beatrice is a real person. And yet Dante wants us to understand them also as representing "something else." Dante is "Every Man," in the sense of every Christian pilgrim. Virgil is primarily human reason. Beatrice is God's wisdom and love. In other words, the historical realities are not absorbed into symbolism, but they do contain in themselves other meanings.

One might object that the whole *Comedy* is a fiction, an imagined journey to imaginary places. True, it is a poetic fiction. Dante the poet knows this, but his poetry is based on the real state of persons and things. In the same letter quoted above he states that the literal subject of the work is the "state of souls after death," but he adds that "according to its allegorical meaning the subject is man, as by good or ill deserts, in the exercise of the freedom of his choice, he becomes liable to rewarding or punishing Justice." These realities of God's justice, human freedom, and the rewards and punishments of the other world are the realities of Christian faith. That basic faith is presumed throughout.

Dante is no less a poet because he views reality through the eyes of Christian faith. Some modern literary critics deny the category of "pure poetry" to Dante's *Comedy*. They claim that the *Comedy*'s purpose is primarily didactic or edifying in the religious sense and therefore is not poetry as such. To be sure, the *Comedy* is a sacred poem, but it is poetry nonetheless—perhaps the highest form of poetry since it embraces *all* the dimensions of the human soul and *all* its experiences of this world and even of the transcendent world.

Dante was a Christian poet, but always a poet. Throughout the *Comedy* he mingles real persons with fictional persons derived from classical poetry. The "allegory of the poets" is also present throughout. The fictional creations of Virgil and Ovid, the Latin poets who inspired Dante so profoundly, are to be found in Hell, Purgatory, and Paradise. Dante draws no neat dichotomy between pagan poetry and biblical faith. His poetic genius draws on the poetic geniuses so familiar to him. Dante was not like Savonarola, also a Florentine, who, some two hundred years after Dante, set out in a burst of unenlightened zeal to burn all the treasures of pagan literature. Dante loved the classics. He appreciated the heritage of Greek and Latin literature and was truly a Christian humanist. Dante's humanism served a higher master: his Christian faith. The classics played an ancillary role. They were the handmaidens, like all pagan philosophy and literature, of the queen, which was Christian faith and theology.

According to the Hebrew poets and prophets, Jesus, the early Church Fathers, and the medieval theologians and mystics, the vision of faith interpreted all visible reality as a symbol of God's goodness, beauty, power, and wisdom. The created universe was not a meaningless puzzle or a mute mystery: it spoke to man, delighting him and generating in him understanding, praise, and love of its Creator.

In this context Dante often used the metaphor of the book. The book of Scripture is God's written word, His self-communication to man; but the entire universe is also a book, written by the Creator, full of meanings inserted by Him for man to discover. The discovery of the full meaning of the book brings man his deepest joy because through this discovery he comes to know and love God. In the final canto of the *Comedy*, as Dante gazes on the vision of God, he bursts into these verses:

> O abounding grace whereby I presumed to fix my gaze through the Eternal Light so far that all my sight was spent in it.
> In its depth I saw ingathered, bound by love in one single volume, all that is dispersed in leaves throughout the universe: substances

and accidents and their relations, as though
fused together in such a way that what I tell is
only a simple light. The universal form of this
knot I believe that I saw, because in telling this
I feel my joy increase.

(Paradise, XXXIII, 82-93)

Here we can appreciate the "allegory of the theologians": the created universe is a volume whose many
pages can be understood only when they are seen bound
together by God's love. This way of seeing the universe
increases Dante's joy because he sees it all as symbol or
real expression of God's love. Such a religious interpretation of reality was typical of the medieval Christian. It
was somewhat obscured, however, in the Renaissance
when the emphasis shifted from the universe as religious
symbol with God as its center to the universe as the object of study and investigation with man as its center.
Man became the measure of all things and the universe
a place to discover and conquer for man's sake alone.

Today's emphasis on technology and the discovery
of space seem to be more in the spirit of the Renaissance.
The universe is used by the consumer for his own pleasure and profit (and perhaps destruction) rather than as a
book which speaks to man about God and leads him to
praise and adoration.

Even in such exalted moments as his glimpse of the
beatific vision, Dante the poet expresses himself in the
metaphors of classical literature. In the same final canto
Dante attempts to convey the experience of the vision
but finds that the memory of it fails him. The vision has
faded like a dream. He uses two metaphors to express
this: the melting of the snow by the sun (an image from
nature) and an image drawn from Virgil's *Aeneid,* the

leaves of the Cumaean Sibyl which, when scattered by the wind, lost the message written on them by the Sibyl:

> From then on my vision was greater than speech can show, which fails at such a sight, and at such excess memory fails. As one who sees while dreaming and after the dream the passion remains imprinted and the rest returns not to the mind; such am I, for my vision almost entirely fades away, yet does the sweetness that was born of it still drop within my heart. Thus is the snow melted by the sun; thus in the wind, on the light leaves, the Sibyl's oracle was lost.

(Paradise, XXXIII, 55-66)

Thus Dante the poet always remained the humanist, aware of his debt to the classical poets, reworking their metaphors and allegories to express his own unique experience. The "allegory of the theologians" and the "allegory of the poets" were often juxtaposed and blended by Dante throughout the *Comedy* even at its theological climax. For Dante was both a sensitive poet and a profound theologian. His vision was a complete one because he grasped the divine in the human and was able to express it in the most exact and profound language: poetry.

My first teacher of Dante in Rome, Professor Giovanni Fallani, introduced me to this interpenetration of poetry and theology in Dante's work. The insights of many other modern writers and poets have confirmed this. Daniel Berrigan in his incisive commentary on Dante's Purgatory, *The Discipline of the Mountain*, makes this quite clear; and Rosemary Haughton in her brilliant *The Passionate God* hits the mark exactly by describing the poetry of passionate love as the "accurate language of theology."

Modern psychology, especially the tradition of Carl Jung, has also probed the importance of symbols, images, metaphors, and allegories. Dante's basic metaphor of the journey from the dark wood, up the mountain, to the white rose has been analyzed by Jungian psychologists as an archetypal symbol of the human process of individuation, the journey toward self-discovery and self-fulfillment. This voyage often takes shape in dreams as the climbing of a mountain. The ascent, according to Jungian interpreters, is the ascent from the unconscious to a clearer vision of the ego, an elevated stage of consciousness. Many of the other symbols in the *Comedy*, such as the three circles representing God, are also explored by the Jungian school, as "symbols of transcendence," man's search for his highest goal, the full realization of the potential of the individual self.

Helen Luke in her *Dark Wood to White Rose* investigates the content and meaning of Dante's symbols in the light of Jungian psychology. Her analysis is very enlightening and helpful in understanding the depth of Dante's symbols and metaphors. Dante's metaphors thus speak to the unconscious depths of the human psyche, apart from their use in the Bible, Christian theology, and classical literature. They are universal and cross the barriers of time and cultures to express what is timeless in human experience.

While reading the *Comedy* we must be aware of its rich metaphors. A knowledge of our own dream symbols and an appreciation of the archetypal symbols that humanity has constantly used to convey transcendent meaning can help us to penetrate the depths of Dante's *Comedy*. A thorough acquaintance with biblical symbolism is also a useful, if not indispensable, key to understanding the work. The same can be said of the classical poets, the

Church Fathers, and the medieval theologians and mystics. In the *Comedy* we discover a basic symbol, such as the sun, which is common to a great variety of religious and secular traditions. Trees, flowers, birds and other animals are also among the common symbols of profound, hidden spiritual realities.

Although Dante was well versed in the technical language of the philosophers and theologians of his day—the language of Scholasticism—he deliberately chose to express his most intimate experiences of self and of God in the language of the poets: metaphor and symbol. This is also the language of the mystics, a language often mistrusted by the rigid, official interpreters of Church doctrine because of its vagueness and the danger of its misinterpretation in an heretical sense. Nonetheless it is the preferred medium for those whose profound spiritual experience cannot be expressed within the narrow framework of approved dogmas and formulas. The language of poetry will always best convey such deep religious experience because that experience is not only intellectual but also emotional and affective.

Dante's language is the language of the great mystics of the Christian tradition: St. Augustine, St. Bonaventure, St. Bernard, Richard of St. Victor, and many others. The language of the mystics is the language of love, since the very essence of mysticism is the soul's love-illumined quest for the Absolute and her union with that Absolute, Who is God.

In his letter to Can Grande, Dante mentions the mystical experiences of the prophets St. Paul, St. Augustine, and St. Bernard. He alludes to their extraordinary visions and defends his own extraordinary vision of Paradise as a revelation that God grants even to sinners. In Dante's words, "He Who makes His sun rise on the evil and on the good and sends rain on the just and the unjust (Matt. 5:45) sometimes in compassion for their conversion, sometimes in wrath for their punishment, reveals His glory in greater or less measure, as He wills, to evil-doers, be they ever so evil." Dante thus humbly confesses himself to be a sinner, but God in His compassionate mercy has given him a gift: a mystical experience. Dante has shared this gift with us. Let us gratefully accept it and journey with him through the experience of the dark forest in order to arrive at the bright vision in the white rose.

Part Two

HELL

Introduction

(*Canto* I)

T he *Comedy* begins on the brink of tragedy. Dante is lost in a dark forest. He has lost his way, encounters ferocious beasts, and is terrified by the darkness, loneliness, and imminent dangers to his life. He is describing his loss of direction and objectives: a sense of meaningless existence, a frustration over goals not reached or simply unattainable; in brief, an experience of emptiness and anguish.

Dante's opening verse suggests that it is *our* life, not just his, that is the subject of this crisis. He invites all of us, young or old, to identify with his personal crisis. Dante is sharing his individual experience, presuming that his fellow pilgrims in life have had similar experiences.

Dante's experience, like all human experiences, is complex. The dark wood with its horrible beasts is the metaphor Dante chooses to express this state of his soul. He also uses the image of a dangerous, stormy sea, another traditional metaphor suggesting imminent destruction. A third image, the desert, is blended with the other two. All these images powerfully convey the human experience of fear and dread of wild forces which forebode evil.

Scholars for centuries have investigated the meanings of the dark wood of Dante and have analyzed *ad nauseam* all the possible interpretations of that metaphor. The opinions range from his political disappointments to carnal sins with women and men. Perhaps there is some truth to all the opinions. Dante's crisis was a combination of many factors; for example, his unjust banishment from the family and city he loved; the miserable conditions of the Holy Roman Empire and the Church (specifically the failure of both Pope and Emperor to fulfill their God-given tasks of guiding the world); his wanderings from city to city as a beggar, literally at the mercy of generous patrons who supported him; his career as poet and public leader in disrepute; and his excessive love for worldly wisdom, fame, and pleasure. But Dante frankly admits that he actually "abandoned the true way," even though he was in a drowsy, semi-conscious state at the time.

But the "true way" to where? In Canto I, as he finds himself in the valley of the dark forest, he perceives a mountain lighted at the top by the rays of the sun. The sun is a metaphor for God. The earthly Paradise is at the top of the mountain. It is human happiness, peace, and joy, the place created by God for man. Dante has lost his way to the mountain. He has forsaken the right path and has been detoured by false promises of happiness. All of this is only suggested in the first canto. At the top of the mountain Beatrice will make this only too clear for Dante. The important point to notice here is that even in the dark valley Dante does not completely lose sight of the mountain lighted by the sun. There is still a faint glimmer of hope left in his soul, darkened for the most part by fear and trepidation.

Dante's crisis then is not total despair, but his faith and hope are dim and weak, almost overwhelmed by his present anguish. Who will help him? Who will come to his aid? He turns to begin the journey to the mountain, but he is confronted by three wild beasts which block the path. These beasts, a leopard, lion, and she-wolf, allegorically mean three basic sins: self-indulgence (lust), violence (pride), and greed (avarice). These external beasts are really the internal forces which detain a person from reaching the mountain. They hold a person captive of his own passions and selfish drives. They are the enemy within. We will see that they symbolize the three major divisions of Hell.

Throughout this terrifying encounter with the three beasts Dante still doesn't lose hope. He notices that it is morning and the season is spring, the season of hope:

> It was the beginning of the morning, and the sun was rising with the stars that were with it when Divine Love first set those beautiful things in motion, so that the hour of the day and the sweet season gave me cause for good hope.

> (*Canto* I, 37-41)

As Dante's mood oscillates between fear and hope, he focuses his attention on God, the Divine Love, Who set the sun and other stars in motion. It was traditionally believed that God created the universe in the springtime.

The thought of God, the Creator and Lover of all His creatures, gives Dante hope of escaping from this dreadful impasse.

Thus at the very beginning of the *Comedy* Dante points to the real source of hope in his life: God as love. That vision of God and the joy atop the mountain had almost disappeared from Dante's life. Something within him blocked the path to that mountain. That something was the grotesque and terrifying reality of moral evil, sin, which takes many forms and confronts the person who is courageous enough to look honestly at the beasts within himself.

It requires courage to admit one's powerlessness over the human tendency to sin. The hidden powers of lust, pride, and greed are indeed realities deeply rooted in us. Modern psychologists may call them by sophisticated and innocuous names, but theologians have traditionally called them the roots of all sin. They pervert our basic goodness and disrupt our wholeness. Dante and all of us have to face them fearlessly and courageously.

However, Dante at this point lacks the courage. The beasts drive him back down into the darkness of the deserted place. But someone does come to his aid. It is Virgil, the Roman poet whom Dante had loved and cherished from his childhood. Virgil as a loving father and teacher helps Dante by telling him that he must take "another road" if he is to escape the wilderness and the beasts. Virgil promises to guide Dante on this other road which will take him to Hell and Purgatory, but a "worthier soul" must lead him to the city of God.

Virgil further explains that the most insidious and malicious of the animals, the she-wolf, can be vanquished only by another animal, the greyhound. The greyhound feeds on "wisdom, love, and virtue" and will eventually chase the wolf back to Hell again, from where "envy had let her loose." Although the greyhound has been interpreted in various ways over the centuries—as a good emperor or pope or some other historical figure—I think that it is best interpreted as God's Holy Spirit, since the qualities of wisdom, love, and virtue are divine attributes and gifts. Only God can entirely conquer evil. Evil is conceived of as a wild beast let loose by Satan because he envied man. Moral evil is a horrible, destructive force unleashed by the spirit of evil itself. It is not God's creation; however, it can be overcome completely only by God's wisdom, love, and power, the actions of His Holy Spirit.

The reason that I favor this interpretation is that in Dante's time, as we have noticed, there were enthusiastic reformers who expected the dawn of a new age, the epoch of the Holy Spirit, when the Church and the Empire would be restored to goodness and wholeness. Among these reformers were the Spiritual Franciscans, who were inspired by the writings of Joachim of Fiore. Dante was apparently influenced by the Joachimists and the Spiritual Franciscans. Together with them he eagerly awaited reform and a new age of the Spirit, which would end the corruption caused by human greed.

The Persons of the Drama
(*Canto* II)

Both the first and second cantos of *Hell* are really an extended introduction to the whole *Comedy*. Like an orchestral overture, all the main themes of the entire work are sounded. The theme of the journey, its goal, its initiators and its main guides are presented to us in these two cantos. The plot of the drama is introduced, but it is still in a very nuanced, subtle form.

Dante begins the journey accompanied only by his guide, Virgil, who has explained that he will take Dante through the "eternal place where you shall hear the hopeless shrieks of the ancient spirits in pain." Dante protests that he is not worthy of such a journey: he is neither Aeneas nor St. Paul, both of whom visited the netherworld. Virgil wisely perceives that Dante's protest is nothing but cowardly fear. We see already the role of reason (Virgil) which unmasks our real motives and feelings.

To reassure Dante, Virgil then explains why he comes to Dante's aid. A beautiful, blessed lady had descended from Paradise to Limbo (where Virgil was located) with an urgent request. The lady was Beatrice. She spoke of her "friend" (*amico* in Italian, a word derived from *amore*, love) who was in trouble on the desert shore. She was afraid that he had already gone too far astray for any help. Her motive is love. She tells Virgil, "Love moved me." We recall that in the first canto God Himself is the Divine Love (*amor divino*) which first moved the stars. Beatrice is moved by that same love. The meaning and role of Beatrice are apparent: she is an incarnation of divine love. She descends from God, Who is Love, and bears that love to Dante.

Beatrice then tells the whole story of what transpired in Heaven. Mary, "the kind lady in heaven," took pity on Dante and asked St. Lucy, Dante's patron saint, to help him. Lucy in turn asked Beatrice to help the one who "so loved you that for you he abandoned the vulgar crowd." This "chain of command" might seem curious to us today, but it was (and still is) traditional Catholic faith that the saints in Heaven have concern for those on earth and by their prayer can aid them. The hierarchy of intercession is imagined here in the style of the royal courts at the time: the queen made her requests to the first lady of her entourage and the commands were passed down the line. This "courteous" manner was typical of the protocol of medieval courts.

In recent years many theologians, especially those who promote a "feminist theology," have stressed the feminine side of God. In an attempt to balance the traditional "maleness" of God and the strongly patriarchal aspect of the Christian religion, these theologians have rediscovered the many feminine images of God in the Judeo-Christian tradition. Medieval piety had such a reverence and veneration for Mary, the mother of Christ, that some historians have even inaccurately termed it "worship." However, the theologians of the time carefully distinguished "worship," which is reserved only for God, from the "veneration" which is given to Mary and a lesser form of reverence given to the Saints. But in popular piety Mary was often given an almost divine role as protector, fount of mercy, heavenly queen, and universal mother. We may say that she imaged forth that "feminine" aspect of God, Who is in fact mother, life-giver, and nurse to all His children.

The tender mercy and maternal compassion of God was usually perceived in Mary, the mother of God and queen of Heaven, who watched over her children, all the members of Christ's Church. This childlike devotion to Mary was really an unconscious perception, as Carl Jung observed, of the "other side" of a God who was too often portrayed in art and preaching as a remote, unapproachable, awesome judge. Mary, then, mirrored forth this maternal aspect of God in popular religion. That is not to say that the theologians and mystics had forgotten these aspects of God and of Jesus. Some medieval mystics, such as Julian of Norwich, often addressed Jesus as a tender mother. Hymns to Jesus by St. Thomas Aquinas, St. Bernard, and others also contain similar sentiments.

We should notice that these three ladies who come to Dante's aid are not a trinity which replaces the Blessed Trinity. They are human instruments of the one Divine Love, God. Lucy addresses Beatrice as "the true praise of God," another hint at the allegorical meaning of Beatrice. Mary's role as queen of Heaven and intercessor will be developed later in the final cantos of Paradise. All three ladies are "God-bearing" images for Dante. One of the most ancient titles for Mary in Christian tradition was the Greek word *Theotokos*, meaning "god-bearer." The English rendering, "Mother of God," is more familiar to us, but this translation could be misleading. The authentic theological meaning of it is that Mary was in fact the mother of Christ, Who is both God and man. Only He is *the* incarnation of God's love for the world. Some human beings, such as Mary, cooperated in unique ways as channels of God's incarnate love. Beatrice was such a channel for Dante.

On a psychological level we could also explore the meaning of Beatrice for Dante. The medieval cult of the woman in the courtly love poetry certainly influenced Dante. The idealized lady, the object of the troubadours' worship, was perhaps, as Jungian psychologists suggest, an unconscious symbol of the feminine aspect of every human soul, its *anima*. In Jungian psychology the *anima* (as opposed to the male form, *animus*) is the personification of all "feminine" tendencies in a man's psyche: intuitions, vague moods and feelings, capacity for love, receptivity to the irrational, and his very relation to the unconscious. Thus the idealized woman of the courtly love literature was really the personification of the man's *anima*. In one version of the Holy Grail legend the bearer of the Grail is named *Conduir-amour*, French for "guide in love matters." She was the guide for the knight.

In the *Comedy* Beatrice is Dante's guide toward the God of love. She is Dante's *anima*, the mediator to this inner world. It is through her that he comes to know himself fully as one loved by God and eventually comes to loving union with God. (The same could be said of Mary since in Dante's time the troubadour cult of the ideal woman was often "spiritualized," purified, and fused with devotion to Mary.) The three ladies in Heaven, images of God's compassionate love, have pity for Dante and take the initiative to help him out of his misery. When Virgil relates their loving concern, he convinces Dante to change his fear and cowardice into trust and assurance that the hard journey ahead is really motivated by God's love and will bring only good to him. Dante changes and the transformation is expressed in one of the most beautiful metaphors of the *Comedy*:

> As little flowers, bent down and closed by the night chill, raise themselves and open themselves on their stems as the sun brightens them, such in my fainting courage I became. And so much good courage rushed into my heart that I began to say, as one set free, "Oh how compassionate was she who helped me, and how courteous were you, so quick to obey the true words she spoke to you! By your words you have made me so eager to come with you that I have returned to my first purpose. Now let us go, for a single will is in us both; you are my leader, my master, my teacher."

> (*Canto* II, 127-140)

These words tell us that the hard journey into confrontation with the evil and murky depths of our personality must be undertaken fearlessly if we really seek healing and wholeness. But we need both a wise human guide (Virgil) whom we trust, as well as a deep faith in the abiding love and grace of God (the three ladies). God wills the painful process for our ultimate welfare, our salvation. There are no shortcuts to the top of the mountain. We must first descend into the dark abyss of ourselves where we fear to tread. This is the only way to true freedom and growth into wholeness.

The Entrance to Hell
(*Canto* III)

Through me you enter the sorrowful city; through me you enter eternal pain; through me you enter among the lost people. Justice moved my High Maker; the Divine Power made me, the Supreme Wisdom and the Primal Love. Before me no things were created, except the eternal ones, and eternal I endure. Abandon every hope, you who enter.

(*Canto* III, 1-9)

This famous inscription over Hell's gate ominously sounds a note of utter finality and despair. It sends shudders down our spine. The eternal pain of Hell! How can we reconcile this with our conception of a loving God, rich in mercy, compassion, and forgiveness? It is no easy matter since the Scriptures consistently present both His infinite mercy and his relentless justice.

Some commentators have been misled into thinking that there was a mean streak in Dante, that he was a cruel, vindictive person who vented his anger and revenge by placing certain individuals in Hell. That would be missing the point of the allegory: the individuals there are images of the sins which they deliberately chose. Neither the Scriptures nor Church dogma had ever assigned any particular human being to the eternal pain of Hell, and Dante was always faithful to these teachings. The individuals whom Dante encounters in Hell represent the sins which they chose in this life. In fact, Dante often expresses pity for those individuals, and his empathy causes him to faint at the sight of their suffering. Virgil even has to reprimand Dante for his pity, since it is really a compromise with evil and an affront to God's justice.

God's justice made Hell, as Dante states. The Trinity, described as Power (The Father), Wisdom (The Son) and Love (The Spirit), made Hell not out of spiteful revenge for Satan's rebellion but simply because the very nature of God demanded it. The meaning of these words, as Dante admits, is hard to understand. The theologians have attempted to probe the meaning of God's justice and have usually come to this understanding: God gave His intelligent creatures (angels and humans) free will; they freely chose evil, the opposite of God; in this sense God created Hell and its possibility. God's power, wisdom, and love cannot be indifferent to moral evil. Evil is a perversion and deformity of His good creation. Evil is chosen by the free will of intelligent beings.

This theological explanation might seem like "fancy footwork" which evades the real problem: the mystery of the very existence of evil. Dante was well aware of the depths of this mystery and was haunted constantly by this question of God's justice and created free will. In Paradise he will pose this question and receive some deeper insights into the mystery.

At the entrance to Hell Virgil advises Dante to leave aside all fear and cowardice. He tells him, "You will see the miserable people who have lost the good of the intellect." This expression sums up the real meaning of those in Hell: they have lost God. "The good of the intellect" is a phrase borrowed from Aristotle, who taught that "truth is the good of the intellect." For Aristotle human perfection consisted in the contemplation of truth, the "good," or object of desire, which satisfied the human quest. Although Dante uses a philosophical phrase, the content of his meaning is profoundly theological and Christian. This will be more apparent in Paradise, where the blessed souls enjoy the Beatific Vision, the full contemplation and enjoyment of God.

The words of John's Gospel, "This is eternal life: to know You, the one true God," are really the basis for Dante's Christian interpretation of Aristotle's philosophy. The human soul (the "intellect") reaches her full happiness and perfection (its "good") only when she reaches God (the "truth"). This is the inner thirst and quest—the *eros*—which stirs within all of us. It can never be satisfied by this or that object, this or that knowledge or pleasure, this or that accomplishment or achievement. The ultimate "good" is God alone.

The Christian concept of "knowing" God is not just an intellectual experience. It is a total experience of the human person who knows, loves, enjoys, and is enraptured in an ecstatic union with God. The damned, who have freely chosen "lesser goods" rather than the greatest one, have condemned themselves to the loss of that highest good. And they receive for all eternity what they have chosen in time. The torments and punishments of Hell are images of what they have elected. The lustful, for example, are eternally driven by hurricanes, an image of their choice for the irrational passions and turbulent drives of lust. These "punishments" are not so much the application of a strict "eye for an eye, tooth for a tooth" law of retaliation as the direct effects of the choice which these persons made. The *real* torment of the damned is the loss for all eternity of the highest good, which they refused to choose. They refused to believe enough, to hope enough, to love enough. They preferred instant gratification with "junk food" to the fantastic banquet prepared for them by God. This is their eternal misery.

Before entering Hell itself Virgil and Dante pass through Hell's vestibule, a dark, starless place of horrible shrieks and torments. There the wretched throng aimlessly follows a whirling, nameless banner. Virgil explains that these souls were those who refused to make a choice for good or for evil, for God or for Satan. They were for themselves. Neither Heaven nor Hell wants them: they are beneath contempt. Both God's mercy and His justice disdain them. One of their torments is to be forever stung by gadflies and wasps. They, who were never really alive, are continuously stimulated into action.

Even though Virgil tells Dante to "look and pass on," since these souls are not worthy of further attention, it is worthwhile to reflect on the meaning of this passage. I think it is a particularly relevant passage for our present age. Dante is describing through these images a possibility of the human person, and thus a possibility for each of us. It is the possibility of not becoming a responsible person: of following aimlessly the latest fad, of becoming part of a nameless crowd instead of thinking, choosing, and acting as an individual. It is the apathy and indifference spoken of in John's *Apocalypse*: "Because you are lukewarm, neither hot nor cold, I will vomit you out of my mouth."

Today many fads and trends in our country, with their emphasis on "me first," on being "comfortable," and on satisfying present desires, seem to echo this basic lack of commitment to anything or anyone outside of ourselves. It is a malaise of apathy and neutrality which apparently affects American society in general. It can be noticed in a general refusal to take stands on moral issues. Whatever satisfies a short-term need becomes acceptable, rather than what is morally right.

As a result, it is no longer a question of what is good or evil, but rather of what we are "comfortable with." As long as there are no conflicts, we become complacent with any situation, any standard or banner. We lack enthusiasm because we are simply *too* comfortable with the material things of life. The Russian author Solzhenitsyn, in a speech he once made at Harvard during a graduation ceremony, put his finger on this spiritual malaise of America and was excoriated for his criticism by "comfortable" Americans. Socrates in ancient Greece was sentenced to death because he had become a gadfly to his apathetic society. He tried to stimulate his contemporaries intellectually and morally, but the masses preferred comfort to the truth.

This moral neutrality is, in the last analysis, a refusal to love. Love is really the basic component of Dante's cosmos. It determines all Dante's classifications of vices and virtues. These neutral souls are as close to nothing as anything could be and still exist. They have removed themselves from reality by depriving themselves of love, and thus they deprived themselves of all activity. By their turning away from God they severed the bond of love which would have allowed them to be real persons with identities, choices, and actions. Instead they are eternally what they chose: an anonymous crowd of outsiders, eternal sitters on the fence.

In the vestibule of Hell Dante recognized one cowardly spirit, the man who made "the great refusal." Many of the early commentators identify this person as Pope Celestine V, the simple, saintly monk who abdicated the papacy after only five months, to be succeeded by the notorious Boniface VIII. Celestine was canonized in 1313 as St. Peter Celestine. Although this has been the most common interpretation, there are good reasons to identify this person as Pontius Pilate, the Roman governor who refused to take a stand for or against the innocent Jesus out of fear for his own career. Pilate's selfish neutrality would naturally be in Dante's mind on Good Friday, the day of his entrance into Hell, especially since other actors in the drama of Jesus' crucifixion, such as Caiaphas and Judas, are met in Hell.

The central importance of Christ's crucifixion is always before Dante's eyes throughout the *Comedy*. In Canto XII of *Hell* for example, Dante refers to the rocky debris of that circle as the result of the death of Christ on the cross, when the earth quaked and rocks were rent. Christ the victor then descended into Hell to take the spoils of his victory: those who had hoped for His coming. In spite of the resistance of Satan's devils, Christ was victorious. Dante states that at the crucifixion "the universe felt love." Christ's love for the universe collided with Satan's hatred and chaos erupted. In this context Dante alludes to an ancient philosophical theory, found in Empedocles and Aristotle, that alternating periods of universal destruction and construction were caused by the supremacy of hate or love. For Dante love, or the lack of it, is the determining factor for the condition of the cosmos.

Dante concludes Canto III with the unforgettable scene of the damned being ferried across the river Acheron (Greek for "without joy"). They are deposited on the shores of Hell. Michelangelo's rendition of this scene in his Last Judgment in the Sistine Chapel does artistic justice to Dante's poetic art of visualization. Dante compares the damned to the dead autumn leaves falling from the trees: a metaphor borrowed from Virgil, but adapted with ingenious creativity in this context. These souls "curse God, their parents, the human race, the place, time, and seed of their begetting and of their birth." They are consumed by hatred, the antithesis of love. And yet, as Dante observes, "They are eager to cross the stream, for Divine Justice so spurs them that their fear is changed to desire."

This is important to notice because Dante always stresses that Hell is the soul's choice. People in this life hate the sin which makes them miserable, but yet they are addicted to it and wallow in it. A person's constant addiction to sin can create a hell even in this life so that the bitterness and misery of it become somehow sweet and desirable. Constant habit blinds and hardens a person to the alternative of a better choice. The many little choices for sin gradually harden the heart so that repentance becomes virtually impossible. Choice for evil becomes almost irrevocable. And *that* is hell! Notice how the damned blame God, their parents, and the whole human race. Sin results in a resentful isolation from all community.

The Value of Humanism
(*Canto* IV)

We now come to the first circle of Hell, Limbo. Here there are no cries of torment, but there are sighs of sadness. They come from the virtuous pagans born before the coming of Christ. Since they did not receive baptism, the gateway of faith, they are "suspended" in this Limbo, a word meaning "border" or "hem." Their sadness, however, has no element of torment. Virgil, who is one of them, describes their fate in this way: "without hope we live on in desire."

Many of the great theological issues, discussed from the beginning of Christianity down to our times, are touched upon here: the salvation of non-Christians, God's justice and love, the value of humanism, the universal dimension of Christ's death and resurrection. All these theological themes are interrelated, and were also among the topics discussed recently at the Second Vatican Council. Currently they continue to be discussed by the Christian laity as well as by theologians.

God's will for the salvation of all humanity is certainly an axiom in the Scriptures. But the Scriptures also speak explicitly of the necessity of faith and baptism— formal membership in the Church, the Body of Christ. What should we think then of the fate of those born before Christ and the eternal destiny of the millions born after Him who have never heard of His salvation? Various solutions have been offered over the centuries, including the theologians' invention of Limbo. Scripture nowhere explicitly mentions any such state. Limbo would be a "border state" between Heaven and Hell: neither the torment of Hell nor the joy of Paradise. Dante echoes this conception when he describes these souls as "neither sad nor joyful." Those who practiced the "natural" virtues and led good lives are thus not condemned to eternal pain. That would be contrary to God's justice.

But what about God's love? Is it so limited that only a few are saved? In this canto Dante raises this question. Virgil answers that shortly after his arrival in Limbo a

Mighty One, crowned with the sign of victory, came there and rescued the shades of our first Parent, Abel his son, Noah, Abraham, Moses, David, Israel, Rachel and many others. He took them and made them blessed, but before these "no human souls were saved." Christ's death and victorious descent into Hell were thus the turning point in the history of human salvation. This was the accepted theology of the Church: salvation was granted only to those who had faith, whether it was in His future coming (the faith of the Chosen People in the Messiah) or in His coming as an event of the past (the faith of the Church).

Some of the greatest theologians, such as St. Thomas Aquinas, were not so simplistic or rigid in their interpretation of this generally accepted Church teaching. Thomas wrote of "implicit faith" and "baptism of desire," thus opening the door of salvation to the pagans who had not received the explicit revelation of Christ but who lived according to their conscience and implicitly believed in a God "who would deliver mankind in whatever way was pleasing to Him." The teaching of the Second Vatican Council on this subject seems to echo Thomas's broad interpretation, which respects the necessity of faith as well as God's loving will for human salvation.

Dante himself elsewhere in his *Comedy* mentions some pagans who nonetheless escaped Limbo and reached salvation in Paradise. We might wonder why Virgil, his revered teacher and guide, is left in Limbo together with all the great poets, philosophers, scientists and other noble pagans of the ancient world. The answer seems to lie in Dante's allegory. Virgil and the other souls are images of "something else." That "something else" here is Humanism, the pursuit of human knowledge and natural virtue.

Classical Humanism was dear to Dante's heart. He never lost his high respect for it. Evidence of that is given here: these "great spirits" dwell in a "noble castle" (Fame), surrounded by seven circles of walls (the seven Liberal Arts). There is light here—the only circle in Hell where there is any light—and verdant meadows. The noble spirits have not lost the beauty of nature or the light of this world. They enjoy a "natural" light, the light of human reason, and a "natural" state of peace, but not the ecstatic joy of Paradise. Dante's concept of justice is seen once again: they receive only what they freely chose—a purely natural bliss.

Dante is making an important statement here. Traditional theology uses the terms "natural and supernatural" or "nature and grace" to express this distinction between the limitations of human potential and the boundless extent of the divine gifts of faith, hope, and charity. Humanism is good, worthy, and valid; but it is limited. It may be optimistic about a certain happiness in this world, but it lacks the transcendent dimension of rapture and ecstasy which only faith, hope, and love can give because they are "supernatural" gifts from God.

In the last twenty years in America there has been a proliferation of movements which promise happiness and fulfillment. Most of them are based on the premise of humanism: fulfillment can be found within our own human potential. We can "make it happen." We are creators of our own destiny and happiness. Although there is some truth in this, sooner or later the limitations and inadequacies of human nature have to be faced and accepted. It is no wonder then that during the same period in our country there has been a quest for "something more"—the transcendent. There was a rush to Oriental gurus in the sixties and a rush to join religious cults in the seventies and eighties—evidence of the human desire for the Absolute, for the Mystery. Likewise, the modern infatuation with the supernatural in horror movies and science fiction is a symptom of this basic human craving.

Dante understood that humanism with all its praiseworthy intentions and achievements does not fully satisfy the human heart, which remains restless until it rests in God.

Dante's evaluation of humanism is in the spirit of many of the Church Fathers, such as Justin Martyr in the second century and Clement of Alexandria in the third. They valued the treasures of classical literature and philosophy as a "preparation for the Gospel." Classical literature in their view served as the "sacred scripture" of the pagans. They recognized the inherent truth in the Greek philosophers and mythmakers, and rather than reject the humanistic heritage as a work of Satan, as some unenlightened Christian teachers had done, they gave a positive evaluation of it.

St. Thomas Aquinas in the medieval period also promoted the study of Greek philosophy, especially Aristotle, and as a result was often the target of criticism and even condemnation for his allegiance to such pagan culture. Thomas, of course, was enamored of the truth and was convinced that truth was found in Aristotle as well as in other pagan philosophers. Dante was certainly a follower of Thomas in this respect. In Canto IV he pays tribute to Aristotle as "the master of those who know," and salutes with the highest respect Socrates, Plato, and other philosophers, poets, and scientists of the Greek, Latin, and Arabic cultures.

Dante's attitude toward classical humanism can clearly be seen in his conception of Virgil throughout the *Comedy*. Virgil is the image or metaphor for the whole classical tradition of humanism. The interaction between

Virgil and Beatrice in Canto II is a good illustration of
the relationship between human nature (Virgil) and divine grace (Beatrice). Beatrice addresses Virgil in the most
"courteous" terms and requests that he help her in the
work of Dante's salvation. She also promises to praise
Virgil often before the throne of God. But Dante adds that
it is "through her alone that the human race rises beyond
all that is contained within this world."

Virgil in Canto IV mentions that the fame of the
great pagans "gains *grace* in heaven, which thus advances
them." Clearly Dante conceives of nature and grace in
complementary terms: they are not hostile to one another
as evil is to good. On the contrary, human nature has an
openness, receptivity, and potentiality for enhancement
from God's grace. Divine grace does not annihilate the
basic, created grace of nature, the fundamental goodness
of God's creation. Rather, it brings to completion a work
already good in itself. Divine grace (Beatrice) descends
from God's love in order to elevate humanity to divine
status and dignity: the "supernatural" order, in theological terms.

Many modern theologians prefer to avoid this traditional terminology of "natural" and "supernatural" since
it obscures the primordial grace of created nature, which
is fundamentally an emanation of God's nature. Besides,
this terminology often tends to view the natural in a
negative light, as if nature were so tainted by sin that it
is radically corrupt and God-forsaken. Dante's stance
avoids this negative appraisal of human nature. His beautiful description of the creation of the human soul in
Canto XVI of *Purgatory* shows a positive approach to this
good creation of God and its orientation toward good:

> The simple little soul, after the fashion of a lit-
> tle child weeping and laughing, comes forth
> from God's hands, Who fondly loves her even

before she exists. She knows nothing except
that, proceeding from a joyous Maker, she turns
eagerly to what delights her.

(Purgatory XVI, 85-90)

This may be the most poetic, and theologically the
most exact, description of the creation of the human soul
that there is. Dante describes creation as an act of love
from the Creator and Lover of humanity. The human
soul, generated from a joyous Lover, is naturally oriented
toward the love of whatever is good.

The Carnal Sinners
(Canto V)

It is not surprising that the beginning of Hell proper,
its first circle, focuses on the theme of love. According to
Dante, the human soul was created by a loving God and
was oriented toward God as the only object which fully
satisfies that need to love. The souls in Hell, of course,
have lost their way toward God, but they are still driven
by love. It is now a tormented and frustrated love, since
they have lost the "Good" of the intellect, God. But yet
this God-given love, which the human spirit still somehow retains in Hell, has a certain ill-fated vitality which
moves us readers, as well as Dante the traveler, to sympathy and pity. The proverb, "Love makes the world go
round," contains a profound truth. Even in Dante's *Hell*,
love is the prime motivation of souls, but it is a love gone
astray and directed to the wrong objects: the ego or some
selfish appetite.

At first reading, the tragedy of Paolo and Francesca,
so dramatically and artfully told by Dante in this canto,
moves us to sympathy for their fate. Dante, the dramatic

poet and storyteller, is perhaps at his best here. Certainly this canto is among the best known and has inspired many painters and musicians. The pathos of Francesca's story, the sweet, majestic poetry of her words on love, her delicate courtesy toward Dante—all combine to make an unforgettable impression on us. Who can forget Francesca's sad words, "There is no greater sorrow than to recall, in misery, the happy time"? Tchaikovsky's symphonic poem *Francesca da Rimini* translated those words into a hauntingly beautiful melody.

We are easily led into feeling sorry for Francesca. After all, it was only one act of adultery and the poor creature just did not have time to repent. Her cruel husband caught them in *flagrante delicto* and mercilessly killed them. She literally seduces us into taking her side by blaming her cruel husband, the passion of the moment, or even God himself, Whose justice relegates her and Paolo to eternal torment.

In many respects the person of Francesca is an image of Dante's own soul as it was in his youth. We must keep in mind that Dante often represents his inner life objectively in a feminine figure that moved him. Francesca is Dante's *anima*, the feminine side of his psyche, the capacity to love in a personal way. Francesca's words on love are in fact reminiscent of Dante's early love poems, his *canzoni*, which celebrated love in the spirit of the troubadours. Dante then was in love with love itself.

The Romantics of the nineteenth century often cited these words of Francesca's as a sublime expression of the beauty, power, and eternity of love, which, in her words, "excuses no loved one from loving . . . which still does not leave me. Love led us to one death." But the Romantics were seduced into a superficial interpretation of this canto. It is easy to be seduced by the sentiments of Francesca. As Virgil wrote in his *Aeneid*, "The descent to

Avernus (Hell) is easy." Francesca shows the way into Hell. She is a seductive embodiment of the love that constitutes the life of the "lost people" in Hell.

Dante the poet, not Dante the traveler in the literal story, is also the theologian and teacher who is both subtly and explicitly making quite another statement here. Francesca and Paolo are in Hell. Their love led them not only to a violent death in the world but to the second and far worse death, eternal separation from the Highest Good. True, the two lovers are eternally together—what they chose in the earthly life—but their passion is now eternally unrequited. They are driven like birds by a furious whirlwind (the image of their passion), which never gives them rest. The place is completely dark and the hellish storm is like a sea in tempest. Why? These carnal sinners "subjected their reason to lust," as Dante learned at the beginning of this canto.

Their love for another was not the pure love that is God, even though Dante uses the same word *amor* to describe both kinds of love. Just as the English word "love" is capable of many meanings, so too in Italian, *amor* is often used to mean both *eros* and *agape*. As we have noted already, eros generally denotes the basic, natural desire for good, a drive which may settle for almost any object perceived as good. It is spontaneous and blind; it needs the guidance of reason and good judgment; and to reach its perfection it needs the further aid of God's grace, which transforms it into agape, a pure, out-going love which does not seek self-fulfillment as its primary goal.

Only God is agape itself, as the New Testament states, but God communicates and shares Himself with His creatures by freely bestowing that divine capacity on them. It would be interesting to compare St. Paul's famous hymn to love (agape) in his first letter to the Corinthians with Francesca's hymn to love (eros). They are complete opposites.

Francesca's love was an eros that went astray and degenerated into lust. It was self-indulgence rather than real love. It forgot responsibilities to others (in this case, to her husband and to Paolo's wife) and slipped into an immature kind of love, so characteristic of the many "affairs" portrayed today in modern television soap operas and cheap supermarket romances. It was actually a romance (a love novel) which she and Paolo were reading together: the Arthurian legend of Lancelot's adulterous affair with Guinevere.

The romance served as a seducer (a "pandar," or "pimp" in modern slang), which was the occasion, or go-between, in their sin of adultery. One thing led to another as they read about Lancelot kissing his lover. Dante discreetly avoids any details which might excite our prurient interests. But it is important to notice that Francesca blames her fate on the book, on its author, on her husband, and even on God. She says, "If the King of the Universe *were* our friend. . . ." She also takes spiteful delight that her husband is in a section of the lowest pit of Hell, *Caina*, the place for those who betrayed their own kin. Francesca thus cannot repent. Instead, she is frozen in self-pity, irresponsibility, blasphemy and revenge. She is the image of self-indulgence which cannot forgive or ask for forgiveness. She is selfishness personified.

Dante, the traveler and listener to her story, was moved to pity and fainted. He fell "as a dead body falls." We must remember that Dante the pilgrim is only at the beginning of his enlightening journey through Hell. At this point he is very sensitive and sympathetic toward the fate of the damned. He has much to learn. His human compassion has to come to terms with the ugly reality, the deformity and monstrous malice of sin. He has to learn that in order to see reality as it is there must be sound judgment and no compromise with evil.

The Right Attitude toward Evil
(*Canto* VIII)

Feelings and emotions can cloud one's clear vision of the truth unless reason and conscience guide them. Dante the wayfarer soon learns this truth. In Canto VIII Dante and Virgil are crossing a muddy marsh, the river Styx, in order to reach lower Hell. Dante speaks with one of the damned souls who is covered with mud. It is Filippo Argenti, a man of violent wrath and arrogance whom Dante had known in Florence. Filippo asks for sympathy, but Dante answers: "Remain in your weeping and sorrow, accursed spirit, for I know you, even if you are all filthy." As Filippo tries to get into the boat with them, Virgil casts him off, saying, "Away there with the other dogs." Then Virgil embraces Dante, kisses him and says, "Indignant soul, blessed is she who bore you!"

We recognize these last words, "blessed is she who bore you," as words from the Gospel (Luke 11:27) which a woman addressed to Christ. Thus Dante is beginning to acquire a Christ-like attitude: righteous indignation, an intolerance for evil, and sound moral judgment. Christ is being reborn in Dante's soul.

Today we may find Dante and Virgil's words and actions too harsh and repressive, lacking in understanding and acceptance. That is because today's society has been saturated by a pseudocompassion (the "I'm O.K.; you're O.K." psychology) which often tolerates the most outrageous behavior in both children and adults. But righteous indignation—the right kind of anger—is really motivated by love. True love cannot tolerate evil for the loved one.

Righteous indignation, then, is the right and Christ-like attitude toward evil. We recall Christ's harsh words about Herod: he called him "that fox" to express His anger at Herod's rapacious exploitation of his own people. We can also recall his wrath directed at the money changers in the temple who had perverted the house of prayer into a den of thieves.

The Journey of Ulysses
(*Canto* XXVI)

This canto ranks with Canto V as one of the most memorable in Dante's *Hell*. In many ways both cantos are similar: both contain pathetic stories of personal tragedy and both are autobiographical, describing Dante's youthful life and his middle period, respectively. Francesca's narrative in Canto V corresponds to Dante's passionate pursuit of love itself, and Ulysses' account here describes Dante's passionate quest of "knowledge and virtue."

Dante's version of the Ulysses story is his own invention. It has some elements in common with Homer's original work; but for Dante, Ulysses is not so much a Greek hero as a despicable deceiver of the Trojans, the ancestors of the Italians. Dante places Ulysses in this circle of the evil counselors. Ulysses, like Francesca, is eternally joined to his accomplice. They had deceived the Trojans together and are now united in a single flame, symbol of the human tongue, which uses intelligent speech to deceive and defraud others. Dante, however, focuses mainly on Ulysses' final journey and especially his manner of death.

The sources for Dante's version of Ulysses' death are unknown. It has been suggested that Dante knew of a voyage in 1291 of the Vivaldi brothers, who sailed from Genoa past Gibraltar, never to be heard of again. The brothers were seeking a route to India, a venture undertaken by another Genoese navigator two hundred years later, Christopher Columbus. Some interpreters of Dante's Ulysses have seen in this story a harbinger of the Renaissance, the age of discovery and thirst for new horizons. This was a common interpretation in the nineteenth century, the age of scientific progress. Alfred Lord Tennyson in his beautiful poem *Ulysses* seems to echo this interpretation. His Ulysses bears many resemblances to Dante's version.

Dante, however, is more concerned with the inner journey, the journey of the soul. The soul of Ulysses in quest of the unknown is a mirror of Dante's soul in his middle years. Dante then was consumed with a desire to know. His unfinished work, the *Convivio*, was testimony to that insatiable thirst, that cult of human reason, that unrestricted confidence in human potential. Ulysses confesses in his tragic tale that nothing "could conquer in me the longing I had to gain experience of the world, and of human vice and worth." Not even fondness for his son, devotion to his aged father, nor the love due Penelope, which should have made her happy, could restrain Ulysses from setting out on his journey of exploration.

Ulysses in his small boat with a few companions sailed past the pillars of Hercules (Gibraltar), considered then to be the limits of the hemisphere. He refused to deny himself in this life—poetically called "the brief vigil of our senses"—the experience of a world beyond. He exhorted his men not to live like brute animals but to follow virtue and knowledge, the ideals of the Greek humanistic culture. They came in sight of a mountain which filled them with joy, but the joy was soon turned to grief. A tempest arose and closed the sea over them, "as it pleased Another."

Beneath Ulysses' story we can detect the basic theme of human eros. In Francesca's case it was the eros of human affections and physical desires. Ulysses' eros is intellectual: he seeks intellectual fulfillment of his desire to know everything. In both cases, however, eros became egotism and self-worship, which drove them to abandon all commitments, except love of self.

Ulysses, like Francesca, ignores the realities of time and place, his own responsibilities, and commitments of fidelity to his wife and family. It is truly a "mad flight," as Dante so succinctly describes his journey. Ulysses insanely and impatiently abandons everyone and everything in order to "do his own thing." He loses awareness of reality and its attendant duties. He lacks the patience to wait for God's good time and in his tragic end is forced to recognize that God's will is really what determines reality.

Ulysses' journey seems to parallel the story of Adam and Eve's sin in the earthly paradise. They refused to wait on God's will. Their desire "to have it all" at once led them to grasp at the tree in the garden. That tree of "the knowledge of good and evil" symbolized the experience of and the power over everything—the divine prerogative. Their impatience with their condition as limited creatures led them to desire to be like God with unlimited power and knowledge. This pride and arrogance is called "original sin" by theologians. It is obviously at the root of all sin.

This is, in essence, the tragedy of Ulysses. He tried to reach the mountain of joy and human fulfillment by a "mad flight." The journey there requires patience and acceptance of God's will for us now, trust in His goodness to give us what we need as we travel along the way. There are simply no shortcuts to perfection. There are no easy, instant "trips" to perfect joy.

Dante in his own life had to learn that his "mad pursuit" of knowledge was like Ulysses' "mad flight." The rational soul has its limits and must be content with steady progress and, at times, setbacks, and failures. Dante left his *Convivio* unfinished because he realized that he was on the wrong track, pursuing an unattainable goal with only a small, frail vehicle, his rational soul. His soul was certainly driven by love for knowledge, but this good eros did not take into account the limitations of human nature itself, his place and time in the world, and all the contingencies of reality which are somehow— who knows why?—willed by God.

This same fundamental eros for the "total experience" seems to be deeply rooted in many aspects of modern life. It manifests itself, for example, in the insane abuse of drugs and alcohol that is supposed to lead to a "trip," an "escape," an "ultimate experience" but instead often leads to tragedy. This eros is deep within ourselves and good in itself, but we can deceive ourselves into thinking that the ultimate is possible here without waiting patiently for God's time and plan. That original sin is always somehow lurking in the shadows of our souls. Only faith— the work of Beatrice— can shed full light into those dark corners and tell us to wait and trust.

The Lowest Pit of Evil
(*Cantos* XXXII-XXXIV)

Thus far we have not given much attention to the basic metaphor of descent. Dante's downward journey through Hell takes him from one degree of evil to a lower one in a continuous descent through the perverted "hierarchy" of evil. The circles of Hell represent sins in their order of gravity. The least serious sins are seen in the beginning and gradually an increasing malice is perceived in the succeeding circles. Thus, sins of incontinence, like Francesca's, are the most natural, the easiest to commit, and the least harmful. But then come the sins of violence, then fraud (Ulysses' sin) and at the very bottom of Hell the gravest of all, treachery.

Dante does not invent this classification of sins. He generally accepts the classifications found in the moral philosophy of Aristotle and in the Christian theology of St. Augustine and St. Thomas Aquinas. We might add that his personal experience of evil—either suffered or personally committed—confirmed these categories. In any case, the outline of the gravity of sin is a rather accurate picture of the possibility of the human soul's descent into evil.

The word "gravity" is a key word here since it unlocks the metaphorical meaning of the journey downward. Gravity in the physical sense of an object's seeking its proper place was a metaphor used by St. Augustine in his doctrine on love. Dante was very much influenced by Augustine in this concept of love. According to Augustine, love is the inner weight that drives the soul to seek its proper place. We recognize Augustine's dependence here on Plato's concept of eros. Augustine believed that our rest is our proper place. All things naturally seek their place of rest: fire ascends and a stone moves downward. Augustine used this metaphor to describe the soul's upward movement to God, its peace in the heavenly city, Jerusalem. (The name of the city means "vision of peace.") Augustine addressed God in these words:

> In Your gift we rest; then we enjoy You. Our rest is Your gift, our life's place. Love lifts us up to it, and Your good spirit raises our lowliness from the gates of death. In Your good will lies our peace . . . My weight is my love; wherever I am carried it is my love that carries me there. By Your gift we are set on fire and carried upward . . . because we go upward to the peace of Jerusalem.

> (*Confessions*, XIII, 9)

The gift, of course, is God's gift of *agape* (pure love), which directs human eros upward. Otherwise eros could fall into sin and descend like dead weight or a heavy stone. This metaphor of the weight of sin, its heaviness or "gravity" is really the symbol that shapes the whole structure of *Hell*. The degrees of sin are the gradations of an increasing weight. Dante alludes to this in Canto XXXII: "And as we were going toward the center to which all weight collects. . . ." He is referring to the center of the earth, the bottom of the pit, where the center of evil, Satan, is found.

The bottom of the pit is described in these last three cantos of *Hell*. It is a frozen lake named Cocytus, which holds the souls of the treacherous. Treachery in Dante's conception was the worst kind of fraud. According to Dante, fraud is a sin which "kills the bond of love that nature makes." But treachery is worse, since it destroys the intimate bond of mutual trust which holds together members of a family, a city, a political party, or a benefactor and the recipient of such kindness. Treachery undermines love and perverts it into a destructive force against the very person who loved and trusted us.

That is why the treacherous are relegated to the very bottom of Hell, the hollow center of earth, to where all heaviness—all evil and sins—converge. And here the downward movement reaches its dead end. Here the souls who refused to follow their innate capacity to love and thus to move upward have now lost all movement, since they are eternally frozen in the immobility of Cocytus. Cocytus, the frozen lake, is a powerful image since it represents so well the cold paralysis of the refusal to love. It is the image of total frustration. The human soul, created to love and interact, is here forever immobilized and confined. There is no community or love here: only isolated souls in solitary confinement.

In these last cantos Dante witnesses the most hideous and grisly scenes of Hell. In the section of Cocytus called Caina (named after Cain, who killed his brother) are located the traitors to their own kin. Dante notices two shades who are so pressed together that the hair of their heads is intertwined. They raise their faces to Dante, who notices that "their eyes, which were moist before only within, welled up with tears which ran down over the lips and the frost bound each to each and locked them even tighter." But nonetheless they continue to butt each other like two billy goats. These two on earth were brothers, sons of a wealthy count, who fought over their father's inheritance and killed each other. They are eternally consumed with rage and hatred.

While Dante and Virgil move along over the icy lake, Dante's curiosity about the identity of one of the traitors prompts him to ask the soul to identify himself. The traitor refuses. Dante tries to entice him by offering him the fame of being mentioned in his travel notes. (Dante obviously had no false modesty about the greatness of his own work.) Still the soul refuses. Dante then seizes him by the hair of his nape, but the traitor persists in his refusal to reveal his name. Dante twists his hair and even pulls out some tufts. Meanwhile another traitor nearby betrays the identity of the poor soul. Once a traitor, always a traitor! This is the inexorable law of Hell: one remains forever what he has chosen.

It is significant that Dante the traveler inflicts punishment here. Dante has now almost completely identified himself with the will of God, which is perfect justice. At the beginning of the journey, when he was overcome by the sad fate of Francesca, he identified with Francesca's suffering and could not accept her fate. Now he is capable of accepting the will of God and even participates actively in the penalties of the damned.

We now come to the most gruesome and horrible scene in the *Hell*: Count Ugolino eternally gnawing at the skull of Archbishop Ruggieri. At the end of Canto XXXII Dante had noticed "two frozen in one hole so close that the head of the one was a hood for the other; and as bread is chewed out of hunger, so the upper one sank his teeth into the other where the brain joins with the nape." Canto XXXIII begins with these chilling words: "From his savage meal the sinner raised his mouth, wiping it on the hair of the head he had laid waste behind." The count is willing to tell his story, which will be a renewal of his desperate grief, provided that the telling of it will produce "infamy to the traitor whom I gnaw." He then speaks and weeps at the same time.

The resemblances to the encounter with Francesca and Paolo are many: like the two lovers, Ugolino and Ruggieri are together for all eternity; like Francesca in the first circle, Ugolino is the spokesman for both and renews his grief while he weeps and tells the story of his death. The differences, however, are quite obvious: Francesca and Paolo had been moved by passionate love; whereas, the count and the archbishop had both been traitors to their own countrymen (the Pisans) and the archbishop, whom the count had trusted, betrayed his one-time companion in treachery. His horrible means of betrayal is "the desperate grief" which is renewed in the count's narrative. The archbishop had locked the count and his four sons in a tower and starved them to death!

The count tells this grim story of his last days in one of the most moving narratives of the entire *Comedy*. We are touched by the father's compassionate love for his children, as he watches them die of hunger before his eyes. His despair and frustration are heartrending. The children, on seeing their father's grief, even offer their own flesh for his nourishment. This only aggravates his helplessness. We readers are at the point of tears when Dante suddenly ends the narrative. The count immediately returns to his ghastly meal and "seizes the miserable skull with his teeth, which were as strong as a dog's on a bone."

This abrupt shift back to his eternal "activity" chills our feelings of sympathy into the rude awakening that this man is basically driven by cruelty and hatred. He is beyond repentance. His natural love for his children had been real in his earthly life and still persists in eternity, but that naturally good love has been rendered futile by his all-consuming passion of hatred and revenge. The

basic sin of treachery has taken over his soul and he now
remains frozen in that sin.

Dante is telling us that sin is the only real death to
the soul: it is the ice which immobilizes and dehuman-
izes us. It frustrates even the natural love which remains
forever unfulfilled within us. Dante's characters in Hell,
such as the count, speak and move; but their speech and
movement are motivated by evil purposes. In this case
the count is willing to add to his own suffering only if it
will cause more harm for the archbishop. The signs of
life, movement, and the rational activity of human speech
are perverted from expressions of love into expressions of
hatred. The count's perverted desire for the infamy of the
archbishop has only boomeranged. Readers over the centuries remember this canto as the story of Count Ugolino. *His* inhuman cruelty is immortalized!

The end of the journey into evil reaches the very
source of evil, Satan himself. According to Scripture,
Satan is at the bottom of all evil. He is the unknown
source of the mystery. The Judeo-Christian mythology of
evil has personified evil in this figure. By mythology, I
mean the representation in persons, stories, and symbols
of realities that simply cannot be expressed otherwise.
This "personal" aspect of evil is represented in the figure
of Satan, or Lucifer, the most beautiful of God's creatures, who by rebellion became the most ugly and even
an ugly copy, or parody, of the divine beauty and majesty.
He was not content with his condition as creature and
rebelled against his Creator. To continue his rebellion he
envies the goodness and beauty of human creatures. His
envy moves him to unleash his fierce beasts (the animals
in Canto I) on humanity.

Dante now arrives at this source of evil, but does not
encounter any majestic figure or heroic person, as we find

in Milton's poem. Instead, the "impersonal" aspect of Satan is stressed. All the aspects of Satan are negative: denials of some positive goodness. This was the traditional conception of evil: non-existence or negation of some good.

The Christian philosophers, such as Augustine and Thomas, had followed the classical Greeks in this notion of evil. Being in itself was good, beautiful, and true. Non-being, or evil, was the lack of these inherent qualities. The eternal mystery of evil consists precisely in this: how can something that is harmful, ugly, and false even have existence? Augustine and Thomas pointed to the freedom of the created will which is capable of choosing the opposite of good. The reason for the choice? One's selfish pride: the desire to be God. This seems to be the partial answer to the mystery, as the Scriptures and Christian tradition interpret it.

Dante's vision of Satan in many ways corresponds to his vision of God in the last canto of *Paradise*. Satan becomes in a perverse way what he desired to be: the Triune God. He is represented with three faces on one head, since he "aped" the divine Trinity. His four wings are not beautiful with plumes but ugly like a bat's. The flapping of the wings is not the creative, life-giving activity which God's love produces, but rather it generates the ice and immobility of the frozen lake. Satan's action is a counterproductive action which eternally freezes and produces paralysis—the very opposite of God's warm love which created all things in the springtime. Here it is eternal winter—no light, no joy, no life, no good movement.

In order to understand more fully Dante's representation of Satan it is helpful to be familiar with an ancient art form of the Church: the icon. The icon, or sacred image, was still in Dante's time the traditional way of expressing eternal truths in art, although a more natural, realistic style of painting, influenced by Cimabue and Giotto, was becoming fashionable in Dante's Florence. The icon had its own rigid style of symbolizing the eternal world of God and His saints. The solid gold background, for example, represented the eternity of God's kingdom. The highlights of light on the faces of Christ, the saints, and the angels depicted the divine glory which emanated from them. The colors also had symbolic value.

Today we are exposed to a glut of images across the television screen and to a display of flashy commercial advertisements almost everywhere. We may have become desensitized to the profound meanings of color and pattern. We may have lost the art of looking at a picture and perceiving its meaning. Because of our overexposure to superficial images we may have become somewhat unmoved and obtuse to the significance of meaningful images.

Dante's picture of Satan is similar to the icons of the Middle Ages which were very Byzantine in style. The Byzantine influence on Italian art can still be appreciated in the paintings and mosaics of the churches in Florence, Venice, and Ravenna. Dante no doubt often feasted his eyes and his faith on those magnificent works of liturgical art. His use of color reveals an acute sensitivity to the art of the icons. Here in his picture of Satan he paints the colors of Satan's three faces: a flaming red, a sickly yellow, and black. These colors are a distorted symbolism for the three persons of the Trinity.

The red of Satan's face is the crimson of anger and hatred, the counterpart of divine love, the Holy Spirit. The anemic yellow is the symbol of weakness, the opposite of divine power, the Father; and the black is ignorance, the contrary of divine wisdom and light, the Son of God. These colors subtly bring to mind the inscription on Hell's entrance, where the three divine persons were described as power, wisdom, and love. The inscription there, like the icon here, suggests a final, eternal mystery. There is something inexplicable and impersonal about both the image of Satan's face and the inscription over Hell's gate. They both point to the ultimate mystery: the nature of God and its complete opposite, the nature of evil.

At the sight of the whole picture of Satan's kingdom, the City of Dis, its icy lake, the gigantic size and hideous features of Satan, Dante is completely at a loss for words. The sight overwhelms him as he gasps, "I did not die and did not remain alive." Dante at this point confesses that his words will fail to relate adequately the experience of it all. Dante the traveler and Dante the writer coincide here in this unspeakable experience, just as they will coincide at the ineffable vision of God in the last canto of *Paradise*. This vision of Satan, the depth of evil, corresponds to the beatific vision, the acme of goodness. Both experiences are indescribable because both mysteries transcend the human capacity to grasp them.

Dante then notices that Satan is masticating three persons: Brutus, Cassius, and Judas Iscariot. Brutus and Cassius had betrayed their friend, Julius Caesar, the symbol of the Roman Empire, which was believed to have been ordained by God for human happiness on earth. Judas betrayed his friend Jesus, whose Church was in God's plan to be the guide to man's eternal happiness. To Dante, these traitors had thus tried to frustrate God's will for human happiness and peace. Now here they are eternally betrayed by Satan. The irony of it all! And Satan himself, the first rebel against God, actually accomplishes God's will and justice by punishing the traitors to the empire and the Church. The poetic justice is perfect.

We should notice also that Brutus and Cassius had betrayed the personal love and trust of their friend and benefactor, Caesar, because in their minds they were serving a great cause: the good of the state. They were probably also motivated by their own ambition and envy. Judas, too, motivated by avarice and self-aggrandizement, was an idealist who envisioned "the good of the many" as the result of his betrayal of Jesus. All three traitors served a principle or ideal to which they sacrificed a beloved friend.

The image of Satan eternally devouring these three men brings us face-to-face with the essence of evil: the betrayal of personal love between individuals. The ultimate treachery to God and to the universe is to prefer some principle or selfish pursuit to mature love of the other. Dante has come to see that evil is the refusal to love in a selfless way. This eerie truth was found at the dark center of the earth. But Dante's arrival at the dead center is only the beginning of his long journey. He now follows his guide, Virgil, out of the pit in order to come forth "to look once again upon the stars."

Thus Dante concludes *Hell* with the words "the stars," which also conclude each of the other two canticles: *Purgatory* and *Paradise*. The stars indicate the ultimate goal of the journey: Heaven. Dante has gone through Hell, looked closely at evil in all its deformities, and is now prepared to ascend. It is time for rising and rebirth. It is now Easter morning.

PURGATORY

Introduction

During his journey through Hell Dante was not spared the shocking and chilling vision of what sin actually is: a gradual and total distortion of the human person; a paralysis of the wonderful, innate power to love; and a transformation from being an image of God into the image of savage beasts and ultimately into the image of Satan. But *Hell* was only an introduction to a long process; it was the first leg of a long journey. The experience there was indeed a suffering—a pathos—which enlightened and shocked Dante into exploring the brutal reality of sin and its relentless devastation to the beauty of the human person. The passage through Hell was indeed a profound learning experience, beneficial and necessary for Dante.

However, mere knowledge of evil and its effects is not enough. Such knowledge could discourage and lead one to the despair of the damned, who remain victims of their own bondage to sin; who escape from evil by hopelessly plunging themselves further into it. But there is a way out—not by the short escape route of acquiescence or apathy but rather by the long, slow process of purgation or conversion. That is the meaning of the second leg of Dante's journey, *Purgatory*.

This is a new kind of journey: a journey of further enlightenment, but more importantly, a journey of change and conversion. Purgatory, literally the center of the *Comedy*, is the experience of Dante's spiritual development and growth. The main action of the drama of Dante's soul takes place here.

Purgatory is the gradual ascent and growth of Dante's spirit (and our spirit with him) in the recovery of its true nature and its authentic self. During this climb of the mountain of Purgatory Virgil is still Dante's guide. His role, however, gradually changes and he yields to other guides. At first Virgil is the all-knowing father, then he becomes the teacher, and finally, the philosopher. His lessons are really paraphrases of Aristotle's moral philosophy, as interpreted by the Christian philosopher and theologian St. Thomas Aquinas. Once Dante has learned and become "free and whole," Virgil relinquishes his role as Dante's guide to Matelda, who in turn prepares Dante for another lady, Beatrice.

The climb up the mountain is really a journey to Beatrice. Virgil with all his wisdom and virtue is still a metaphor of human eros, that upward thrust toward personal fulfillment, which nonetheless never reaches the final goal without the aid of another power, the descending love—agape—of God, represented by Beatrice.

The following outline, based on Francis Ferguson's more detailed scheme in his book *Dante*, may be helpful for our understanding of Dante's itinerary:

The Plan of Purgatory

Cantos	The Pilgrim's Literal Journey: Times and Places	Dante's Guides	The Allegorical Journey: Soul's Movement into God
I-IX	First day: shore and base of mountain	Virgil as father	Soul's movement outside of self; awareness, but inability to grow
IX-XIX	Second day: gateway and first four terraces—pride, envy, anger, sloth	Virgil as teacher, philosopher	Soul's movement into self: repentance of seven capital sins—forms of perverted love; love is put into order—directed to proper goals, in proper measure
XIX-XXVII	Third day: last three terraces— avarice, gluttony, lust	Virgil and Statius	
XXVII-XXXIII	Fourth day: Earthly Paradise	Matelda and Beatrice	Soul's purified *eros* meets *agape*.

This outline appears to fall short of the final goal of the journey: above and beyond one's self. And so it does. The fourth day begins with the sunrise, which symbolizes Beatrice's arrival. She then gradually unfolds her splendor, which reaches its zenith at noon. It is only then that the real journey "above" begins, as Dante ascends with Beatrice to guide him into Paradise. Beatrice's appearance in the Earthly Paradise is still only an allegory. If we recall the four levels of meaning which Dante outlined in his letter to Can Grande, we know that the allegorical meaning yields to the *anagogical*, that is, the meaning in terms of the "above". The last leg of the journey is the entrance "into God" in Paradise proper.

Beatrice is God's revelation and love, allegorically expressed in *earthly* signs and symbols. These signs and symbols are expressed in the faith and sacraments of the Church, which are only shadows that point to the reality above. These shadows, adapted to our present, earthly state, are valuable gifts which communicate to us a share in the reality which they signify; but they are only the beginning of the journey above ourselves. They introduce us here and now to the end which is reached only in God. Beatrice, then, is the true revelation of God, but not the full revelation, since—like faith—she reveals partially; she can only lead Dante into the full vision in Paradise.

It is only at the top of the mountain in the divine forest of the Earthly Paradise that Beatrice appears. She then continues the process begun by Virgil because only she (Divine Wisdom, Revelation, and Love) can guide Dante to the final goal, the Heavenly Paradise. Only in that Paradise does the human journey come to its completion, because, according to Dante, to become complete the human person must be enlightened by the vision of God and be at one with Him in perfect love.

Purgatory corresponds in many ways to the pattern found in St. Bonaventure's famous work, *The Journey of the Soul into God*. It is a journey in three stages, based on the soul's movement of love: first, the movement "outside of self"; then the movement "into one's self"; and finally the move "above one's self." This journey in Dante's plan takes place during the three days and three nights on the mountain. On the fourth day Dante arrives at the summit in the divine forest where the climax of the drama unfolds: his encounter with Beatrice.

The very concept of Purgatory may seem outmoded and strange to readers in the closing decades of the twentieth century. One simply doesn't hear much today, even in Catholic circles, about the "souls in Purgatory." The official teaching on Purgatory has for centuries been a typical "Roman Catholic" belief, generally rejected by Protestants as well as by Orthodox Christians. Although there is little (if any) *explicit* evidence in the Scriptures about Purgatory, still a belief in such a preliminary purification process was deemed necessary for entering eternal glory. This concept developed during the earliest period of the Church, during the time of the Council of Florence in 1439 and still later during the Council of Trent from 1545 to 1563. In the fifteenth and sixteenth centuries it was a much disputed question between Roman Catholics and Eastern Orthodox Christians at Florence and between Catholic and Protestant Christians at Trent. But it is beyond our scope to trace here a history of the Church's doctrine on Purgatory.

Some modern theologians recently have attempted to sift through the historical and cultural conditions of the Church's teaching on Purgatory in order to arrive at the essence of the belief. In their "revisions" and speculations they have generally agreed on these basic insights:

baptized Christians usually do not complete in their lifetime the full process of baptism—the complete death to sin and resurrection to a completely new life in Christ; therefore most Christians die before becoming perfected in love and in some way must complete this process. This completion or purification takes place after physical death, out of time and space, as we understand these categories.

In fact some theologians today understand "the experience of death" as that very purification process. It is not so much a second chance for repentance as a first chance for those who have already repented and accepted God's loving forgiveness to see in a truly objective way (in the light of God's light) how little they have loved and responded to His love.

Purgatory, then, would be something like being exposed with all one's failures at love (essentially our sins) to the full light and heat of God's love. It would be a painful experience; but yet something we desire since the encounter with the all-knowing and all-loving God would so enlighten and attract us that we would see perhaps for the first time what our sin is and we would want to pass through the purifying fire of God's love. This concept of death and purgatory as a kind of second baptism—or, more precisely, a completion of the first—can be found also in some of the early Church Fathers.

It was for this reason that the early martyrs (even those who were only catechumens and, therefore, not yet formally baptized) were so venerated by the Church. They imitated Christ's love perfectly; their love of God had reached perfection before their death. Their martyrdom was "the witness" to their perfect love, and so the Church considered them as having entered immediately and directly into God's glory and eternal blessedness.

The story of St. Stephen in the Acts of the Apostles is a good example.

The Church from the earliest time also considered our present state as pilgrims to be a continuous conversion process, or purgatory, since we must always be aware of our failures and sins and repent of them. This is dying to the "old self." At the same time we must turn to the loving God and wait for His grace to change. This is being born again to the "new self." We know that throughout this process we are constantly being loved and saved by Him. Our conversion—our dying and rising with Christ—is always somewhat defective during our earthly pilgrimage since we do not become completely transformed into Christ. The conversion process remains a work of ours, but it is simultaneously a work of God's grace.

A baffling mystery? Of course. Some of the Church Fathers called it "synergy": the working together (cooperation) of God's grace and human effort. Dante expressed this in his *Purgatory* through the poetic metaphors of day and night. During daytime the souls on the mountain pursue their work of purifying themselves under the light of God's grace, the sun; but during the night they must wait and rest. Even then, however, God continues to work by speaking through dreams, which instruct and enlighten the souls. The entire process, both day and night, is enlightenment, instruction, change, and growth. The interplay of God's activity and human effort is really the action of Purgatory.

Contrary to some misinterpretations of Dante and of Catholic theology in general, salvation is not earned by humans. Human freedom cooperates with God's healing power, but salvation is primarily a work of God. Perhaps the analogy of the surgeon's work in the healing process can help clarify this mystery. The surgeon uses all his skill and instruments, but the healing itself is God's work. The Scriptures provide another analogy in the farmer's work. It is the farmer who plants and irrigates, but it is God who makes the crops grow.

This interaction of God's activity and human effort is clearly the basic pattern of each of the seven terraces of the mountain of Purgatory. God's work is represented by the angels, traditionally the agents who carry out His will. Initially the guardian at Purgatory's gate marks seven "P's" on Dante's forehead. The letters symbolize the seven capital sins (*peccati* in Italian) or wounds (*piaghe*) of sin, which must be eradicated. Then there is an angel on each of the seven terraces, who, after the human efforts, pronounces one of the beatitudes (Christ's words from His sermon on the mount) over Dante, erases a "P" from his forehead, and directs him upward. The words of the angel are really Christ's words. His word is always effective, powerful, and healing.

The human activity also follows a basic pattern: examples of the virtue to be acquired—the positive aspect—are first presented to the soul. This is a kind of "whip" which drives the souls to repent of their failure in that virtue—the negative aspect. Their repentance is their learning how they lack that virtue. This discipline (the original meaning of the word is "learning") takes the form of some appropriate physical pain. For example, the proud are bowed down under huge, heavy stones. Then examples of the opposite sin are presented. This is the "rein" or "bit" which restrains the souls until they have suffered enough. This psychological tension between the whip and the rein is the suffering which the souls patiently endure.

Thus they grow to love the virtue and hate the sin. But since they are painfully aware that the roots or

wounds of that sin are still within them, they must wait
and repent until they *know* that they are finally freed of
it. They can then breathe a sigh of relief, await the angel
for their dismissal, and then move upwards. The entire
process is a gradual freedom from the grip of the capital
sins.

Contrary to another misunderstanding of Purgatory,
the souls are not "punished" for their sins. For that matter the souls in Hell are not punished for their sins: they
endure the penalty of sin itself, the sin they freely chose.
The damned even take on the nature of that sin for all
eternity. But in Purgatory the souls "re-suffer" for a time
the nature of their sin; they don't become it. They purge
themselves and rid themselves of it. In Purgatory there is
time, just as there is time here on earth. Where there is
time there is also hope for repentance, growth, and salvation. In timeless Hell there is no growth or change. The
souls there are eternally locked into their sin because
they refused to wait and suffer through repentance here
on earth. They preferred to wallow in their sin and as a
result they became completely possessed and victimized
by it.

Thus, the state of patient suffering—Purgatory—is
not "some place out there" where souls are tormented by
fire for their sins. That is a popular misconception which
still lingers in the Catholic imagination. Without alter-
ing the Church's teaching on the reality of a state of Purgatory, Dante poetically creates a mountain-island at the
other side of the earth's sphere, at the very opposite pole
of Jerusalem, the place of Jesus' death and resurrection.
He thus establishes a direct correspondence to the paschal mystery of Christ.

It is there on the mountain that the souls, saved by
God's grace, through baptism and repentance, continue

their baptism into Christ. Jesus Himself referred to His death and resurrection as a baptism. But Dante is more interested in his own and *our* need to continue the baptismal process of growth and development. That is his conception of the spiritual life: growing awareness, continuous change, movement and development into the perfect image of God, Christ.

We will notice that on the first terrace the first example of humility is Mary at the Annunciation. She humbly received God's word through the angel and conceived Christ. The Christian pilgrim at the very beginning must also become humble in order that Christ may be born again in his own soul. Mary, the perfect disciple, who learned humility, is an example of this virtue, as well as of all the virtues, for the Christian pilgrim.

Dante always understands the virtues and their opposite sins in terms of love. The sins purged on the mountain are either perverted love, defective love, or excessive love. On the first three terraces pride, envy, and wrath are cleansed. These vices are basically a love of self perverted into hatred and contempt for one's neighbor. Then comes sloth, a failure to love any good object in proper measure. The final three sins, avarice, gluttony and lust, are forms of excessive love for objects which are good in themselves but which had become primary and not secondary goods. They had not been subordinated to the soul's first object, God alone. Thus the work of purgation is, in essence, the "re-ordering" of love: putting our loves in their proper order. Today we might call the process a "reorganization of our priorities."

The virtues, on the other hand, are actions of "well-ordered" love, directed to their proper objects in proper measure. We detect here echoes of Aristotle's teaching on the nature of virtue as a *via media* between two extremes, but Dante's conception is basically biblical, rooted in the teaching of the Hebrew prophets and Jesus on the proper hierarchy of love for God, self, neighbor, and other "objects."

Many Church Fathers and theologians developed this basic concept of morality as the dynamics of love. St. Augustine, whose influence on Dante was enormous, had developed this theme throughout his writings and life. His famous dictum, "Love and do what you want," although sometimes misconstrued when taken out of context, was his succinct summary of the essence of Christian living. In the context he explained that "love" meant love directed and ordered to its proper objects. His saying highlights the wonderful freedom and carefree exhuberance of authentic love.

The Beginning of the Journey
(*Cantos* I-III)

Dante begins his *Purgatory* with the metaphor of a navigation over the sea. The sea of Hell had been a very "cruel sea." He has escaped from that sea and that "dead, blind air." He now invites his readers to join him on a different voyage to a different shore. It is the shore seen, but not reached by Ulysses: the island-mountain which rises out of the sea.

The time is early morning of Easter Sunday. Dante's description of the pre-dawn light and the colors of the sky is perhaps one of the most beautiful examples of lyrical nature poetry in world literature. It is also a skillful use of "pathetic fallacy," that poetic figure of speech which ascribes human traits or feelings (pathos) to inanimate nature. Canto 1 abounds in pathetic fallacies: the sea of Hell had been "cruel"; the "sweet," sapphire-blue sky now delights Dante's eyes and heart; the planet Venus "gives strength for love and makes the whole east laugh"; the heavens "rejoice" in the four stars. The sea "playfully" shimmers as the morning light dances on its surface.

There is an exact correspondence between the mood of nature and the feelings they arouse in Dante's soul: delight, stirrings of love, joy, and play. Dante is like a child looking about with wonder and innocence at these new sights and sounds. The contrast is so striking after the darkness and gloom, the filth and shrieks of Hell. Here there is only gentle light, sweet colors, serenity, peace, and life—an atmosphere that reminds one of the pure, delicate colors of a Fra Angelico painting or the simple, natural backgrounds of a Giotto painting.

The opening scene, besides being a seascape and a landscape, is really a mindscape: a picture of Dante's spirit which, after such a horrible experience, is being refreshed and gently caressed by the simple beauty of nature. Since it is Easter morning, the memory of Jesus newly risen from the realm of death was in Dante's mind. Dante too—like Christ—is awakening to the gentle light after the harsh darkness; to soft, pastel colors after the gloomy, sickly colors of Hell; to serenity after chaos.

In this totally new atmosphere of delicate beauty Dante focuses on the planet Venus, "the fair planet that strengthens for love and makes the whole east laugh." He thus subtly hints at the source of all this gladness: love. Dante the pilgrim, however, is still filled with his child-like mood of delicate feelings and perceptions. On this first day he does not yet understand the arduous climb that will purify love. At this stage we the readers also relax with Dante and feel with him the lyrical delight of this new atmosphere.

Dante and Virgil then meet a venerable old man. It is the famous Cato of Utica, statesman and Stoic philosopher, who committed suicide in 46 B.C. rather than fall into the hands of the conqueror Julius Caesar, whom he considered to be a tyrant. Many philosophers of the ancient world esteemed Cato as a champion of liberty, and Dante also praised him in many of his works as one "who chose to pass out of life as a free man rather than without liberty to abide in life."

Cato, whose face is illuminated by the four stars (the four natural virtues of Stoic morality: prudence, justice, fortitude, and temperance), is the warden of Ante-Purgatory. In the allegorical meaning he symbolizes moral freedom, which will be the goal of Dante's ascent of the mountain. Cato seems stern and harsh, perhaps because the moral virtues of Stoicism are rigid when compared with the gentle grace of divine love. Nonetheless, Virgil appeals to Cato's love for his wife, Marcia, in order to gain his favor and entrance to Purgatory.

This appeal is significant since in his *Convivio* Dante had presented Cato as an allegory of God's merciful love. Cato's wife, Marcia, had abandoned him to marry a close friend of his, but later asked to be taken back as his wife. He accepted her back. For this act of forgiveness Dante considered Cato a symbol of God's mercy which welcomes back the repentant sinner. All of this background is relevant to the meaning of Cato and of Purgatory itself. Purgatory is the experience of acquiring true freedom from the bonds of sin, but it is also the experience of growing in divine love.

It is also noteworthy that Cato, who had cast off his mortal flesh by suicide, will be clothed in radiance "at the great day." This is no doubt an allusion to the resurrection of the body and a rather clear, though implicit, indication that Cato, a pagan and a suicide, will be glorified and saved on the last day. Perhaps this is a reference to Jesus' parable of the last judgment which teaches that the one criterion at the last day will be the same for all: our love and compassion for others. Love never ceases to be the secret law of Dante's universe. It is also the foundation and wellspring of his spirituality.

Cato directs Virgil to gird Dante with a reed and to wash his face of the filth from Hell, since Dante's eyes had been obscured by its mist and dirt. They must go down to the very base of the island, where the waves beat gently against the shore and reeds grow in the soft mud. These gestures are deeply symbolic and filled with many biblical overtones. The descent to the lowest level, the girding with the reed, and washing, all suggest baptism, humility, and new birth.

The reed—a tall grass—was a biblical symbol for humility, that frank honesty about our human frailty. Putting on the reed (the acquisition of humility) is an absolute condition—the *sine qua non*—for any progress of the spirit. The reed also recalls the reed used by the soldiers to humiliate Jesus in His suffering, still another allusion to His passion and death. Dante is amazed that after Virgil plucked the reed, another one sprang up miraculously. This signifies humility as the lowly source of wonderful leaps in spiritual growth and life.

Dante's eyes must be washed clean from the filth of Hell. This at first might seem superfluous, but Dante is telling us that the constant viewing of evil has its insidious "after-effects." It taints our moral vision and renders us somewhat insensitive to the real malice of evil. For example, the constant portrayal of violent crime, adultery, and other irresponsible sexual activity on our television screens today does have bad effects on our psyche. Our sensitivities to its real nature are gradually dulled to a non-reflective acceptance and tolerance of it all. Ironically, American society is shocked by the alarming increase in violent crime, adultery, divorce, illegitimate children, epidemics of venereal disease, vandalism and so on. But the point is that images of evil subtly sow the seeds of evil actions. Jesus taught this same truth: one must purify one's eyes in order to render the whole person pure.

Dante the poet continues in Canto II the lyrical mood of Canto I by describing the white and red cheeks of "beautiful Dawn," which turn to orange in old age: a remarkably exact description of the changing colors of a calm, beautiful sunrise. Dante and Virgil walk along the deserted shore like "people pondering the road, who go in heart but stay in body." This mood of delay is suddenly interrupted by a sight coming across the water. It is God's angel ferrying across the souls of the saved to the shores of Purgatory. This crossing corresponds in its joy and hope to the sorrow and despair of Charon's ferry service across the Acheron in Hell. The souls here are all singing joyfully together Psalm 114, an ancient Passover song, which began with the words, "In the exodus of Israel from Egypt. . . . " The ancient Jews sang this song to commemorate that marvelous act of God's love: the deliverance of His people from the slavery of Egypt. The allegorical meaning of the Exodus theme which dominates *Purgatory* was described by Dante in a letter to Can Grande. The Exodus of the Israelites from a state of slavery to freedom in the Promised Land is an allegory of the soul's liberation from sin to new life and happiness.

The people of Israel throughout their Exodus—the crossing of the sea of reeds, the journey through the desert, the crossing of the Jordan—were pilgrims going toward the Promised Land. The Exodus was a pilgrimage toward a sacred goal. Here in Purgatory the top of the mountain, the Earthly Paradise, is the goal of the new pilgrims, Dante and Virgil. In fact, here for the first time in the *Comedy* Dante refers to himself as a pilgrim. When the newly arrived souls ask directions to the summit of the mountain Virgil responds, "We are pilgrims even as you are."

Dante then recognizes one of the souls whom he tries in vain to embrace. It is Casella, an old friend from his youth in Florence. Casella, a musician, had put some of Dante's love poems to music. Dante asks Casella to sing one of those love songs "which used to calm my every desire." Casella honors the request and begins to sing Dante's celebrated "Love that discourses in my mind." Dante, Virgil, and the other souls begin to relax and enjoy the sweet music until Cato abruptly reprimands them all for their delay and negligence of the real task at hand: "to strip themselves of the filth of sin in order to appear before God." They all scatter like doves who, having been peacefully feeding in the fields, are suddenly frightened away by the arrival of something dangerous.

This apparently simple episode is fraught with meaning. It is certainly not a condemnation of the pleasures of music. It is, however, a rejection of the inordinate passions of Dante's youth and middle age: his passion for the poetry of love and his passion for philosophy, both manifestations of human *eros*. In his *Convivio* Dante wrote a commentary on this favorite love poem of his and interpreted it to mean that he was then in love with Lady Philosophy.

Here in this episode the delay to listen to this sweet music of love and philosophy means that these former pursuits of Dante had prevented him from loving his heavenly lady, Beatrice, who personified Divine Wisdom. Thus, this present delay is a recall of his former delay or, more exactly, his detour from the right path. He had neglected his real lady after her death and had let the sweetness of poetry and philosophy calm all his desires. Cato's harsh words dispel Dante's dreamy mood and awaken him to the real purpose of his presence in Purgatory. The metaphor of the innocent, unsuspecting doves suggests that the pilgrim Dante is still at the childlike level of emotions and not yet at the level of serious reflection, understanding, and action.

As Canto III opens, Virgil feels the sting of remorse for their negligent delay and Dante begins to grow fearful and apprehensive about the unknown venture ahead of them. Virgil, like a caring father, reassures him that he will not abandon him. They then encounter a group of souls who slowly move along like timid sheep. The sheep imagery is no doubt related to the Exodus theme since God's people were often described as a flock of sheep in the Scriptures. God led the children of Israel out of Egypt and went before them in the desert journey as a shepherd leading his sheep. Dante refers to these souls as a "happy (or fortunate) flock," since they are among the saved.

These sheep, however, had been astray on earth because they had lived for some time outside the fold of the Church. They had been excommunicated and had delayed their repentance until the last moment. Now they must delay their climb of the mountain. They are now also like sheep without a shepherd since at their head is Manfred, a notorious and colorful king in the Middle Ages, who had been excommunicated by two popes for his political and military resistance to the temporal power of the papacy. Manfred was a Ghibelline, the illegitimate son of the even more notorious Frederick II, king of Sicily, whom Dante has encountered in Hell among the Epicureans. Manfred was very much like his father in his fondness for carnal pleasures, his patronage of the arts, his tolerance of the Saracens, and his contempt for the clergy-ridden Church.

Manfred tells the story of his final repentance, death, and the dishonorable burial given his body by the local bishop of Cosenza. Like the poignant stories told in *Hell*, this is one of the monumental narratives in *Purgatory*. In the most moving terms Manfred recounts how he abandoned himself to God's mercy:

> Horrible were my sins, but the Infinite Goodness has such wide arms that he receives all who turn to Him. If Cosenza's shepherd, who was sent by Pope Clement to hunt me down, had read well that page in God, the bones of my body would still be at the bridge near Benevento, under the stone monument. Now the rain washes them and the wind stirs them, beyond the Kingdom near the Verde [Green] River, where he transported them with tapers quenched. By curse of theirs no one is so lost that the Eternal Love cannot return, so long as hope keeps its flower of green.

(*Purgatory* III, 121-135)

What a profound and elegant statement of God's merciful love! The biblical imagery shines through the words: God as the one good shepherd and the loving father, prodigal in His mercy, Who embraces the returning son with open arms. There is also a play on the Italian word *faccia*, which could mean a human face or a page of a book. The bishop of Cosenza had not read well both faces of God (His justice *and* His mercy), which are presented in the pages of the Scriptures. Dante, the master poet and theologian, mixes both metaphors with supreme art and theological acumen.

The thorny question of the Church's excommunication and its validity for all eternity is treated here in the light of God's infinite and eternal love. According to the theologians whom Dante had studied (St. Augustine, St. Thomas Aquinas, and St. Bonaventure), ecclesiastical excommunication cannot deprive the sinner of communion with God as long as that person is willing to repent and turn to Him wih hope and trust in His mercy. Communion, as Bonaventure explained, is of three kinds: corporal, spiritual, and sacramental. An excommunicated Christian may be physically separated from full membership in the Church and from Holy Communion (the sacrament), but yet remain spiritually in communion with God and the Church. St. Thomas stressed that love (charity) is the bond uniting all members of the Church. "It is the life of the soul just as the soul is the life of the body. It has no end for 'charity never fails' (I Cor. 13:8). . . ."

Dante was no rebel against the divinely-given authority of the Church, nor was he a fanatical reformer who rejected the necessity and relevance of the institutional Church. He adopted the sound teaching of the approved theologians of the Church. Their theology flowed primarily from their intense love of God. The mystery of God as love is the root of all theological reflection and thus holds the primacy over decisions of popes and bishops who may err in their personal judgments and applications of Church discipline. We are not discussing here their role as official teachers of Church dogmas on faith and morals.

Dante's metaphorical use of the color green is very effective in this canto. The handsome, flamboyant Manfred always dressed in green. The pope and bishop had his body dumped on the bank of the river Verde (green), but Manfred had died full of hope, symbolized by the color green. While there is still life (green signifies life), a soul may turn to the God of eternal love, Who is always faithful to the repentant sinner. His love eternally gives hope and life.

At the end of Canto III Manfred requests Dante to seek his good daughter, Constance, once he has returned to the world. Manfred wants his daughter to pray for him so that his long sentence of delay be shortened. Such a concept of prayer may appear at first naïve and even cheap and self-serving; but it is based on a deep, faith-inspired understanding of the efficacy of prayer. It is essentially rooted in the concept of the Church as the communion of saints: those members still in their pilgrimage on earth are united to those who have died by the bond of charity, the eternal life of the Church. Thus by prayer all the members express their love for one another. Dante often alludes to this love-inspired action of prayer throughout *Purgatory*. In Canto VI Dante explains that God's justice is not abased by prayer, that "fire of love," which accomplishes in a moment what normally takes a long time. Authentic prayer, then, is an expression of that love which pleases God because that is His very nature: love.

The Pilgrimage of Love
(*Canto* VIII)

It is now the evening of the first day on the island of Purgatory. Dante and Virgil have wandered aimlessly at the base of the mountain in the Ante-Purgatory. They still do not know the right way to the summit. Their mood becomes nostalgic as Dante and Virgil recall their native cities in Italy, Florence and Mantua, respectively. In their wanderings they meet another troubador poet, Sordello, who, like Virgil, is also from Mantua.

The themes of wandering, pilgrimage, and homesickness become the focus of Canto VIII, in which Dante describes the novice pilgrim pierced with love and homesickness. He apparently is describing himself. Dante captures this sense of sadness and homesickness in the opening verses of Canto VIII by describing the hour of sunset. He heightens this melancholic mood by describing also the sound of the evening church bells.

> It was now the hour that turns back the longing of the navigators and melts their hearts as they recall the day they bid farewell to their sweet friends. This hour pierces the new pilgrim with love, as he hears from afar a bell that seems to mourn the dying day.
>
> I then began to annul my sense of hearing and gaze on one of the souls who rose and signaled with his hand to be heard. He joined and lifted both palms, fixing his eyes on the East, as if he said to God, "I care for nothing else." The hymn, *Te Lucis ante* came from his lips so devoutly and with such sweet notes that it rapt me from myself. Then the rest joined him sweetly and devoutly through the whole hymn, keeping their eyes fixed on the heavenly wheels.
>
> Reader, here sharpen well your eyes to the truth, for the veil is now indeed so thin that certainly to pass within is easy.
>
> (*Purgatory* VIII, 1-21)

This passage was a favorite of the romantics of the nineteenth century, and the English romantic poet Lord Byron gave a beautiful rendition of this passage in his *Don Juan*. The romantics, however, appreciated only partially this profound passage. They understood the pathos and nostalgia as poetically conveyed here, but they failed to follow Dante's recommendation to the reader. Dante, the poet and theologian, is moving us to a new level of perception while Dante, the pilgrim, is simultaneously breaking through into this new stage of awareness. Dante is telling us a religious truth which pierces the "thin veil" of poetry.

To tell this truth Dante skillfully employs several metaphors, such as the hour of sunset, the *Angelus* bell, the sea journey, and the liturgical hymn. He recreates the pensive mood of sunset when sea travelers turn their thoughts to the loved ones they have left behind. This homesickness (*nostalgia*) is the dominant mood. But he introduces several religious symbols to suggest quite another homesickness: the yearning of the Christian pilgrim for his true homeland, God Himself. It is primarily religious nostalgia that Dante has in mind: the soul's longing for God. In the preceding canto he established this mood of religious nostalgia with the souls' chanting of the Vesper hymn, *Salve Regina*, which describes Christians as "exiled children of Eve in the valley of tears." The souls in Purgatory are still exiled from their true home.

Now another liturgical hymn, the *Te Lucis ante Terminum*, gives a further clue to Dante's intention. The opening words of the hymn mean: "Before the ending of the day, Creator of the world we pray. . . ." It is an ancient Latin hymn sung at the end of the Church's liturgical day. This hymn, sung by all the souls, has the rapturous effect of lifting Dante out of himself. The gestures and prayer of one of the souls become Dante's own experience: "God, I care for nothing else but you!" This is what Dante means when he describes himself as the new pilgrim who is pierced (literally, "stung") by love as he hears the church bell and hymn and sees the sunset and souls in prayer. Prayer is truly the "heart in pilgrimage," that incisive expression in George Herbert's poem, *Prayer*. Prayer is the hopeful cry of thirst from the pilgrim's heart.

This canto focuses sharply on the dominant theme of love which pervades the realm of Purgatory. All the souls are pilgrims pierced with love for their true homeland. We recall Augustine's doctrine on love as a weight which moves objects to their proper resting place. This love we perceive as the driving force within us, but it is really God within us drawing us to Himself.

Dante represents this activity of God by the arrival of angels winging through the evening air. Their robes and wings are green, "like newborn leaves." Once again the theological virtue of hope is symbolized. Hope is *the* mood of Purgatory. It is essentially the childlike trust we place in God for our future well-being and salvation. By hope we are born again like new, translucent leaves on a spring tree. The green angels have descended as an expression of God's provident love. They will show the pilgrims the right path to the mountain and protect the pilgrims on the way. Their first task is to frighten away the serpent, the ancient symbol of evil, who lurks in the valley as it grows dark.

After this episode one of the souls addresses Dante in these words: "May the light that leads you on high find in your will as much wax as is needed for the climb up to the enamelled summit." This is another of Dante's felicitous metaphors which expresses that unfathomable mystery of the cooperation between God's grace and human effort. God's grace is the flame of light which leads upwards, but the wax of the candle—the willingness of the human soul to be consumed by divine love and light—

is also needed. When the two work together the ascent to the green summit will be accomplished.

The First Dream
(*Canto* IX)

After a busy first day in the Ante-Purgatory, Dante, the weary pilgrim, lies in the green, flowering valley and gazes on the rising moon. He feels the "heaviness of Adam" (the weakness of human flesh) yielding to sleep. Sleep overcomes him as a kind of death which he obediently accepts; but it will free him for a new kind of life, the inner life of spiritual growth which will take place in his dream.

Dreams in ancient cultures, including the Judeo-Christian tradition, have often played an important role as vehicles of a deeper and clearer perception of truths which were not perceived or articulated during one's conscious experiences. Dreams, the inner world of the unconscious, were believed to be revelatory and prophetic of mysterious truths. Often dreams were interpreted as being God's activity of enlightening the human soul and communicating His secret wisdom and His otherwise unknown will. Dreams were the voice of God in the unconscious life: an analogy to the human conscience, God's voice in the conscious, moral life.

Dante was no stranger to these ancient intuitions. He believed that the dreams nearest the morning are the most true and prophetic. Modern dream psychology, especially in the Jungian tradition, has confirmed many of Dante's beliefs and interpretations. Modern psychology has made us aware of the often neglected importance of dreams as sources of self-knowledge, spiritual enlightenment, and growth. Dante's three dreams in Purgatory describe what is happening to him at the deepest levels of his psyche. They express through images his own spiritual journey into himself and into God.

Dante dreams that a fierce, golden eagle swoops down from the sky, snatches him away, and carries him up to a scorching fire. He compares himself to the mythical Ganymede, the beautiful Trojan youth who was kidnapped by Jove's eagle and carried up to Jove, who had fallen in love with this handsome boy. Upon awaking, Dante finds himself transported above the valley to the entrance of Purgatory proper. Virgil explains to the frightened Dante that while he was sleeping a lady named Lucia carried him in her arms up to this level on the mountain.

To understand the meaning of the dream we have to explore the symbolic content of the pagan and Christian images which Dante employs here and elsewhere in the *Comedy*. The eagle, for example, suggests several different, yet interrelated meanings: it represents the Roman Empire, God's justice, and baptismal regeneration. The association with Ganymede recalls the myth of the Trojan youth who was taken up by Jove's eagle to be his cup-bearer on Mount Olympus. All of these different symbols, like pieces of a mosaic, fit together into a coherent and meaningful picture. Dante often refers to Heaven, the City of God, as Rome, where "Christ is a Roman." The Trojans were the legendary ancestors of the Romans.

Putting these pieces together we begin to see the allegory: God (represented by Jove) loves Dante (represented by Ganymede) so much that He snatches him from the earth to be His cup-bearer in Heaven (Mount Olympus). The cup has many associations in Christian faith: Christ referred to His suffering and death as "drinking the cup";

the cup of the Eucharist holds the wine, His precious blood; the Holy Grail in medieval legends symbolized the human quest for God.

In medieval symbolism the eagle, like the phoenix, was believed to regenerate its youthfulness in fire and thus became a symbol of baptism. The eagle, symbol also of God's justice and Rome, carries Dante to the purifying fire (God's justice) on high (Rome, the eternal city of God). Allegorically, the human soul, loved by God for its original beauty, must undergo a cleansing or purgatorial fire—the baptism of fire—before entrance into the heavenly city.

The contrast between the fierce eagle of the dream and the gentle St. Lucy of the literal story is an allegory of the rigorous justice of God and the tender love of God. Lucy, we recall, was one of the ladies who represents God's love, grace, and light. God's justice and His love are really the two faces of the one God, as Manfred told us earlier. The allegory tells us that His justice, which frightens, is only a function of His love which carries us to Him. Fire has this twofold symbolism: purification and love.

The dream's truth is a profound intuition into our lovableness in God's eyes. He is enamored of us because He first sees our inherent beauty and worth. Moved by His passionate love (portrayed in the myth of Jove's love for Ganymede), He takes us to Himself by way of a purifying fire since He wants us free and pure of the evil which has contaminated us and rendered us less beautiful. The suffering of death to sin is the cup which we must bear. Baptism, the process of purifying suffering, is the purgatorial fire which the soul must endure. This "baptism" is a fire which burns off the selfish neuroses and perversions of human eros. In brief, Purgatory is the transformation of our eros (with all its impurities) into perfect love, agape.

Dante is fearful of that fire—the scorching sensation in the dream woke him up—just as we all fear moral change and the loss of what we think is good and even necessary for us. But Dante learned to "let go and let God" carry him. A childlike passivity and dependence, a yielding to His powerful, yet gentle, grace is necessary for our transformation into wholeness and arrival at the summit. Dante's first dream reveals all these gems of spiritual wisdom to us. This dream brings Dante (and us) to a new breakthrough in consciousness. We become more aware of our own goodness and beauty, of God's love for us, and of our need to undergo change fearlessly and confidently. We grow in the conviction that we are being carried by God's maternal arms through the bitter experience of purgation, which is willed by Him only because He loves us and wills our perfect beauty, wholeness, and fulfillment.

Pride

(*Cantos* X-XII)

After the dream and the flight upwards Dante and Virgil encounter the guardian angel seated at the top step of the entrance to Purgatory proper. The three steps leading up to the angel are each of a different color: pure white, blue-black, and flaming red. The white step is polished like a mirror; the black one is cracked and rough; the red step is like bright blood. These colors and textures symbolize the prerequisites for entrance into Purgatory: honesty, contrition and love. They are the dispositions necessary for a "good confession" in the Catholic tradition. The love here is the ardent desire to make amends for the harm caused by sin. It is an essential component of true contrition, which literally means "brokenness." We are broken in spirit when we honestly admit that we have broken the bonds of love. We want to repair them. That's what the sacrament of penance is about: candid self-revelation (the mirror image), painful sorrow (the brokenness), and ardent love (the blood).

The angel holds the two keys entrusted to him by St. Peter. The gold one symbolizes God's forgiveness and the silver one the Church's sacramental ministry. Both are needed to open the gate, but the gold key is far more precious. After the angel inscribes the seven "P's" on Dante's forehead, he opens the gates. A wonderful, joyful song erupts: the *Te Deum Laudamus* ("We praise Thee, O God"). This liturgical hymn was believed to have flowed spontaneously from the lips of St. Ambrose and St. Augustine when Augustine was finally baptized after his very wayward life. It is certainly appropriate here as Dante enters Purgatory, his baptismal process.

Once inside the gate Dante sees images carved in stone which portray examples of humility. The sculpture shows Mary humbly receiving from the angel "the decree of peace, which for many years had been wept for." This decree opened heaven from its long ban. Mary's humble words, "Behold the handmaid of the Lord," turned "the key to open the Supreme Love." God, the Supreme Love, became man at that moment in Mary. The long-awaited peace between God and man took flesh through Mary's humility. Christ, our Peace, the supreme expression of God's love, came to us through His humble servant Mary.

Mary's humility reveals the true nature of humility: honest, joyful acknowledgement of one's condition as servant in relationship to God. This is the very opposite of pride, which pretends to make the creature the Creator. Just as pride refused to accept the condition of creaturehood, so humility willingly recognizes the truth of the creature's complete dependence on God. Humility is not self-debasement or servile fear; it is rather the creature's honesty and respect for the truth.

Humility empties the soul of delusions of grandeur, of a sick egocentrism; and transforms the soul into a virgin soul, an empty womb, which awaits the powerful activity of God's love. When we are filled with self-love there is no room for God's love to operate within us. If Christ is to be born within us, we have to be empty, receptive, and open. The humble Christian—like Mary—becomes the womb for God. The empty desert of our souls is then transformed into a garden flowing with living water and blossoming into flowers and life-giving fruit.

When Dante sees the souls of the proud, bent under the heavy burden of huge stones, he reflects on the "sickness" of pride:

> O proud Christians, wretched and weary, who, sick in mental vision, put trust in backward steps: do you not perceive that we are worms, born to form the angelic butterfly that flies to judgment without defenses? Why does your mind soar on high, since you are, as it were, imperfect insects, even as the worm in which full development is lacking?

(*Purgatory* X, 121-129)

This metaphor of the caterpillar's transformation into a butterfly describes beautifully the Christian's metamorphosis from his puny, earthly condition into splendid, heavenly beauty. The humble Christian accepts his present condition without resentment and anger. Humility is a patient waiting, yet a waiting filled with hope of final transformation and ecstasy. Pride is essentially an arrogant impatience with our present creaturehood.

The souls of the proud then pray in the words of the perfect prayer, the Lord's Prayer. It is fitting that this prayer be the prayer of the proud since the opening phrases recognize God, *His* Rule and *His* Will as the supreme value. The proud must learn that they as individuals are *not* the center of the universe. They too are asked to say "Our" Father rather than "my" Father. In Dante's paraphrase of the Lord's prayer, he has the proud say:

> Our Father, Who art in Heaven, not restricted there, but through greater love for the first of Your creatures;
>
> Praised be Your name and Your power by everyone, since it is fitting to give thanks for your sweet outpouring.
>
> May the peace of Your kingdom come to us, for we cannot attain it of ourselves, with all our striving, unless it comes.
>
> Just as Your angels sacrifice their will to You, singing hosannas, so may humans do with theirs.

(*Purgatory* XI, 1-12)

These words, not found in the Gospel text, are intended to make the proud realize that human creatures are not the highest in the hierarchy of created beings and are thus not the only, or first, objects of God's love. God dwells in Heaven with the angels, those "first effects" of His creative love. He is, of course, not limited to any particular place, but He dwells there out of "greater love" for the angels.

This "measuring" of God's love may appear arbitrary or capricious, and thus contrary to God's nature. But it is based on a theological and philosophical conception of creation as a participation in being. God alone is "Being Itself" (as St. Thomas stated), Who shares Himself through His act of creation. Created beings are beings which receive limited shares in God's Being. God's sharing of Himself in the act of creation is really the overflowing abundance of His love, which wants to give of His own goodness to others. He creates these "others" in a rich variety of ways.

Human creatures receive "more" of His goodness and perfections—a greater share in being—than animals, plants, or minerals. Angels participate in *being* more than do humans. Thus God loves the angels more since the angels share more of His goodness. This conception has nothing to do with selfish emotions or favoritism: it is the ontological reality of the created universe. The proud have to accept the truth of this reality and their proper place in the scale of created beings.

Dante's paraphrase of the Lord's Prayer has many other appropriate additions which are adapted to the learning needs of the proud. For example, they say "May the peace of Your kingdom come to us, for we cannot attain it of ourselves, with all our striving, unless it comes." Humility is thus the patient expectation of His peace.

The pilgrimage and desert themes are expressed in the second part of the Lord's prayer: "Give us this day our daily manna, without which one goes backward through this harsh desert when he labors to advance." Danta substitutes "manna" for the original "bread" of the Lord's Prayer and refers to the climb up the mountain as a journey through the desert. These paraphrases point to the Exodus experience of the Israelites in the desert where they learned to depend on God's providential food on a daily basis. Humility is dependence and trust in the loving God Who provides us with what we need day by day through the desert experience of this life.

The last petition of the prayer is also evidence that the proud are learning humility. They pray to be delivered from the Evil One, but add: "This last petition, dear Lord, we make not now for ourselves, for there is no need, but for those who remain behind us." This final note reveals that the proud not only recognize the lordship of God but also the existence of others and their needs. Here we see again prayer as an expression of love for others and a liberation from self-love. Prayer is a transition from selfish isolation into a communion with other members of God's family. Humility and prayer free us from the bondage of sick egotism and enable us to be healthily dependent on God and unselfishly loving of others.

Satan, "who was created nobler than any other creature," is the prime example of pride. His refusal to be dependent was the cause of his downfall, "like lightning from Heaven." He is the archetype of evil since the root of all sin is pride, the *hubris* of the creature who insists on being God. In the pit of Hell Dante described him as "the one who *was* so beautiful, but now is so ugly." (The Italian word for "was" expresses a definite, absolutely past time.) Pride, the root of sin, deforms our created beauty, and metamorphoses us into hideous monsters aping God.

As Dante leaves the first terrace, the angels sing, "Blessed are the poor in spirit," the first beatitude given by Jesus in His Sermon on the Mount. Poverty of spirit is the end result of Dante's sojourn on the first terrace. The angel erases the first "P" from his forehead. The pilgrim has learned humility, that emptiness of spirit and desert of the soul, which waits on God patiently and cares for one's fellow pilgrims in the desert.

Envy
(*Cantos* XIII-XV)

The landscape of the second terrace is bleak, bare, and rocky. There are no beautifully carved marble scenes, as on the first terrace, for this is the land of the blind. There are no images but only voices, which serve as the whips and the reins. The atmosphere corresponds to the nature of envy: blindness of the spirit. (The Italian word for envy, *invidia*, means "not seeing.") The souls here have their eyelids sewed up so that they do not enjoy the sun, because in their lives they were blind to God's goodness, "which makes His sun rise on the evil and on the good." (Matt. 5:45) These words from the Sermon on the Mount are the leitmotif of the terrace.

The envious are sitting pathetically in their darkness, supporting one another with their shoulders. This corrects their lack of mutual support on earth. We begin to perceive what envy is. By seeing only the good things of one's neighbor the envious person becomes blind to his neighbor as a person and hates him. Envy is a sadness over the good gifts which God has generously given to others. It is a resentment against God because we have not received those same gifts. It is also a blindness to the gift we have received and to the Giver of all gifts.

Envy, which can be traced ultimately to an inordinate self-love (pride), has the unique quality of not offering any satisfaction or pleasure, except perhaps the perverse joy of seeing one's enemy in misery. It produces only sadness and darkness, depicted in the drab, rocky nature of this terrace. It is a perverted love which must be healed by learning how to love unselfishly.

The voices of the angels on this terrace utter "courteous invitations to the table of love." These voices are the whip, "whose cords are drawn from love." We notice again that the "punishments" of Purgatory are ultimately motivated by God's love. The first voice echoes the words of Mary at the marriage feast of Cana: "They have no wine." This indicates Mary's selfless concern for the embarrassed, poor couple who did not have enough wine for their guests. Another voice says, "Love them from whom you have suffered wrong." This is another echo from Jesus' Sermon on the Mount. The whips for the envious are examples of love for one's friends *and* enemies, because God's love embraces both. He makes His sun shine on all. Envy tries to put limits on God's love, but it limits only the envious, closing them into a world of blindness and isolation.

During his stay on this terrace Dante shares with us some candid remarks about himself. He admits that his own eyes have offended little with looks of envy, but adds: "Far greater is the fear that holds my soul in suspense of the torment below (the terrace of pride), so that already the load down there is heavy upon me." He honestly confesses that he is a proud man, who after death will have to serve time on the first terrace. Some of his biographers have alluded to his haughtiness. It's good to hear it from Dante himself. Although he acknowledges traces of all the seven capital sins within him, he is aware that certain ones have dominated him. These are pride, wrath, and lust. Dante shows us that the first step toward personal wholeness and spiritual progress is to identify the dominant roots of sin within us. Otherwise we remain in the dark forest, trapped and victimized by the beasts within us, condemned to regression and spiritual atrophy.

As Dante and Virgil leave the terrace of the envious, the angel of fraternal love sings, "Blessed are the merciful." Virgil then explains to Dante the real nature of envy: it is a selfish desire to possess, a refusal to share good things with others. Envy is a love for the good, which resents any "partnership". It is the ugly, sinful side of eros, which is not transformed into agape. In Virgil's words, "For as many more there are who say "ours," so much the more of good does each possess and the more of charity burns in that community."

When Dante fails to understand this, Virgil points out to him that his soul is still set on earthly things and so remains in darkness about the true light. Virgil further explains that the true light, the ineffable goodness, Who is God, shares Himself with others. That is His essence: giving, sharing, loving. The souls in Paradise live a life of continuous increase in love because they continuously share the goodness of God and reflect it, like mirrors, to one another. Virgil admits, however, that he really cannot satisfy Dante's desire to understand this, since only Beatrice can guide him into this truth.

We might reflect here on the evils that private ownership, capitalism, and powerful industrial corporations have inflicted on our planet earth: the devastation of the land, its beauty and its wild life; the pollution of the waters and the air; the merciless exploitation of the poor. All these are manifestations of the grip of envy which still holds the earth in darkness. Many individuals still cling to selfish eros, preferring this darkness to the light of agape, which would set them free to share all the good things with all the people. It is no wonder that revolutions, inspired by Communism and Socialism, strive to restore the common sharing of the earth's good things. Such political ideologies—in theory, at least—are not far removed from the Christian vision of agape.

PURGATORY: FROM CANTO XVII

The Great Discourse on Love
(Cantos XVII-XVIII)

After the terrace of envy Dante and Virgil ascend to the terrace of wrath (Canto XVI) where smoke and mist cloud the air—symbols of the darkness in which anger wraps the soul. One of the souls there, Marco Lombardo, gives a brief discourse on the reasons why there is so much corruption on the earth. This short discourse is a prelude to the lengthy discourses of Virgil in the next two cantos.

145

Marco introduces the themes of human free will and the innate love for good: the causes of human corruption or human goodness. He clearly states that corruption and evil in the world cannot be blamed on the influence of the stars (astrology) or on some blind fate. In his words, "If the world today goes astray, in *you* is the cause!"

Marco then explains how the good, loving God created the simple human soul in an innocent state; but the human soul, attracted by some trifling good is often deceived and needs a guide to know the proper, higher goods to be loved and pursued. These guides or curbs were provided by God in the institutions of the State (under the rule of the Roman emperor) and the Church (under the rule of the pope). However, the leadership of both institutions had become corrupt. The sword (the temporal rule of the world) has been joined to the shepherd's staff (the spiritual guidance of the pope). We detect here Dante's own criticism expressed in Marco's words.

Virgil and Dante then emerge from the mists of wrath as the angel of meekness pronounces: "Blessed are the peacemakers who are without evil wrath." They then ascend to the next terrace, the place of the slothful, those "who were slow to love the good." It is here, the place of delay, that Virgil and Dante slow down to rest. It is literally the mid-point in the soul's ascent of the mountain and the mathematical center of Purgatory and of the whole *Comedy*. It is not, however, the dramatic center of Purgatory. That is the meeting with Beatrice.

Cantos XVII and XVIII contain Virgil's discourse on the nature of love, the central theme of the *Comedy*. These two cantos are a magnificent summary of the wisdom of classical humanism. They express in the language of Aristotle and Plato the great achievement of human philosophy. Virgil, as the spokesman for the classical tradition, sums up here the deepest insights into love as being the inner dynamic of the entire universe. He explains in Aristotle's words the nature of love as the intrinsic movement driving all beings toward their natural goals. All beings in the cosmos—the inanimate, the plants, the animals, the humans—are drawn by this natural instinct (love) toward their ends (their goals). Aristotle, the biologist as well as the psychologist and metaphysician, understood this inner dynamic of growth and development. The seeds of our modern theory of evolution and the concept of man as a microcosm are found implicitly and sometimes explicitly in his philosophy.

This supreme achievement of human philosophy is nonetheless only a stage in Dante's spiritual growth, although it represents a very high plateau. Virgil expresses in his discourse the highest peak of human philosophy, which is not only the love of wisdom but also the wisdom of love. Love (*eros*) is the inner force of all life in the universe, and consequently also of man, the cosmos "in miniature." It is at the root of all human virtue or vice, since love, the attraction for the good, moves the free human will to choice and action.

Love becomes perverse when the free will chooses the wrong objects. These perversions of love are the sins of pride, envy, and wrath, which were purged on the lower terraces. Sloth is the slowness or retardation of the soul's activity of love. It is "defective" love. On the upper terraces of Purgatory "excessive" love for good objects is cleansed and set aright. These are the sins of avarice, gluttony and lust.

This analysis of the human soul and its movements certainly rings true to us even today. We are all driven by love for what appears good to us. We desire that good and strive for it, although we are sometimes deceived and misled by what appears to be our true good. This striving is the basic *eros* deep within us that is never satisfied in this life on earth. That is why Virgil's discourse, intellectually profound and psychologically accurate as it is, does not satisfy Dante's needs. Virgil once again confesses his limitations of knowledge and perception. He tells Dante that Beatrice, "the noble virtue," will speak to him further on this subject of love and free will.

Human eros, naturally good and wholesome, is a point of arrival in Dante's inner journey, but it is also a point of departure toward greater heights. The wisdom of humanism (Virgil) is a peak of achievement in self-knowledge, but it is nonetheless inadequate and deficient. This self-knowledge is certainly deep and dynamic, containing many sound psychological insights; but it is simply too intellectual and logical. It is too "cut and dried"— too clear and reasonable. It lacks the nuances of the complex emotional, subconscious, and unconscious aspects of the human person, known to us somewhat through the studies of modern psychology. But above all it lacks the passion, the "madness," and the ecstasy of love.

These "irrational" dimensions transport the human soul out of itself into a world beyond the merely rational world—a transcendent world. Beatrice must be the guide into this other world, since she—divine, supernatural wisdom—enlightens the soul with faith, strengthens it with hope, and enflames it with the passionate, ecstatic love of God. Beatrice, the woman—Dante's *anima*—will integrate his masculine, rational *animus* and complete it with the mysterious, the transcendent, the divine.

At the end of Virgil's discourse Dante expresses this weakness and inadequacy of human eros and wisdom through the subtle metaphor of the moon. He describes the moon as "a bucket all burning," a striking metaphor which describes the brightness of Virgil's light, but at the same time it expresses the moon's paleness and semi-darkness if compared to the brilliant light of the sun, which symbolizes Beatrice. The moon, associated with the amorous, ambiguous, and often perverted moods of the human psyche, is a fitting symbol here since it expresses the general weakness of the flesh (human eros). At the end of the canto Dante yields to the death of sleep once again, and must in sleep await further enlightenment.

The Second Dream
(*Canto* XIX)

The second dream, which concludes the second day on the mountain and serves as a transition to the third day, is quite different from Dante's first dream. In that dream he was a mere youth; in this one he is a mature man. In this second dream, a pale, ugly, deformed woman appears to him. He gazes on her, and his gaze transforms her into a beautifully formed woman with a warm glow. As she sings, she identifies herself as the sweet Siren who lures sailors by her song away from their course to their destruction, just as she had led astray Ulysses' mariners. Then another lady, "holy and alert," appears and scolds Virgil (also in the dream) for his inactivity. Virgil then seizes the Siren, rips open her garments, and exposes her hideous, putrid belly. The stench wakes up Dante.

This dream contains some of Dante's most profound and subtle insights into human psychology. There have been many interpretations of this dream; but in my own understanding of it I am particularly indebted to Dorothy Sayers and Helen Luke, who have given remarkable analyses of it. It is interesting to note that the dream itself comes immediately after Virgil's very rational discourse on love and precedes the purgation of the three sins of inordinate eros: avarice, gluttony, and lust. These sins of "concupiscence" are rooted in the excessive appetite, or love, for the secondary "goods" which human eros desires as if they were the primary good.

After the well-defined clarity of Virgil's rational discourse, the dream presents us with the assertion of the mysterious, "irrational" unconscious. As Helen Luke has so keenly observed, the rational component of the human soul—its *animus*, or masculine principle—must be balanced and complemented by the feminine principle, its *anima*. The activity of the anima often occurs in dreams. In this dream there is an interaction in Dante's soul of his reason (Virgil), his "fantasy" (the transformed woman), and his intuitive sense (the alert woman).

It is difficult to identify precisely the figure of the transformed woman. Dante later refers to her as "the ancient witch." She is first of all a symbol of the illusive attraction that the three sins of concupiscence exercise on the imagination. Dante observes that it is his own gaze that transforms the ugly woman into an attractive one. His own unsatisfied and unfulfilled love (*eros*) bestows a beauty on her which she really does not possess. Dante's own fantasy deceives him. What he actually does is project his selfish desire for pleasure on the object before him. The woman becomes what the man Dante wants her to be for his own gratification. Thus she becomes, in Dorothy Sayer's words, "an egotistical fantasy."

A woman often becomes merely a projection of a man's selfish imagination and not a real other person to be loved with mature love. We can readily perceive how true to life this is. The women (and men) presented on the center folds of erotic magazines are not gazed upon as real persons but only as sex objects and fantasies. This exploitation of men and women (and, more shameful, even of children) is prevalent and perhaps all-pervasive in the "Playboy/Playgirl" atmosphere of American society today. The obsession with sexual gratification, money, food, and drink in today's society is in reality an immature fantasy produced by human egotism. The fantasy is always superficially attractive. Just observe how magazines and TV commercials successfully capitalize on this attractiveness by exploiting the unconscious, dreaming public that easily falls prey to the fantasy and buys the products advertised. Today's consumers irrationally purchase products they really do not need. They are led astray by that ancient Siren within all of us.

The "holy and alert" woman, however, intervenes before it is too late. She represents neither Beatrice nor Lucia but rather an indefinable instinct for what is true and good. She is the inner sense of good counsel that moves reason (Virgil) to strip the fantasy and expose it for what it really is. Notice that reason is now within Dante at this stage of his spiritual maturity. The dream reveals to Dante that reason, once acquired and developed, can be misled by the allurements of the sensual appetites. Reason must be put on alert by that instinct and must act promptly. The rational wisdom of Virgil (the masculine animus) must be integrated and complemented by the mysterious wisdom of intuition (the feminine anima) before Dante can reach wholeness and maturity.

Carl Jung's more systematic twentieth-century studies on the meaning of dreams substantiates a great deal of Dante's own thirteenth-century "dream psychology." The medieval theologian-poet and the twentieth-century psychiatrist agree on many basic aspects of the intricate dynamics and the timeless nature of the human psyche. This affords us an example of how the same truths about ourselves can be discovered by keen minds from different cultures and different epochs of human history.

Avarice
(*Cantos* XX-XXII)

After the dream of the Siren the angel of zeal, with outspread wings like a swan, turns Dante and Virgil upwards. They are ready to ascend. Dante is still uneasy about the strange dream of the Siren, but Virgil assures him that he has learned how to free himself of the Siren's enchantment. He invites Dante now to turn his eyes to another lure—the one which God offers in the eternal spheres. Dante then compares himself to a falcon who turns at the call and spreads his wings with desire for the food which draws him upward.

We notice here a transition from the second day, when Dante learned to understand himself through Virgil's wisdom. Now that self-knowledge has been gained, Dante realizes that his unsatisfied love has yet to be quenched. The third day's mood is haste and yearning after the full satisfaction of that inner desire. The terraces of the third day (avarice, gluttony and lust) correspond to this "spiritual" desire, hunger, and thirst. The bird images and the metaphors of flight suggest the upward *élan* and speed toward the goal of this yearning. Dante is being unconsciously drawn upward to his first love, Beatrice.

On the terrace of avarice he notices that the penalty for the greedy is the most bitter one that he has so far seen on the mountain. The people there are lying prostrate on the ground, turned face-downward, as they weep and recite words from Psalm 119: "My soul has cleaved to the ground." Dante speaks with one of the souls, Pope Adrian V, who sadly narrates that his eyes during his life in the world were fixed on earthly things rather than on those above. Divine justice now sinks these souls to the earth which they had desired. Adrian tells Dante that "Just as avarice quenched our love for every good, so justice here holds us tightly bound hands and feet, motionless and outstretched."

Dante kneels down out of reverence for the dignity of the papal office, but the former pope persuades him to stand up, saying to him: "Get up, brother, do not be mistaken: I am a fellow servant with you and with the others of the One Power." Adrian then quotes the Gospel text, "They will not marry in the Kingdom of Heaven," signifying that earthly roles will give way to a new family relationship in God's Kingdom. As pope (the vicar of Christ) he had been "married" to the Church, but now he is a brother to all the members of the Church.

In Dante's mind the sin of greed is the evil which has contaminated the whole world. He angrily proclaims: "Accursed be you, ancient wolf, who have more prey than all the other beasts, because of your hunger endlessly deep!" He further inveighs against avarice when he comments on the greed of a French king, Charles the Lame, who sold his own daughter: "O Avarice, what more can you do to us, since you have drawn my race to yourself that it has no care for its own flesh?" Again on the subject of greedy French kings he mentions Philip the Fair who, in Dante's time, had taken "his greedy sails into the temple." This is a reference to Philip's outrageous treatment of Pope Boniface VIII, whom Philip's troops had physically assaulted and held captive. In spite of Dante's bad feelings toward Boniface, he still regarded him as the vicar of Christ. In the person of Boniface Christ was once again given vinegar and gall to drink and crucified between thieves. Dante compares Philip to a "new Pilate" who inflicts cruel punishment on Christ.

Dante's acute penetration into the malice of greed and his justified anger at the evil that greed inflicts on the world are just as relevant today, if not more so. We are no strangers to the greed and corruption of individuals who hold positions of leadership in the secular and religious realms. Our world today is torn apart by constant wars, economic oppression of the poor, hunger, and the denial of basic human rights. In most cases these miserable conditions can be traced to the greed of a few individuals, large corporations, or nations. As Dante so poignantly observed, greed "quenches the love for every good." It devours the human soul and renders it immobile, incapable of loving other humans and God. It binds the whole human person, "hands and feet," so that he cannot reach out in love to others.

After reflecting on other examples of avarice (the conclusion of Canto XX), Dante feels the whole mountain quake. A chill of terror grips him. He doesn't yet know the cause of the mountain's sudden quake. He then hears the voices of all the souls singing, "Glory to God in the highest," the joyous hymn of the angels at Christ's birth.

Canto XXI begins on a note of deep curiosity about the meaning of the quake and the song:

> The natural thirst which is never quenched except by the water of which the poor Samaritan woman asked the grace, was tormenting me and our haste was urging me along the encumbered way behind my leader. . . . And behold, as Luke writes for us that Christ, newly risen

from the grave, appeared to the two who were
on the way, a shade appeared to us, saying "My
brothers, may God give you peace."

(*Canto* XXI, 1-13)

This is an important turning point in the drama of
the journey. For the first time Dante's natural thirst is
presented in a *Christian* context. It is the thirst which
can be quenched only by the living water of Christ's
grace. The reference to the Samaritan woman's meeting
with Christ (John 4) and her request for water gives us the
clue to the meaning of Dante's thirst. We begin to perceive that the secret longing of the human heart (its eros)
can be satisfied only by the gift of Christ's love (agape).
Throughout Cantos XX, XXI, XXII there are many subtle
allusions to Christ's love, expressed in His death and
resurrection. These allusions keep reminding us that it is
Christ's love, like a hidden magnet, that is constantly
drawing Dante's soul upward.

One of these allusions is the sudden appearance now
of the first Christian guide to the pilgrim Dante. This
"shade" is described first of all in terms of the risen
Christ, Who encountered the two travelers on the road to
Emmaus that first Easter Sunday (Luke 24:13-31). This
new guide is Statius, a pagan poet who had converted to
Christianity in the first century. Statius is the image of
the Christian convert who has risen to new life in Christ.
He answers Dante's questions about the mountain's quake
and the joyful song. These phenomena happen, he explains, when a soul on the mountain feels free to ascend.
The joyous song accompanies the ascent since Christ is
being born again in a Christian's soul.

Statius further explains that a soul rises only when
it feels cleansed:

When some soul feels itself cleansed, so that it
may rise up and set forth to mount on high,
such great shouts resound. The will itself at-
tests its own purity. Amazed, the soul that is
free to change its place finds that its mere will
suffices for liberation. True, it wills always,
but can gain nothing as long as divine justice
keeps its desire set toward the pain as once it
was set toward the sin.

(*Canto* XXI, 58-66)

This is one of Dante's keen psychological insights
into the meanings of conflict, guilt, purgation, and liberation. It also clarifies the meaning of the purgatorial process itself. We see that Purgatory is not a series of punishments imposed by an external tyrant on the soul which
must satisfy the anger and offended majesty of a demand-
ing master. On the contrary, it is self-purgation, undertaken willingly. The soul perceives her need for cleansing and change, and willingly endures the conflict until
she knows that she is free to accept fully God's love and
mercy. Thus freed, she then proceeds in her pilgrimage
toward God, Who wills her complete freedom and beauty.

The Spiritual Hunger and Thirst
(*Cantos* XXII-XXIV)

Statius then reveals himself to Dante and Virgil. He
tells them that he was a poet in the time of the Roman
Emperor Titus, "who avenged the wounds from which
flowed the blood sold by Judas." This is another allusion
to Christ's sacrifice of love. It focuses our attention once
again on the central event and the very meaning of hu-

man history according to Dante's Christian vision of faith. As we shall observe throughout these cantos and through to the end of Purgatory, Dante's understanding of history plays a vital role in the development of the *Comedy* as well as the development of Dante's inner life.

Statius proceeds to tell Dante and Virgil about the inspired source of his poetry: Virgil's *Aeneid*. As yet he does not know that he is standing before Virgil. He refers to Virgil's work as the "divine flame" which kindled the "seeds of my poetic fire." Virgil's poetry was "mother and nurse" of his own poetry. He expresses a deep desire to have known Virgil in his own lifetime. At these words Virgil's glance at Dante (It must have been a wink!) tells him to be silent, but Dante can't conceal a smile, which gives Virgil's secret away. There follows now one of the most moving "recognition scenes" in all literature, as Statius stoops to embrace his teacher's feet. Virgil courteously rebukes him in these words:

> "Brother, do not do so, for you are a shade and
> a shade you see." And he, rising, said, "Now
> you may comprehend the measure of the love
> that burns in me for you, when I forget our
> emptiness and treat shades as solid things."

(*Canto XXI*, 130-136)

This scene and the words spoken contain a depth of meaning which we should pause to explore. Here are three poets who have not known one another personally in their earthly lives. They are united here, however, as fellow travelers and share a community of mutual respect and love as poets and friends. Dante and Statius have known Virgil through his works. His works had been the nourishing mother, the inspiration and teacher, for both Statius and Dante. Dante at his first meeting with Virgil in Canto I of *Inferno* had given a similar tribute to Virgil in the words, "May the long study avail me and the great love that had led me to search your volume."

Virgil, in Dante's mind, represented the peak of humanistic culture and wisdom. Virgil's role in the development of the human spirit symbolizes the peak of humanity's striving for truth, goodness, and beauty. He is the image of the best in the human quest for knowledge and virtue, the personification of the highest ideals of the wisdom and justice of secular Rome. He lived and wrote when the secular world was ripe and ready for the descent of divine wisdom and love in the person of Christ, Who was born in the Roman Empire at the zenith of Rome's "humaneness," the era of the *Pax Romana*, the reign of peace. Thus, secular humanism prepared the way for the Incarnation of Christ, the Prince of Peace, Who is the secret meaning of all human history.

The friendly exchange between Statius and Virgil continues as Virgil responds: "Love, kindled by virtue, has always kindled other love, if only its flame appears outwardly." These words indicate how these poets, removed by time from one another, are yet united by a love, which may be shadowy (they are shades here); but it points to the reality of Christ's love. Recall that Statius is a shadowy figure that represents the risen Christ. Virgil (human eros, the love for wisdom and virtue) expresses his love for Statius. Authentic human love—either for wisdom, virtue, or another human person—is always a shadow of that perfect love, (agape), which appeared outwardly in the death and resurrection of Christ. All the truly "humane" movements of human history and of individual human spirits have been faint shadows of that reality. Virgil's exaltation of Roman virtue, incarnated in

Aeneas's *pietas* (that loyalty to the gods, to one's family and to Rome), was an authentic expression of the secret yearning of the pagan world for the full expression of love, Christ's agape.

This concept of history as a progressive movement of love towards its fulfillment in Christ is expressed by Statius in his personal history of conversion to Christianity. Virgil's words were the light and inspiration which led him to Christ. He addresses Virgil in these words:

> You it was who first sent me toward Parnassus to drink in its caves, and it was you who enlightened me to God. You were like one who goes by night and carries the light behind him. The light profits not himself, but makes wise those who follow him. You did this when you said, "The ages are renewed; Justice returns and the first age of man; a new progeny descends from heaven."
>
> Through you I was a poet. Through you, a Christian.
>
> (*Canto XXII*, 64-73)

Virgil's words quoted here were from his Fourth Eclogue, considered by many Church Fathers and medieval theologians as a prophecy foretelling the birth of Christ. The words of Virgil look forward to the return of the "golden age" of humanity, the dream of the classical poets, when mankind once lived in peace and prosperity and in harmony with all of nature. In many ways Virgil's words echo the prophet Isaiah's idyllic descriptions of the Messianic age, when the wolf and the lamb, the lion and the little child (named Immanuel) would play together in a harmonious world of abundance and peace (Isaiah 7-11).

Virgil's role is compared to the role of St. John the Baptist, the forerunner of Christ. Just as John was a dim lantern in the night leading to the bright light of Christ, so Virgil (classical humanism) was the guide for Statius to Christian faith. Dante's understanding of the role and function of classical literature, philosophy, art, and government—the whole humanistic tradition—is nowhere so clearly stated. All of these noble expressions of the human spirit were leading humanity toward a goal. Imperfect and sometimes even mixed with gross errors, they were nonetheless the strivings of human eros for its unknown fulfillment in Christ.

Virgil, together with all the great lights of human philosophy, science, and literature, was unconsciously following the deep inspiration of the love for "the Good" which drove them to discover and create. They brought the world so close to the flame of love which burst forth in the incarnation of Christ. They, like the Hebrew prophets, sowed the seeds of faith, hope, and love, which reached maturity in the harvest, the coming of Christ. They were the precursors, the figures and shadows, which guided humanity toward the full reality, the fulfillment of all human desires: the love of Christ. They expressed their "natural thirst" for the supernatural waters of Christ's abundant grace.

This natural thirst and hunger we can discover within ourselves and in others as well as in the many movements toward good in our modern world. Such movements may not bear the name "Christian," but they are radically Christian in their orientation. The life and works of people like Mahatma Gandhi and Simone Weil— to name only two—come to mind here. The people who promote peace and justice, the abolition of nuclear weapons, the end of hunger and oppression, are all inspired by this same human eros. The relentless efforts of scientists to find cures for "incurable" diseases, the silent, unpublished work of physicians and nurses who care for the sick, the creations of writers, poets, and artists, are all manifestations of this inner drive. Whether they carry the name "Christian" or not is irrelevant. They are all outward expressions of the loving spirit of Christ, which inspires them all. "The Spirit blows where it wills."

This deep desire is beautifully expressed by one of the souls on the terrace of the gluttonous. It is an old friend of Dante, Forese Donati, whom we know from Dante's biography. Their relationship occurred during the "dark forest" of Dante's life. The poetic correspondence between Dante and Forese reveals a somewhat unseemly aspect of Dante's life at that time. Dante now recalls with sadness what their life together had been and "what they had been for one another." But that is all over now, since Virgil had turned Dante from that way of life. Forese speaks here as one who has received the grace of repentance. He now sees his life and Dante's in a new light, the Christian light.

Forese is repenting of the sin of gluttony and, like the other souls on this terrace, he is wasted away and famished as he gazes on a luxurious, yet unattainable, tree laden with fruit and a clear spring of water falling from a high rock. These are the penalties of this terrace: the hungry, thirsty souls cannot reach the fruit or water. Forese then addresses Dante:

> From the Eternal Counsel power descends into
> the water and into the tree, whereby I thus
> waste away. All this people who weeping sing,

sanctify themselves in hunger and thirst, for having followed appetite to excess. The scent which comes from the fruit and from the spray that is spread over the green leaves kindles within us a desire to eat and to drink. . . . For that desire leads us to the tree which led glad Christ to say *Eli*, when he made us free with His blood.

(*Canto* XXIII, 61-75)

These words of Forese finally reveal to us in clear terms this "natural thirst" and hunger which Dante has been referring to all along. The physical desire for food and drink is really an image of the spiritual hunger and thirst for God which is deeply rooted in every human soul. The tree here on the terrace is reminiscent of the tree in the garden described in the book of Genesis. That tree was delightful and attractive, but unattainable.

The tree in Eden held the forbidden fruit, which Adam and Eve could not attain, except by sin. Their arrogant pride and their selfish desire to be like God led them to eat that fruit which God had specifically forbade them to eat. They grasped for complete knowledge, power, and life (equality to God) without waiting for God's bestowal of these gifts. The tree of disobedience and sin, however, in the "fullness of time" became the tree of the Cross on which Christ humbly and lovingly submitted to His Father's will. The sin of humanity was transformed by suffering and sacrifice into an act of love for God and humanity.

Forese's desire to suffer hunger and thirst is thus an imitation of Christ's desire to give Himself in sacrificial love to the Father and to humanity. Forese's willingness to suffer is a pale shadow of Christ's gladness when he

cried Eli ("My God!"), as He shed the blood which liberated mankind from the guilt of sin and reconciled man
to God. Dante refers to Forese's desire to suffer now as
"the sorrow which weds us anew to God." This profound
meaning of the human thirst and hunger unfolds itself as
the secret desire to be united to God in love.

This desire willingly endures the suffering because it
knows now the meaning of suffering: the purification of
"other loves, thirsts, and hungers" which distracted us
from the ecstatic gladness of pure love for God our Father
and for our human family. Forese expresses the bitterness
and the sweetness of the suffering with a very effective
metaphor: he now "drinks the sweet wormwood of the
torments." Wormwood is a plant which yields a bitter oil
used in absinthe. This bitter-sweet motif is the underlying "joy-in-suffering" of the souls in Purgatory.

As Dante passes through this terrace, another Italian
poet, Bonagiunta, recognizes him. Bonagiunta had been a
critic of the new style of poetry which Dante had followed; but now he praises Dante and his poetry, and recognizes that the "sweet new style" was more concerned
with truth and inspiration than with mere style. Dante
then explains to Bonagiunta his theory of poetry, and in
these few words tells us his basic motivation for writing
poetry and also the content of his poetry:

> I am one who, when Love inspires me, takes
> note, and goes setting it forth after the fashion
> which He dictates within me.

> (*Canto* XXIV, 52-54)

At this point of the drama Dante the pilgrim and
Dante the poet speak with one voice: the love of God is

the chief force which moves him in his journey and moves him to the art of writing poetry. We have just learned in the preceding cantos that the half-understood desire which drew Dante and the other souls up the mountain was in fact that same desire—the love of God—which led Christ to His sacrifice. The love of God, as we have noted so often, is the secret magnet pulling all the pilgrims upward. Dante recognizes that it is also the primary source of his poetic inspiration. It is God Himself Who dictates and inspires Dante to create his poetry. Poetry for Dante was not mere aesthetic contemplation or a pleasurable pause which is aware of nothing else. We recall Cato's stern reprimand of that kind of poetry when Dante and Virgil paused to listen to Casella. For Dante, poetry was first of all an obedient listening to God's love which speaks not only through nature but also through human history and in particular through human love.

Dante's theory of poetry, then, approaches very closely the traditional Christian understanding of the inspiration of Sacred Scripture. It was generally believed that the Scripture writers received inspiration in the manner of a dictation from God. Their interpretation of reality was thus not a merely human vision but a vision of faith: God's love was speaking through them and enlightening them as to the hidden meaning of all reality. St. Augustine had compared the Scriptures to "love letters" from God.

Dante's poetry, then, should be called "sacred poetry," since Dante attributes the source of his inspiration not to himself or to some special talent of his but to God Himself. It is a transcendent poetry which contemplates everything with the eyes of faith and sees all in the light of God's grace. The whole created universe is contemplated in Dante's poetry as a book written by God's love. Only God can give the true interpretation of that book. Therefore He inspires poets like Dante to see with His eyes.

The Passage through Fire
(*Cantos* XXV-XXVII)

The three pilgrims finally arrive at the last cornice of the mountain, the terrace where lust is purified. The souls here must pass through a wall of fire. This is the only time, contrary to the traditional image of Purgatory as a place of fiery torments, that fire is the medium of purgation. The souls, as they pass through the flames, sing an appropriate liturgical hymn, the "*Summae Deus Clementiae*" (O God of supreme mercy). It is a hymn which celebrates God's merciful love and implores His aid—"His chastening fires"—to expel sinful lust.

No doubt Dante places lust next to the summit of the mountain since it is the sin which most closely resembles authentic love. All souls, no matter what their dominant sin was, must pass through this fire. This is consistent with Dante's theory that sin of whatever kind derives basically from some kind of love. The attraction and desire for some good (eros) is at the root of all human activity, even of sin.

Fire is a most appropriate image here since it not only signifies the passion of lust, but also the purity of love. Burning charity (agape) must purify here the burning eros of the human soul. Fire is also reminiscent of the flaming sword of the Cherubim, the angels who were posted outside the garden of Eden after the original sin (Genesis 3). They blocked the entrance to Paradise. This terrace is in fact at the very threshold of the Earthly Paradise.

On this terrace we notice that both homosexual lust and heterosexual lust are treated equally. In Hell those guilty of homosexual acts were assigned to a much lower and more horrible circle than the heterosexual sinners. Here there are two separate bands of sinners: the homosexuals go in the opposite direction of the heterosexuals. The former shout, "Sodom and Gomorrah," while the latter shout, "Pasiphae enters the cow so that the young bull may hasten to her lust." This latter shout is a reference to a Greek myth about the act of bestiality committed by Queen Pasiphae.

It is noteworthy that while homosexual acts in Dante's time were usually considered "unnatural," he considers lustful heterosexual acts as "bestiality," a much more unnatural act. Both, however, are considered sinful since they were motivated by lust rather than by mature, human love. Authentic human love is by nature an exchange, a reaching out to the "other," a communion and sharing of mutual love, rather than a lustful grasping at selfish pleasure. That is where the good drive of eros goes astray: it turns into itself and becomes a perversion instead of an act of communion. Here on this terrace both bands of sinners meet one another and all the souls exchange kisses in haste. This is a reference to the "holy kiss" of Christian greeting recommended by St. Paul. This friendly, hasty exchange is obviously the corrective of their lingering, lustful kisses on earth.

There is also a somewhat humorous note in this passage. The homosexuals are referred to as those who committed the sin for which Julius Caesar was hailed as *regina* ("queen") by the crowds in Rome. What is being referred to is Caesar's alleged homosexual relationship with King Nicomedes of Bithynia.

After Dante encounters some of the troubadour poets who had been his forerunners in the earthly life, he moves toward the fire as the third day comes to an end. It is near sunset now, but it is morning in Jerusalem, "where the Creator of the sun shed His blood." This allusion to Christ's death once again keeps before our eyes the memory of His sacrificial love.

As Dante approaches the fire, he is terrified. The memory of criminals burned at the stake in his native Florence is still vivid in his mind. He himself had been condemned to that final punishment if he were to return to Florence after his sentence of banishment. Virgil attempts to assure him that the fire brings "torment, but not death." Fear, however, still grips Dante. He stands there "rooted, but with an accusing conscience."

Virgil, the clever father, must entice this stubborn child. He lures him with the words: "Now look, my son. Between Beatrice and you is this wall." Dante compares this moment to an episode from the classical myth about Pyramus and Thisbe, found in Ovid's *Metamorphoses*. It is a touching love story, similar to Shakespeare's *Romeo and Juliet*, in which the two lovers meet a tragic end. Pyramus kills himself, thinking that Thisbe has already perished. When Thisbe finds her lover dying, she tells him that it is really she, Thisbe, who is still alive. At the sound of her name he lifts his eyes to behold her face once more before his death. His blood turns the white mulberry tree into red. Thisbe then kills herself. Dante's allusion to this myth suggests his own experience here: joy at the name of the beloved one, as well as the impending suffering and death which he must endure.

At the name of Beatrice, Dante is enticed "as a child is won over by an apple." Dante then enters the fire as Virgil continues to encourage him by saying, "Already I seem to behold her eyes." Dante moves through the excruciating flame, guided by a voice from the light on the other side that calls, "Come, blessed of My Father." These words will be Christ's words to the just souls at the Last Judgment (Matthew 25:34). They are certainly appropriate here as Dante passes through the purgatorial fire. However, the rest of the quotation, "possess the Kingdom prepared for you. . . . ," is not given here. Perhaps the reason is that Dante must still undergo a judgment before entrance into the Kingdom.

Dante passes through the fire because he is drawn by his love for Beatrice. A deep insight is given us here: only love can make the pain of suffering bearable. His human love for Beatrice is at the same time a response to a divine love that is calling him. The hidden Christ, the light on the other side of the fire, is calling him to Himself through his human love for Beatrice.

After the ordeal of the passage through fire the three pilgrims: Dante, Virgil, and Statius, prepare for rest, since "the law of the mountain takes from them the power but not the desire to ascend." Dante the poet then compares his two guides to shepherds who guard their flock at night. He compares himself to a "she-goat." This strikes us as an odd metaphor here since Dante has just heard "Come, blessed of My Father," the words of Christ at the Last Judgment, where the sheep (the just) are separated from the goats (the damned). Perhaps it refers to the severe condemnation which Dante must endure at the summit. The process is not yet complete for Dante. He is not yet fully "just."

As night falls Dante gazes at the stars, which appear brighter and bigger than usual, a good omen of the approaching splendor of Paradise. He is now on the threshold of another important breakthrough, and his rational soul must yield to the mysterious world of the unconscious. He falls asleep and has the third and last dream on the journey.

The Third Dream
(*Canto* XXVII)

In this third dream the planet Venus, the morning star, is burning brightly. The dominant mood once again is love. Dante sees two ladies in the dream, Leah and Rachel, two sisters from the patriarchal stories in the book of Genesis. Leah is gathering flowers to adorn herself, while Rachel sits before her mirror admiring her beauty. These two Old Testament figures were well-established allegories in the Middle Ages for the active and contemplative lives. Since this dream, like the other dreams, is prophetic of the next scene, we are prepared for the appearance of two ladies on the summit of the mountain: Matelda and Beatrice.

The meaning of the women in the dream has been much discussed. The best interpretation seems to be that both Leah and Rachel are shadows of a greater and transcendent reality. They adorn and admire themselves, signifying that their activity and contemplation are centered on themselves. They are satisfied with those activities.

Their counterparts in the Earthly Paradise are far different: Matelda gathers flowers, but takes delight in the works of God's hands. Rachel contemplated herself, but

Beatrice contemplates the beauty of God's face. The contrast obviously points to an imminent, radical transition in the journey. Dante is about to pass from the natural into the supernatural. He has now reached a plateau in his spiritual progress, but something much greater lies beyond. His human eros must still ascend to a higher plane, to another experience. He is still earthbound (like the goats) and childish in comparison with what he will soon become.

As Dante awakes he finds the brightness of the predawn light, "which gladdens the hearts of pilgrims as they come closer to their home." Virgil again encourages Dante with the words, "That sweet fruit for which mortals search on so many branches, this day shall give your hungers peace." What comforting words to the pilgrim's weary heart after the arduous climb! The peace that will satisfy the many desires of his eros will at last be Dante's. Dante feels the feathers growing for the flight.

Virgil then takes leave of Dante in these moving words:

> Son, the temporal fire and the eternal you have seen, and you have come to a place where I of myself discern no farther.
>
> I have brought you here with understanding and art. Henceforth take your own pleasure for your guide. You have left the steep and narrow ways.
>
> See the sun that shines again on your brow, see the tender grass, the flowers, the shrubs, which here the earth alone produces of itself.
>
> You may sit or go among them until the beautiful eyes come rejoicing which weeping made me come to you.

No longer expect word or sign from me. Free,
upright, and whole is your will, and it would be
wrong not to act according to its prompting.

Therefore I crown and miter you over yourself.

(*Canto* **XXVII**, 127-142)

These words are an extraordinary tribute to the inherent worth and nobility of human nature itself and its
ability to find freedom and wholeness. The human potential to heal itself and reach spiritual health are celebrated
here. The humanistic wisdom and virtue of the classical
tradition, represented by Virgil, are given the highest
praise. Dante has been purified, liberated and made whole.
He has acquired the purity of human nature, that original innocence of the first parents, Adam and Eve, and is
therefore ready to enter the Earthly Paradise. Dante is
now master of himself (symbolized by the crown and the
miter), freed from the evils which pervert the basic goodness of human nature. Dante's guide now is his own purified will and pleasure. Virgil can do no more. He must
now relinquish his role as guide to another one: Beatrice.
He refers to her beautiful eyes, which will soon come
rejoicing.

The Divine Forest
(*Canto* XXVIII)

Dante now enters the "divine" forest. This is really
the garden of Eden, the Earthly Paradise; but Dante purposely calls it a forest to contrast it with the "dark"
forest at the beginning of his journey. This divine forest
is a picture of the purity and innocence of the human

soul as created by God. Dante in the middle of his life had transformed this divine forest of his inner self into a dark forest by his own sins of pride and sensuality. But now that he has been freed from those sins he is able to delight in the marvelous beauty which unfolds before his eyes.

Dante's description of the divine forest is one of the masterpieces of nature poetry. The splendor of a morning in spring bursts before our eyes. This scene makes the beautiful opening scene in Purgatory seem pale, color- less, and lifeless. Here all the senses are delighted. The colors are not pastel, but brilliant. The cheerful singing of the birds harmonizes with the murmuring pines in a sweet symphony. A gentle breeze (the famous *scirocco*) caresses his face. The fragrance of the flowers delights him. It is literally a feast for all the senses. Dante's choice of words to describe this scene are sheer poetry and music. English translations simply cannot convey the musical charm of such Italian words as *augeletti* (little birds), *fiumicello* (little stream), and *fioretti* (little flow- ers). The poet's sensitivity to the beauty of nature is re- vealed as he recalls the scenes of his native Italy, in par- ticular the pine forest at Chiassi, near Ravenna, where he often walked and meditated in his last years.

The forest is devoid of humans—a reference to the Paradise lost by human sin—except for one, a woman gathering flowers and singing. She is Matelda, symbol of human innocence and happiness. Her historical identity is often disputed, but her allegorical meaning is quite clear. She is one of the most charming persons in the *Comedy*: she radiates a joy which is truly infectious. Dante recognizes immediately that she must be a woman in love and addresses her in the words: "Pray, beautiful lady, who do warm yourself in the rays of love, if I may

believe outward looks which are usually the testimony of
the heart. . . ." When she finally lifts her eyes to look at
Dante, he perceives the love which shines forth from
them, like "the eyes of Venus when she was struck by
her son (Cupid)."

She then explains to Dante and the other two poets,
strangers here, the meaning of the place and meaning of
her smile. The forest is "the place chosen as the nest of
the human race." She refers Dante to a word (*Delectasti*)
from Psalm 92 as the clue to her delight and joy. The
verses of the psalm are: "You have delighted me, Lord, by
Your work and in the works of Your hands I will rejoice.
How praiseworthy are Your works, O Lord."

This is the source of her experience of joy and love.
She is in love with God, Who has shown His love to her
in the beautiful works of nature. She is responding with
a love song, a song of praise to the Creator of all this
splendor. The created universe is in essence a revelation
of God. It reflects His beauty and His love for humanity.
The innocent human soul responds with delight, love,
and praise.

This response is not the so-called "pure poetry" of
the aesthetes, who stop short at the mere enjoyment of
it all. It is a deeper awareness of its meaning as a reflection of its Creator. It is a movement of love and praise of
Him. In theological terms it is a response to the "natural"
revelation of God, which elicits this act of praise, worship, and love from the human soul. This response to
natural revelation is not only on an intellectual level: it
touches the human heart and fills it with joy and love.
The natural revelation is "natural" in the sense that all
nature is a mirror reflecting God; and human "nature," as
such, can experience revelation through nature without

the fuller revelation given in the course of history. This is the primordial "grace" of nature, given by God to all at all times and in all places.

Matelda alludes to this "grace" when she explains that the poets of ancient times intuited this gift of God when they sang of the "golden age" of humanity, a time when the "root of the human race was innocent." They had written of this very place where "Spring is everlasting" and "every kind of fruit and nectar" abounded. She is quoting phrases from the famous pagan poets, recognized by Dante, Virgil, and Statius. Dante turns to his fellow poets who smile with recognition and approval. Dante subtly suggests once again that classical culture was the "Scripture of the pagans." God's revelation and truth lived in the dreams and songs of the classical poets.

The Divine Pageant
(*Canto* XXIX)

Matelda, the woman in love, continues her singing, but her song now is another psalm: "Blessed are those whose sins are forgiven," a reference to Dante's innocence. She then addresses him as "my brother" to show how they share the same innocence as God's children. This calm state of peaceful innocence is then suddenly interrupted as a brightness like lightning floods the whole forest. Dante is alarmed as the light grows brighter. He exclaims, "What is this?"

He has just tasted some of the ineffable joys of Paradise; but as something new begins to shine forth, he realizes that these first joys (natural innocence) were only the "first fruits" of eternal pleasure. There is much more to come. His inchoate rapture now yearns for more joys.

Before his dazzled eyes a splendid sight begins to show itself. At first appearance there seem to be "seven trees of gold" moving toward him. He soon discerns them as seven candlesticks at the head of a beautiful pageant. The chant "Hosanna" is being joyously sung. This pageant resembles a medieval procession for the feast of *Corpus Christi* (The Body of Christ). It was, and still is, an annual celebration to honor the real presence of Jesus in the sacrament of the Eucharist. The splendor of those medieval processions can still be witnessed today in many European cities.

This dazzling pageant has broken into the peaceful, natural scene to indicate the arrival of something greater than nature. It is sometimes called the "divine" pageant since it represents allegorically all the divine (supernatural) gifts that descend from God: the Scriptures of the Old and New Testaments, the theological virtues, the gifts of the Holy Spirit, and the sacraments of the Church. All of these are represented as persons, animals, or things. The flames of the seven candles (gifts of the Holy Spirit) paint the sky in rainbow colors. Everyone sings: "Blessed are thou among the daughters of Adam and blessed for all eternity are thy beauties."

These overwhelming sights and sounds continue as a chariot drawn by a griffin arrives. The griffin, a legendary animal composed of part-lion and part-eagle, is drawing the triumphal car. His colors are gold (the eagle part), white and red (the lion portion). The dancing and singing accompany the advancing chariot when suddenly a thunderclap is heard.

Dante's readers in the Middle Ages were very familiar with the kind of symbol and ritual he used; whereas, in our post-Vatican II Church much of the traditional

Catholic ritual has been changed, simplified, or elimi-
nated altogether. To a great extent this has been a real
loss, for the sense of awe in the presence of God's mysteries has often been substituted with the merely ordinary, the emotional, or the prosaic. Our attempts to make
the liturgy more "relevant" have often resulted in empty-
ing it of its mysterious, transcendent dimension. The use
of everyday clothing, popular secular songs, everyday
language—all these innovations strip ritual of its unique
power to evoke the experience of the divine, the "sacred,"
the transcendent.

This pageant in the forest is pure ritual, with all its
evocative beauty and also its rather formal, impersonal
style. The "persons" in the procession are not real persons. Here we see the most formal use of allegory in the
Comedy. The "persons" are merely symbols of divine
gifts. They are somewhat like the first part of the Catholic Mass—the readings from the Old and New Testaments, the hymns, the profession of faith, etc.—all leading up to the Real Presence of Christ in the Eucharist.
This pageant is really a grand entrance rite. It is grand,
since God's gifts—His Scriptures, the virtues, the Church—
are great revelations of His love; but they prepare us for,
and lead us to, a far greater revelation of His love.

The Arrival of Beatrice
(*Canto* XXX)

As the solemn procession comes to a halt, all sing,
"Come, Bride from Lebanon," words from the famous
love song, *The Canticle of Canticles,* in the Old Testament. This love poem was generally interpreted as a song

about Christ's love for His Bride, the Church. Then the whole entourage around the chariot chant "Alleluiahs" as well as "Blessed *(Benedictus)* is He who comes!" These last words, once sung by the crowd at Jerusalem during Christ's triumphal entrance, are also the words sung in the Catholic liturgy as the solemn moment of Consecration approaches.

Dante then adds another chant, taken from Virgil's *Aeneid*: "Give lilies with full hands." These words, a tribute to Virgil, have a deep significance. Here at the most solemn arrival of Beatrice (God's supernatural revelation) Dante quotes words from a pagan poet. Pagan culture thus joins in this great celebration of welcome, for it had prepared for it and yearned for it. The words quoted from Virgil refer to the funeral rite for a noble Roman, Marcellus, who was destined to become Emperor but died in his youth. Lilies thrown on his grave were the tribute to this outstanding, heroic youth. It is significant that these words come immediately before Beatrice's arrival. The earthly Beatrice, who died in her youth, has risen to a new and glorious life. Here the words about Marcellus express all the pathos and sad yearning of the pagan world—and of the whole earth—for eternal life, which was attained by Beatrice.

The contrast between Marcellus's lamented death and the present scene is striking. The present scene is a cloud of flowers rising from the hands of angels as the dawn breaks into spectacular hues of rosy red. This magnificent sunrise accompanies the epiphany of Beatrice. She is clad in the color of living flame (charity), with a green mantle (hope), and a white veil (faith), crowned with olive leaves (triumph and peace). The symbolic colors are familiar to us from the *Vita Nuova*: they are the same colors worn at Dante's first encounter with her.

Many of the other details of this glorious arrival suggest the glorious Second Coming of Christ. The words of the songs certainly suggest the coming of Christ, especially the *Benedictus* (with the masculine ending of the word). And yet it is Beatrice, and not Christ, who arrives. Although we have alluded to the meaning of Beatrice several times before, it is only here that her full significance shines forth clearly.

Several obtuse ecclesiastics—both from the Catholic and Protestant traditions—have been shocked at this apparent blasphemy of equating Beatrice with Christ. This shock stems from a complete misunderstanding of Dante's poetic genius as well as of sound Christian theology, as we have already noted. The figure of Beatrice embraces several levels of meaning. In the literal sense she is the historical young woman whom Dante knew and loved in Florence, a lady of flesh and blood. But this beloved creature has died and passed into a new life, the eternal glory of Christ. Dante now knows her and loves her in a far different way. She is now "in Christ." She, a glorified member of His Body, has been "deified." That is basic Christian faith.

In her earthly life she was indeed a "sacrament," that is, a visible manifestation of God's love for Dante; but now that she has entered Christ's glory, she is more fully a "sacrament" of His love. That is why hymns to Christ are sung for her. Hymns to celebrate the Church as Christ's Bride are also applied to her. She is still the creature, the Bride of Christ.

Without losing her individual personality (She is still the Beatrice Portinari of Dante's youth), she takes on an "impersonal" symbolism as the Revelation of God, His ineffable Wisdom which comes to us in human form, just as Christ in His Incarnation is the Wisdom of God. And just as Christ is the incarnate expression of God's love, so too is Beatrice, through her incorporation into Christ, an incarnation (but not *the* Incarnation) of God's love. She is the God-bearing image of God for Dante.

After the "extraordinary" ritual of the pageant, we see that God's wisdom and love come to us in the "ordinary," the "personal," the "human" form, adapted to our present conditions and capabilities. That's the very meaning of the sacraments. Beatrice, like Christ in the Eucharist, is—in an "ordinary" form—an extraordinary manifestation of all of God's attributes. God reaches us, touches us, loves us through other "ordinary" human persons. The "sacred" is found not only in the Church's solemn liturgy but also in other human persons.

Dante trembles at the sight of Beatrice and feels the mighty power of that first love. He recognizes within himself "the tokens of the ancient flame"—the final quotation from Virgil's *Aeneid*. The context of that phrase was Dido's erotic love for Aeneas, which led to her suicide. Dido, we may recall, was among the carnal sinners with Francesca in the *Inferno*. Her words, quoted at this point, evoke the whole tradition of eros, which gives way now to agape. At this very point in the drama Dante turns to Virgil as a little child might turn to a parent when he is frightened. But Virgil is gone. Human eros has disappeared and agape has arrived. Agape—the fulfillment of all unsatisfied desires. The glory of Rome (Marcellus) and human eros (Dido) ended in death, but God gives the gift of eternal life and perfect love (Beatrice).

As Dante bursts into tears at the loss of his "sweetest father," the great moment—the long-awaited encounter with Beatrice—draws near. The drama has been building up to this climactic meeting with a *crescendo* of increasing hope, love, and awe. Beatrice now speaks: "Dante, because Virgil leaves you, do not weep yet, for you must weep for another sword!"

This is the first and only time that Dante's personal name appears in the *Comedy*. It is obviously a supreme moment in the drama, the most personal one. One would expect tender words of loving welcome from Beatrice after all the sufferings of Dante so far. Instead she shows no sympathy for Dante's loss of Virgil and even announces a far greater pain. Her words are personal, but they are foreboding. She continues in her regal, stern manner: "Look at *us* well: I am, I am Beatrice." The royal plural here suggests unapproachable majesty, while the singular pronoun suggests a personal approach. She now reprimands Dante for coming to the top of the mountain "where man is happy." These are strange, unexpected words, since it was she who descended into Hell in order to save Dante from his misery. She is, of course, alluding to the misery which Dante had freely chosen in life rather than happiness and wholeness which could have been his. Dante becomes fearfully aware that the worst is yet to come from her accusing words. He becomes like a child who feels the brunt of a mother's "harsh pity."

Dante's fear and shame turn him to ice. The angels then sing words of a psalm, "In You, O Lord, I have hoped," to express compassion for Dante. The mention of hope in the Lord begins to melt the ice and snow around his heart, as a flood of emotions pours out of Dante's eyes.

Beatrice then turns to the compassionate angels to explain her sternness. She no longer addresses Dante but talks about him to them. He was a man endowed by nature and grace with the highest gifts. He had the potential in his youth (his "new life") for wonderful deeds. But just as weeds grow better in rich, untilled soil; so, too, evil took root in his good soul. One thinks of the Latin proverb *Corruptio optimi pessima*: corruption of the best person is the worst kind of corruption.

While Beatrice was still living on earth she sustained him with her youthful eyes, but as soon as she passed from death to her "second age"—from flesh to spirit—and acquired a greater beauty and virtue, she became less pleasing to him. His passionate love cooled and he abandoned the true path for false visions of good, which promise much but yield so little. He sank so low that only a journey through Hell to see the "lost people" could save him. That's why she descended to Hell, and weeping asked Virgil's aid as guide to this place. It is now God's will that Dante sincerely repent with tears before he cross the river Lethe, which wipes out all remembrance of sin.

We are surprised at these cold words of accusation from Beatrice. The sweetness and light of the rosy sunrise might have led us to expect a warmer reception. We must remember, however, that Beatrice here is the image of Christ in His Second Coming: His Coming as supreme judge. Christ the lover is also Christ the judge. The sweetness of love is not diminished by the accusing light of judgment. In John's Gospel Jesus is the light of the world, a light which exposes the wickedness of human sin, judges it as such, and condemns it. Judgment is a function of that love that cannot compromise with evil in the beloved. It is a "harsh pity"—the bittersweet attitude of the authentic lover who draws the beloved into pain only in order to bring the beloved finally to a greater good: personal integrity and health. This "harsh pity" of Beatrice is like the medicinal "tough love" practiced by parents for the benefit of their children. This tough discipline can be truly positive and healing provided that its source is love and its administration is moderated by compassion.

Dante's Confession
(*Canto* XXXI)

Beatrice's accusing words are compared to the sharp sword of love which pierces Dante's heart. The stress and tension build up so much within him that he bursts into tears. This breakdown is compared to the hunter's bow which is drawn so tightly that it breaks under such pressure. This metaphor aptly describes the experience of contrition (literally, a "breaking apart") which precedes honest confession. The sinner must reach that breaking point when the inflated ego is completely deflated and broken by the pressure of the truth which had remained half-hidden or deliberately buried in the depths of the soul.

Beatrice's accusation draws the unpleasant truth out of Dante by posing some very pertinent questions to him. She wants to know what desires and allurements distracted Dante from the love of the transcendent Good, which satisfies all possible human desires. She is asking Dante to name the "secondary goods" which distracted him from the love of God. Then Dante finally confesses: "Present things with their false pleasures turned away my steps as soon as your face was hidden."

Beatrice responds that sincere self-accusation turns the grindstone back against the edge. This metaphor implies that the sharp sword of justice is blunted with mercy when the sinner makes his confession. She further warns

Dante to be aware of such Sirens (allurements) in the future.

Now Beatrice comments on Dante's self-accusation. It was indeed truthful, but she wants to elaborate on that truth. She tells Dante that her death should have been an occasion for a deeper love of God, not the contrary. Her buried flesh is now scattered to dust, but she has risen to a new life. She has passed from the flesh to the Spirit.

She tells Dante that "no young maiden or other vain thing with such brief enjoyment should have weighed down your wings to await more shots." She is referring to young birds which are not yet full-fledged and consequently don't know by experience the dangers of the hunters' nets and arrows. But the full-grown bird should know and avoid such snares. In other words, Dante in his mature years should have known better. He now feels like a shameful child before his angry mother. He detects the sarcasm in Beatrice's words when she tells him to lift his "beard" (the sign of mature age) rather than his chin or face. Dante must now look on the face of Beatrice and experience even greater shame and sorrow.

He sees Beatrice on the other side of the stream. She is turned toward the griffin, "which is one sole person in two natures." The symbolism of the griffin is now apparent. The legendary animal (half-lion and half-eagle) represents Christ, Who is both man and God. As Beatrice gazes on the griffin, we are reminded that she is never isolated as an object of worship: she is always turned toward Christ, always pointing to Him.

At this moment Dante feels the piercing sting of repentance. It bites at him and gnaws at his heart. This remorse (literally, "second bite") induces Dante to hate all the things that turned him from his first love for Beatrice.

The "young maiden" and the "vain things" have been interpreted in various ways. Most interpreters consider the maiden to be "Lady Philosophy," the love of his middle years, which replaced Beatrice, the love of his younger years. Other commentators prefer to think of some "flesh and blood" woman. It is difficult to make a choice since the language could be allegorical. Besides, medieval writers did not ordinarily indulge in explicit self-revelations as modern writers often attempt to do for the sake of hoping to produce best sellers. The veiled language of Dante could possibly imply either sins of the flesh, sins of the spirit, or both. In any case, the main accusation is infidelity to Beatrice, who represents God's passionate love.

The substitution of other persons, values, or pleasures as the highest good or the real center of one's existence is the basic sin of Dante. This "dark forest" of Dante's soul was his aberration from his first love, which was the passionate and all-absorbing center of his life. His love for Beatrice had grown tepid after her death. His heart had become hardened. He had lost that fresh, innocent, child-like fascination and love for Beatrice. In brief, he had fallen "out of love." The "false pleasures and vanities" which he pursued did not fill the void left by Beatrice's death. He had not learned that physical absence should have increased his love for the invisible beloved. The "fleshly" Beatrice of history had passed into the realm of Spirit, just as the Jesus of history had passed into the glory of the Father to become Spirit. But Dante's love did not follow her there.

Dante, however, must forget these aberrations and sins. He must heal these bad memories by letting himself be plunged into the water of the stream which separated him from Beatrice. The memory of sin with all its guilt and remorse must be drowned in the stream of oblivion (*Lethe*) before Dante can go look on the twin beauties of Beatrice's eyes and smile. Matelda, Beatrice's handmaiden, pulls him into the water and immerses him completely into it.

This is the second baptism, which, as the word implies, is an immersion or bath in water. The Latin hymn *Asperges Me* is sung as Dante passes through the water. These words are from the penitential psalm *Miserere*, which the Church still uses as a purification rite at the beginning of Mass. It was, and still is, a reminder of baptism and a kind of second baptism: repentance, sprinkling with water (*asperges* = sprinkle), confession of sin, and finally absolution. This was the penitential entrance rite of the liturgy in Dante's time and it remains so in our present liturgy, although there are other options as to the form of the rite.

Dante is then led by other handmaidens of Beatrice to behold the unveiled face of Beatrice. They tell Dante: "We have placed you before the emeralds from which Love once shot His arrows at you." Dante exclaims:

> A thousand desires hotter than flame held my eyes on the shining eyes that remained ever fixed on the griffin. As the sun in a mirror, so was the twofold animal gleaming within them, now with the attributes of one, now of the other nature.

(Canto XXXI, 118-123)

Dante is filled with wonder, stupor, and joy as he finally "tastes that food which satisfies but at the same time causes hunger for itself." He is seeing in Beatrice's eyes a reflection of the divine and human beauty of Christ Himself. The meaning of Beatrice is transparent here.

She is divine revelation, a reflection of God, just as a mirror reflects the splendor of the sun. She is not Christ, but a wonderful reflection of Him.

Beatrice then unveils her mouth, which reveals her second beauty, her smile. If the first revelation—her eyes—gave intellectual light to Dante's mind, this second revelation gives joy to his heart. The smile of Beatrice reveals God's love and affection, just as her eyes revealed His truth and light. Dante is overwhelmed by these revelations and confesses to his readers that all his poetic art fails to communicate the beauty revealed to him at this supreme moment.

The wonder of this moment should evoke in us a sense of awe at the sheer beauty of God's revelation. Most Christians have been exposed to it from early childhood. Christian faith has been shared with us by our parents, teachers, and the Church in general; but rarely does that faith awaken in us a sense of wonder at the marvelous beauty and grace of it all. Beatrice in all her splendor personifies this divine revelation which constitutes the "object" of faith. God's revelation comes to us in a human, personal way (Beatrice) and is addressed to each human person (Dante). It comes to us as an invitation from God, Who is Love. The invitation is an expression of His condescending love (agape), which reaches us through the human: the humanity of Jesus, first of all, and then through His extensions—the Church, the sacraments, and all the members of His Church. It is not surprising, then, that the human person Beatrice, a glorified member of His Church, should be the symbol and channel of God's revelation and love. Since she reflects Christ as a mirror reflects the sun, she is a brilliant light but at the same time she is only a faint shadow of the unseen reality.

This twofold aspect of the Christian experience of faith is clearly shown in the person of Beatrice. Faith is a real light, but also a dark veil which is not penetrated in this life. That's why the Earthly Paradise is not the end of Dante's journey. It is merely a nest for mankind, whose true home is the Heavenly Paradise, the direct vision and enjoyment of God—without veils, signs, and symbols. Beatrice is God's initial revelation—in earthly symbols and allegories which communicate only "something" about the mystery of God's love. The mystery will be fully experienced only above and beyond in the "face-to-face" vision of Paradise. Faith, in St. Paul's words, is a "looking into a cloudy mirror." The beatific vision in Paradise will be clear and direct, without veils and shadows.

The Final Pageant
(*Cantos* XXXII-XXXIII)

As Dante gazes on Beatrice and quenches his "ten years' thirst," the attendants of Beatrice warn him that he is looking "too fixedly." This indicates that the vision of faith in this life should always be understood as the shadow. It is not the absolute reality. The shadow should lead us beyond itself to the reality, the absolute beauty and goodness of God. The Scriptures, the creeds and the sacraments of the Church—all true revelations from God—are nonetheless only pale reflections of God.

Dante next witnesses the second movement of the pageant which had been interrupted by Beatrice's accusation and Dante's confession. The personal encounter between Dante and Beatrice was set between the two phases of the pageant in order to stress the personal aspect of

God's revelation. We now return to the procession, which comes to a halt before a huge, defoliated tree in the forest. The tree suggests the tree in Eden which, because of Adam and Eve's sin, was stripped naked of its leaves and flowers. The symbolism here is rich: the tree is God's justice and goodness which were violated by human sin, that selfish grasping for equality with God.

All those in the procession sadly murmur "Adam," as they gaze on the naked tree. Then they sing praises to the Griffin (Christ), who attaches the wooden pole of the chariot (the Church) to the bare tree. The tree comes back to life and blossoms into bright red flowers, symbolic of Christ's blood. The allegory is clear: Christ, the new Adam, restores by His innocent suffering on the wood of the Cross the covenant of peace which had been broken by human sin, the rebellious pride of Adam. This central event of salvation history—the reconciliation of God and man through the blood of Christ—is celebrated here with the sweetest hymns and music. It is a celebration of Christ's sacrificial love for humanity and His obedient submission to His Father's Will.

The beauty of this scene and its music overwhelm Dante and cast him into a trance or deep sleep. When he awakes he compares himself to the Apostles Peter, James, and John who awoke after Jesus' glorious transfiguration on the mountain. The extraordinary vision of Christ in His glory had plunged those apostles into a state of rapture. Dante claims that his experience was similar to theirs. For a moment he had penetrated into the mystery of Christ's love. He also compares his rapture to the experience of the angels' vision of Christ in the heavenly Paradise. Christ is the "apple tree" whose fruit they continuously hunger for in that eternal heavenly feast.

Dante calls that feast "a perpetual marriage feast" to show that although the beatific vision fills and delights the blessed, the delight and yearning continue and grow. Love is the endless activity of the angels and blessed souls in Heaven because they continuously celebrate God's love for them and their love for him.

When Dante regains his senses after the momentary glimpse of Christ's love, he looks for Beatrice, who is now seated alone at the foot of the blossoming tree. The Griffin has ascended to Heaven and Beatrice is now guardian of the chariot. Her handmaidens tell Dante that he must stay awhile in the forest but sometime in the future he will be a citizen of "that Rome where Christ is a Roman." The allusion is, of course, to Dante's final salvation in the City of God.

Dante then witnesses an allegorical representation of the history of the Church from the time of Christ's Ascension to Dante's own time. The chariot of the Church is invaded by greed and ravaged by heresy. The progressive damage to the Church sinks her to the nadir of corruption in Dante's time when the papacy and the empire betray their divine missions by their greed and lust for worldly power. Here Dante draws on the vivid imagery of the Book of Revelation to express this tragedy. The papacy is represented as the harlot kissing and embracing the giant, symbol of the French kings. The chariot has been transformed into a hideous monster on which the two lovers are enthroned in their acts of mutual lust. Dante paints in lurid colors the picture of the corrupt Church of the fourteenth century. It is noteworthy that Dante uses gestures of love to express the mutual greed of popes and kings. This parody of love shows Dante's consistent concept of sin: misdirected or perverted love. The Bride of

Christ (the Church) had become the adulterous whore of
Babylon, whose sin of perverted love is basically her infidelity to the true Husband, God Himself.

Beatrice then comforts Dante as he looks with shock
and horror at this scene. She tells him that the Church
will recover from her present decadence. She predicts in
very enigmatic language that a leader will come to reform
and save the Church. This seems to be a veiled reference
to the greyhound mentioned in the first canto of *Hell*.
Beatrice then commissions Dante to take this message to
the world. It is an angry message that God's justice is offended by the corrupt behavior of popes and kings, but it
is also a message of hope for the reform of the Church.

Dante, like the pilgrims in his time who carried home
from Jerusalem a staff wrapped in palm branches, is commissioned to carry back this message to the world. Dante
must tell the world that God's Will is not being carried
out there. Beatrice reminds him that her word is divine
wisdom, far superior to his "school" of human philosophy. Human wisdom alone is inadequate to understand
the full dimension of sin, God's Will, and the hope which
she gives him.

Dante's last act before leaving the divine forest is to
pass through and drink the waters of the second stream,
Eunoe, the river which will restore the memory of good
deeds. Only then will Dante be ready to ascend to Paradise. When he tastes those holy waters he is born again
and becomes like new-sprung foliage. He is now "pure
and ready to rise to the stars." The purification process
is complete.

Dante's purgatory was a painful journey through the
sin within him; but it was crowned with the loving gaze
of Beatrice, who judged him, required his repentance and
confession, but also gave healing to his bad memories as

well as remembrance of the goodness within him. Both forgetfulness of evil and remembrance of good are necessary for personal wholeness. Both baptisms are needed as a preparation for the ascent to the higher experience of transcendence.

Perhaps Dante reserved this final step—the remembrance of our good acts—to the very end because such a remembrance comes dangerously close to pride. We are often reluctant to recognize the good that we do because we fear pride, the root of all sin. We thus fall victim to a false humility. Dante always debunked that false piety. He strongly affirmed the truth that we are images of God, that deep down within all of us is an untarnished beauty: the human heart, innocent, loving, capable of good acts of authentic love.

This image is not completely destroyed by sin. It is God's image within us and therefore the basis for a truly "good self-image." It is God's own gift of Himself at the moment of our creation, and it continues since our creation is an ongoing act of God here and now. We have received and continue to receive this participation in God's goodness. We must therefore recognize this and remember this. This remembrance is a necessary step in our transformation and ascent to the stars.

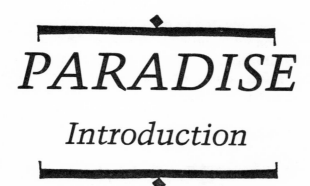

PARADISE
Introduction

Dante's spiritual journey so far has taken us through Hell, a prolonged contemplation of the misery caused by sin, and then through Purgatory, a painstaking process of liberation from that misery as well as a gradual ascent filled with the hope of reaching personal wholeness. Even after the encounter with Beatrice and the twofold baptism of forgetfulness of evil and remembrance of good, the journey is not yet complete. Dante may have attained moral integrity and some intellectual enlightenment—great achievements in themselves—but the "natural thirst" which was awakened in him during this process has not yet been quenched. In fact, it has been increased and intensified.

Dante now desires more than ever his own completion and self-fulfillment. His restless pilgrim heart is even more restless now that he has reached the plateau of moral integrity and wholeness and has lost the "heaviness" of sin. The hunger and thirst for the still unknown bliss of Paradise is felt more keenly. This longing for bliss will be satisfied in the experience of the Heavenly Paradise.

Paradise, the third *cantica* of Dante's *Comedy*, has been and still is the most neglected of the three *cantiche*. Unfortunately, readers over the centuries have found the language and subject matter "too abstract and too theological." The language of the medieval scholastics and mystics, which Dante naturally employs here, has become a foreign language to the modern reader. The concepts expressed also seem too far removed from our ordinary experiences. All this is true. We readers in the twentieth century must do our "homework" in order to understand the idiom and ideas of medieval theology and mysticism. Such study is necessary if we want to understand this cantica as well as the other two.

Dante, however, never abandons his lively, poetic art in order to become a dry, scholastic theologian. Dante the poet continues to appeal to our senses and imagination throughout his *Paradise*. Contrary to some superficial impressions and shallow criticisms, the *Paradise* is not an abstract or boring section of the *Comedy*, unless, of course, we find the experience of joy and bliss boring. It is true that the *Paradise* lacks the dramatic narratives found in *Hell* and *Purgatory*. It also lacks bizarre, grotesque scenes like those of *Hell*, or scenes like the earthly atmosphere of the mountain and the enchanting forest of the Earthly Paradise in *Purgatory*. It lacks the familiar sounds and sights of earth, but it replaces them with other sounds and images of a far greater, although unfamiliar, beauty and majesty. *Paradise* is hardly lackluster or dull.

Dante never forgets that we are dependent on our senses for information and understanding. He does not ignore our need for sensuous images in favor of an abstract dissertation on theology and mystical experience. Dante employs a rich variety of images and metaphors throughout *Paradise*; he describes designs and colors, but above all he focuses on light and music. His nuanced description of the crescendo of light as he soars from the moon all the way to the Empyrean is perhaps unmatched in all of world literature. The imagery of light dominates throughout *Paradise*.

Perhaps one of the great difficulties that prevents the modern reader from appreciating the *Paradise* is a basic mistrust of mysticism and of supernatural visions. Mystical experience is often conceived to be a form of self-delusion or an escape from reality. Dante's vision of Paradise is often dismissed as an ingenious feat of poetic imagination and Dante's mystical experience is sometimes relegated to the area of extraordinary art. And yet Dante claims in his letter to Can Grande that even a sinner such as he can be given by God's grace a glimpse or foretaste of perfect beatitude.

Perhaps underneath the modern misgiving about authentic mystical experience there is an unspoken lack of faith and hope. Perhaps we simply do not believe and hope enough. Perhaps Dante's experience of the joy of Paradise just seems "too good to be true." The modern denial of the possibility of such ecstatic joy is a strange phenomenon, especially in the light of the contemporary glut of books with titles like *Joy of Sex* and *Joy of Cooking*; however, these books have more to do with pleasure than with joy.

The joy that Dante describes in *Paradise* is a complete and inexpressible joy shared by all the blessed, whose minds, hearts, and senses are filled to capacity with delight as well as with active love. It is a joy which totally transcends any joy we can experience in this life.

Naturally it requires an act of faith to believe in such an extraordinary and total joy. Dante presupposes that the reader has this faith. It is a prerequisite for this journey.

It is possible, however, that the modern reader may be attracted to the *Paradise* even if his faith is not so vivid and imaginative as Dante's. There are at least two avenues of approach that can bridge the gap between Dante and the modern reader: Recent advances in man's conquest of space and the popularity of science fiction. Dante's flight to the moon and the other planets reminds us of the "unbelievable," yet real, progress of modern technology in its exploration of outer space; and we realize that what was thought to be impossible and incredible twenty-five years ago is today fact and no longer only science fiction. We need to realize also that the flight to outer space is an appropriate metaphor for the journey into the inner space of the soul.

Dante's *Paradise* introduces us into a strangely different world, but yet a world peopled with real individuals. These individuals have not lost their particular personalities, although their earthly appearance has now been transformed into various kinds of light. They continue to speak, act, sing, and dance; but their personalities glow and sparkle with the intense warmth and light of love. They still express concern for the earth. In fact, their love for the reality of this earthly world is even more real than ever. St. Peter, for example, in the glory of Heaven glows red with indignation and anger, as he denounces the corrupt behavior of Pope Boniface VIII and other popes who are neglecting their pastoral care of the Church on earth. The blessedness of the saints in *Paradise* is not an escape from reality, but rather an "inscape" into the full reality of the cosmos, into the deepest implications of love for the universe.

Dante never takes refuge in some false, "other-worldly" mysticism which denies the reality of the physical world. Even throughout his experiences in Paradise he is always aware of the earth and writes from that perspective. As he enjoys the glorious vision of Paradise he often contrasts it with the misery and sin of this world. He takes our world very seriously, but sees it within the framework of the total reality: a cosmos created and set in a magnificent order by God. Reality is created by God and has God as its center and goal. Reality seems less real and less good to us only when we turn away from its center.

Dante's mysticism, then, embraces all of reality as he knew it. He recognizes within the human person an unfulfilled desire to be at one with this total reality. This is basically man's desire for transcendence: his yearning for what is beyond himself—that something which finally completes him and brings him into harmony with all beings and Being Itself. This experience of transcendence brings man into loving union with God and the entire universe. It seems that this yearning for transcendence is really at the bottom of modern man's fascination with drugs and alcohol and other avenues of escapism. These escape routes (or "trips") seem to express the human desire for the "ultimate experience," but too often they become the *cul-de-sac* of self-centered love. They often lead to misery and despair—the ultimate "bad trip."

The love which Dante celebrates in *Paradise* is a far cry from the ego-centered love of those in *Hell*. The wretched souls in *Hell* had freely chosen themselves as the center of the universe, the highest good. Their selfish love had ended in a dead and timeless paralysis. They remain frozen in their opposition to the Will of God, Who desires our total happiness but yet mysteriously respects our freedom. In *Purgatory*, however, the souls freely recognize other objects of love besides themselves. They grow and change since they have time to do so. They learn how to exercise their freedom with true love. Dante himself learns in *Purgatory* that his earlier passions for love poetry and philosophy were only symptoms of a deeper thirst for a greater good. It is in *Paradise* that he finds that thirst satisfied at last. There his freedom is finally at one with God, the true goal of his labyrinthine journeys. He finds rest, but a rest which is simultaneously a constant activity and free flow of love.

In his *Paradise* Dante developed that fourth level of meaning which he describes in his letter to Can Grande. It is the "anagogical," or "ascending," dimension which reaches up to the final goal of human existence. In his *Hell* he had developed the "literal" level of meaning with realistic descriptions of the individuals in Hell as well as with a description of Hell's vivid scenery and torments. In the *Purgatory* he had developed the "moral" level of meaning by his accounts of how the souls may attain moral integrity; and through the presence of Virgil he provides many lessons on moral philosophy. Then, in the Earthly Paradise, Dante unfolds an "allegorical" level of meaning: the two pageants and the figure of Beatrice reveal another reality beyond the signs and symbols. In *Paradise* the fourth level of meaning—anagogical in approach—is finally reached and enjoyed. These four levels of meaning are present throughout the entire *Comedy*, but each is developed specifically in a separate stage of the journey. Appropriate guides lead Dante through each of these various phases of the pilgrimage. Virgil, as Human Reason, points out the human capacities for evil (Hell) and for good moral development (Purgatory). But Virgil's ability to enlighten Dante must yield to a higher power. Human nature is completed with divine grace, symbolized in Beatrice. Beatrice leads Dante into Paradise. In her, Dante finds his own *anima*, his soul. Virgil, as the masculine principle of reason (the *animus*), could lead Dante only so far; Beatrice completed Dante's journey of self-discovery and self-integration. She leads him into the sacred, the mysterious, the suprarational. She, the eternal feminine, is the spiritual intuition of faith: a light which transcends the merely rational powers of the human mind.

But toward the end of the upward journey through Paradise, Beatrice yields her leadership to another guide: St. Bernard. This third guide, or light, is an allegory for the higher grace of mystical contemplation, the soul's union with God. Bernard, however, is not the last intermediary between Dante and the beatific vision of God. He entrusts Dante to Mary, the living image of the Christian soul in love with her Creator. It is she, the creature closest to the Trinity, who introduces Dante to the final vision and union.

The Trinity of the Divine Persons is not only the goal of Dante's ascent but also the creative foundation of the entire universe and, more particularly, of the individual human soul. All of reality is somehow a reflection of the inner life of the Trinity. That is why Dante's universe is composed of three parts and all three realms are divided into nine sections plus one. Variations on three and one—Trinity and Unity—are found throughout the *Comedy*. Dante's own poetic unit, the tercet, is also an imitation of the primal reality, the Trinity. Dante was familiar with St. Augustine's intuition of man as an image of the Trinity. According to Augustine, the Father knows Himself and that self-knowledge generates the Son, His word or thought. The mutual love "breathed" between the Father and the Son is the Holy Spirit. Augustine sees this same pattern in the human soul: its power to know (the Father); its wisdom (the Son); its love (the Spirit). The unity in diversity of the human soul is thus an image of the Triune God.

The journey into Paradise then should not be such a strange adventure for the modern reader because it is really a journey of self-discovery. The human soul finds herself when she, the image, is reunited to her source or archetype, God. Since we as creatures are not complete until we have re-entered the circle of that community of love (The Trinity), self-discovery and discovery of God are one and the same experience. This "mystical" experience should not frighten us, but rather attract us. The Divine Persons Who created us in Their own image are drawing us back to Themselves. We can of course resist this magnetic force, since we remain free; but if we let go of our fears and self-centeredness we will find ourselves and our real center. We will be at one and in harmony with God and the universe. That was Dante's mystical experience. He did not consider himself to be uniquely gifted with that experience.

His *Paradise* is an invitation to all of us to share that experience here and now. Eternal life, as St. John's Gospel teaches us, begins now. A foretaste of the perfect vision can be ours now, provided that we first work through the pain of hell and purgation. Although the foretaste of Paradise is sheer gift and not a reward for our efforts, it is nonetheless an experience which presumes the hard work of death to the ego. We must lose ourselves in order to find ourselves. This teaching of Jesus is found in all four Gospels. It is perhaps the most important truth about ourselves. When we die to ourselves we find ourselves embraced by the community of love, the Three Divine

Persons. Dante's spirituality is centered on the Trinity, the community of love in which the individual is fulfilled as a person, with the capacities to know and to love fully developed and satisfied at last.

Transcendence
(*Canto* I)

Dante begins the *Paradise* with a moving hymn of praise to God the Creator, Whose glory can be seen throughout the universe; but he confesses in the same breath that he cannot adequately relate the experience of God's glory as it was revealed to him in Paradise:

> The glory of the All-Mover penetrates through the universe and shines forth in one part more and in another less. I have been in the heaven that most receives of His light; and have seen things which cannot be retold by anyone who descends from there because our intellect, as it draws near to its desire, enters so deep that memory cannot go back upon the track. Nevertheless, as much of the holy Kingdom as I could treasure up in my mind shall now be the subject of my song.
>
> (*Canto* I, 1-12)

In these majestic opening words we can detect an underlying desire to be able to express adequately this totally new experience. This desire is similar to a lover's frustration in trying to express the experience of his or her love and admiration for the beloved. The attempt often issues in a song: a love song, a hymn of praise. Such is Dante's experience as his words rise and fall: from the glory of God to his own weakness and inability to express it. This is the lover's sigh.

He is trying to describe what he experienced in "that heaven which receives most abundantly of the glory and light of God." That heaven is the tenth heaven, called the Empyrean, the region beyond space and time, the very abode of God. Empyrean means "flaming with fire"; not with material fire, but as Dante explains in his letter to Can Grande: with a "spiritual fire, which is holy love or charity." What Dante attempts to express is the inexpressible nature of God, Who is the love that moves the universe, penetrates throughout it, and contains it all. Dante, the human lover, is singing about *The Lover*, Who, moved only by love, shares His nature by creating and sustaining the universe.

Dante's opening words echo the experience which St. Paul described in his second letter to the Corinthians. Paul wrote of a man (no doubt himself) who was rapt into Paradise and saw and heard things which cannot be uttered (2 Cor. 12:3-4). It was an experience which went beyond the ordinary, human perception of God. This transcendent experience is the topic of Dante's *Paradise*. Because it is *transcendent*, Dante feels compelled at the outset to invoke the aid of God Himself for the telling of it. At the beginning of *Hell* and *Purgatory* he has called on the inspiration of the Muses, the patronesses of poetry; but now he invokes Apollo himself, the god of poetry and music. Apollo, of course, is a poetic metaphor for God.

Dante alludes to a myth about Apollo who was challenged by the satyr Marsyas to a contest of musical skill. Apollo naturally won. He punished Marsyas for his presumption by having him flayed alive. This reference to

Marsyas's being drawn from the sheath is a metaphor to express how Dante is now taken out of himself—the meaning of ecstasy—in order to be filled with new breath and new life. It is similar to the Gospel metaphor of the new wine poured into new skins. Dante becomes an empty vessel to receive the new wine of God's inspiration, that divine power which alone can express this ecstatic experience.

As Dante invokes God's help for his venture, he exclaims, "A great flame follows a little spark." His prayer, which is the spark kindled in him by God's love, will become by God's power a great flame. His human frailty will receive the power it needs to sing of God's Kingdom. Like the mustard seed in the Gospel parable, Dante's small human potential will be activated by divine energy to produce a work beyond his own capabilities.

After the prayer of invocation Dante turns his eyes to his guide, Beatrice. She has her gaze fixed on the sun like an eagle, believed by medieval legend to be able to gaze directly at the sun. Her action of gazing is reflected in her eyes, which become like mirrors for Dante in which he sees the reflected sun. Once again the allegorical role of Beatrice is clear: to reflect like a mirror the glory of God. It recalls Paul's words that seeing God in a mirror is only a prelude to a greater vision: the face-to-face contemplation of God in glory. Beatrice's role as a light reflecting light will yield to another light later in the journey: the light of glory, symbolized by St. Bernard.

As Dante gazes on Beatrice, he feels like the pilgrim returning home: "the place made for humanity as its proper abode." The Earthly Paradise was only the nest for mankind; now Dante is flying to man's true home. Dante begins to feel transformed as he gazes on Beatrice. This strange transformation he compares to the experience of the mythical Glaucus, a fisherman who tasted the magical grass which made him a "consort" of the other gods in the sea. Glaucus, transformed into a sea god, is the metaphor Dante offers to explain this "transhumanizing" experience.

The inadequacy of human language constrains Dante here and throughout *Paradise* to coin new words, such as "transhumanize," to express this novel event. Dante attributes the experience to God's grace. He addresses God here as the Love Who lifts him with His light. Dante is lifted out of his own flesh (his humanity) and his "transhumanized" soul now begins to feel this extraordinary change. This "passage beyond the human" into the divine is a gift which the soul receives from God's overflowing love. As the rain enlarges a river, so divine grace expands Dante's soul, creating a new capacity in him. This expansion is a new creation. It kindles in Dante a "spiritual high" which he has never before felt. This "keen delight" engenders even more desire for the beauty and splendor of God. Many of the Christian mystics before Dante's time had spoken in similar terms about God's grace, which "deifies" or "divinizes" them. They all, like Dante, attributed this deification to an extraordinary gift of God and not to their own efforts or merits. It is essentially His activity of love which accomplishes the mystical experience.

Dante is overwhelmed with wonder as he feels himself soaring effortlessly with Beatrice upward toward their goal. Beatrice responds to the disturbed, awe-struck Dante in these words:

> You make yourself dull with false imagining,
> so that you do not see what you would see if

you had cast it off. You are not on earth, as you
believe; lightning, fleeing its proper place, never
darted so fast as you are returning to yours.

(*Canto* I, 88-93)

Beatrice sighs as Dante continues to be perplexed
by the novelty of their speedy ascent through space. She
comforts him as a loving mother consoles a "delirious"
child, and explains to him that there are many more
wonders in store for him. She tells Dante that he is merely
returning to his true destiny. The human creature, like
all the creatures in the vast sea of being, is simply returning to its true port. Every creature is directed to its proper
end by God Himself, Who is compared to the archer who
shoots arrows to the target. The human potentials of intellect and love are powers given to man by which he arrives consciously and willingly at his goal; but it is God
Who gave the initial impetus (eros) to His human creatures so that they would eventually reach Him through
their own desire and will.

Beatrice explains that the good direction and impulse
of eros can be diverted by the human creature into the
wrong direction. False pleasures are the attractions which
the human soul can willingly choose instead of its true
goal. This perversion, or detour, of human eros is sin, the
downward, distorted course of a naturally good drive.
Beatrice further explains that it would be just as strange
and unnatural for a mountain stream to go upward as it
would be if Dante should descend now that he has lost
the weight of sin. Dante's being is soaring upward toward
God because it is natural for a being to seek its proper
place. Human eros, freed of the heaviness of sin, simply
flies to its natural destiny: agape. The natural eros of man

soars into the divine agape of God because it is drawn by Him and destined by Him to arrive there for its completion and the satisfaction of all its desires.

At this stage of the flight Dante is still bewildered by the novelty of it all. He is feeling a new wholeness or simplicity which he never felt before: his physical and spiritual dimensions are at one with one another. His humanity is transformed and divinized. He is free of all hindrances and soars to that irresistible magnet, the center of his being. He is at last responding fully to his true identity as he lets himself be drawn by that Love Who draws all to Himself.

The Moon
(*Cantos* II-III)

Dante issues a strange warning at the beginning of Canto II to those readers who may want to follow him in this journey through Paradise. He advises them to turn back if their motives are not adequate. It seems that Dante has in mind those who may be motivated by mere curiosity or a desire for intellectual or emotional thrills. He states one necessary condition for following him in this journey: a desire for the "bread of angels, on which humans here subsist but of which they never become sated." Dante is referring again to that innate thirst or hunger for God which is deep within all of us, although too often we either ignore it, misunderstand it, or misdirect it. It is only when we recognize it and surrender ourselves to it that we are ready for this journey. When we are true to ourselves—to that deep longing for wholeness and for God within us—then we are ready to launch our boats and set sail in the wind of His Spirit toward our true destiny.

When Dante and Beatrice arrive "in the moon," Beatrice tells Dante: "Direct your mind in gratitude to God Who has united us with the first star." Dante, filled with wonder, realizes that he has been enveloped in a kind of cloud, yet a cloud that is dense and firm like a diamond shining in the sun's rays. He calls the moon "an eternal pearl," which receives them as a ray of light is received in the water. All these metaphors help to explain how his body could penetrate into the dense substance of the moon, how one dimension could support the other. Dante's penetration into the moon is a pale image of what is happening to himself: his human nature is penetrating into the divine.

These images accentuate the reality of this first taste of Paradise, and at the same time they indicate the strangeness and wonder of this reality. Dante tells us that the desire to comprehend this mind-boggling reality is similar to our longing to penetrate the mystery of how our human nature can be united to God in the Incarnation of Christ. That wonderful truth, which we hold by faith now, shall be seen in all its clarity above. We should notice that the Incarnation, God's eternal wedding of Himself to our humanity in the person of Christ, is always in the back of Dante's mind.

Some critics have mistakenly pointed out an absence of Christ in the *Comedy*, but they have apparently missed Dante's many allusions to Christ. The "bread of angels," for instance, was a familiar phrase in medieval hymns for Christ in the Eucharist. He, the Bread of Life, satisfies the deep hunger of the human heart. The human thirst for God is satisfied by the water of the Spirit, which He gave to the Samaritan woman, mentioned in *Purgatory* (Canto XXI, 3). We recall how often Dante alluded to that thirst in the journey through Purgatory.

Dante now encounters the first souls of the blessed and mistakes them for reflections in a mirror of physical faces behind him. He turns around to see the real persons, but sees nothing. Beatrice smiles at his childish thought, and in a motherly manner assures him that he should trust in the reality before him. The souls are real substances; their transformed beauty is strangely different, but yet real. Dante, eager to know the identity of the first soul that approaches him, courteously makes his desire known. The soul answers with smiling eyes in these words:

> Our charity does not shut the doors against a just wish any more than He Who wills that all His court be like Himself. In the world I was a virgin sister, and if your memory be searched well, my being more beautiful will not conceal me from you. But you will recognize that I am Piccarda, who, placed here with these other blessed ones, am blessed in the slowest sphere. Our affections, which are kindled only in the pleasure of the Holy Spirit, rejoice in being conformed to His order. And this lot, which appears so lowly, is given to us because our vows were neglected and not filled in some particular.

(*Canto* III, 43-57)

The soul speaking is Piccarda Donati, the sister of Dante's friend Forese. On earth she had been a Poor Clare nun, but through pressure from her family she did not fulfill her religious vows and left the convent to enter a marriage planned by her family. She meets Dante here in the lowest and slowest sphere of the heavens because she and the other souls here were inconstant in their commitment to love of God on earth. The moon, because of its appearance of inconstancy and change, is the image of the inconstant human soul. Although their love of God had been imperfect on earth, here their love has been perfected and they are filled to their capacity with joy.

The souls of the blessed do not lose their individual personalities or the memory of their lives on earth. Their imperfections are recalled, but their guilt and remorse have been completely obliterated. They are so filled with God's love and His light that they see and feel now in a totally different way. The memory of their failures has become an incentive for greater love and gratitude to their all-loving and forgiving God.

Dante the pilgrim, still thinking in earthly terms, is troubled and curious that these souls may somehow resent their "low place" in the heavenly hierarchy. He is not yet aware that all the blessed are filled to their individual capacities. Dante the poet has arranged the souls on different planets to indicate the particular traits that dominated them in their earthly existence. Dante the pilgrim will soon encounter those dominated by erotic love on the planet Venus. He will eventually learn that all the blessed enjoy the perfection of Paradise above in the Empyrean and that they come down to meet him in these lower spheres out of condescending love for Dante, whose limited understanding needs a gradual introduction to the heavenly hierarchy. There is order and differentiation in Paradise, but this diversity in no way obscures the unity of love, peace, and joy which all the souls share—each according to its own capacity.

Piccarda smiles at Dante's curiosity and lack of understanding, but she gladly answers his questions. She seems to burn with "the first fire of love," as she responds:

Brother, the power of love quiets our will and makes us wish only for that which we have and gives us no other thirst. If we would desire to be higher, our longings would be discordant with His will Who assigns us here: which you will see is not possible in these circles if to exist in charity here is of necessity, and if you consider well the nature of love.

On the contrary, it is the essence of this blessed existence to keep itself within the divine will, whereby our wills themselves are made one; so that our being from threshold to threshold throughout this realm is a joy to all the realm as to the King, Who draws our wills to what He wills. In His will is our peace. It is the sea to which all moves, both what it creates and what nature makes.

(*Canto* III, 70-87)

These words of Piccarda, particularly "In His will is our peace," are among the most frequently quoted verses of the *Comedy* and rightfully so. They express the deepest truth about ourselves, the nature of love, and the very mystery and meaning of our existence. Any commentary on them might seem superfluous. The words are actually a very close paraphrase of St. Augustine's words in his *Confessions* (XIII, 9). They express the deepest intuition of all Christian mystics and similar expressions of the same truth can be found in other religious traditions. (*See* p. 100.)

To our human, myopic vision this truth may seem to annihilate our individuality and free will, but if we penetrate this truth with the eyes of faith we will discover that the surrender of our individual wills—the destruction of our proud egos—is really the secret to our true liberation, wholeness, and peace. Our innermost nature is oriented toward love, and love wills what the beloved wills. At the same time we see that the beloved wills what is truly good for us. This mutual attraction of love is the essence of happiness and inner peace. It is the fore-taste of the unspeakable peace of Paradise. This truth can be denied only by someone who has not tasted the true nature of love, someone who has not surrendered to that ecstatic bliss which overcomes the pride of human *hubris*. This loss of self-will is the only real gain—the finding of one's true self, created for love, completed only when totally absorbed by that love.

After Piccarda's words Dante begins to see the light of "how everywhere in heaven is Paradise, even if the grace of the Supreme Good does not rain down there in one same measure." Piccarda then tells Dante of her life on earth, describing the life of a nun as "a waking and sleeping with that Spouse Who accepts every vow which love conforms to His pleasure." She was torn away, how-ever, from that sweet cloister by "men, more used to evil than to good."

Love and Will
(*Cantos* IV-V)

Dante still does not fully comprehend two things: why certain souls have a "lower place" in Paradise and why Piccarda's broken vows place her in this lowest sphere since it was against her will to leave the convent. Beatrice kindly answers both questions. To the first she responds that the most ardent lovers of God, those who are most "into God," such as St. John the beloved disci-ple and Moses, are at one with these souls on the moon.

They all have their seats in the highest heaven, the Empyrean: "They all make the first circle beautiful." But they enjoy "that sweet life in different measure, by feeling more and less the eternal breath." In other words, they all are filled to their own capacity with joy. Each vessel is different, but each is filled. St. Paul's words may apply here: "The sun has a splendor of its own, the moon another splendor, and the stars another, for star differs from star in brightness" (1 Cor. 15:41).

The individual souls in Paradise show themselves to Dante at various levels to indicate their own different capacities and limitations as well as to accommodate themselves to Dante's imperfect understanding of the truth. Dante compares their condescension to the way that God condescends to our human level in the Scriptures. There He is described as having physical parts, such as hands and feet, but such descriptions are allegories. The allegory conveys an invisible truth with sensory images. This condescension of God is an act of His love: He reveals Himself in Scriptures by accommodating Himself to the human level of understanding which is so dependent on sense-knowledge.

But Dante still has a question about the broken vows of Piccarda and the others in her group. Can consent to violence under pressure be an excuse for breaking one's vows? He cannot understand how Piccarda was less than perfect since she was forced to break her vows. Beatrice explains to Dante that Piccarda's "absolute will" did not consent to evil, but out of fear of grave harm she consented to the evil will of her family. The Christian martyrs, on the other hand, kept their wills perfectly intact and suffered even violent death rather than consent to breaking their faith. Piccarda's love for God, then, was not the perfect love that the martyrs exhibited by their willingness to undergo death.

Dante is grateful to Beatrice and compares her words to the "rippling of the holy stream which issued forth from the Fount, from which springs every truth." Dante recognizes Beatrice as a channel of God's truth, which is a gift that flows from His condescending love. He pours out his gratitude with these words:

> O beloved of the First Lover, O divine one, whose speech inundates me and warms me so that it enlivens me more and more. Not all the depth of my affection is enough to render you thanks for the grace. . . . Well do I see that never can our intellect be wholly satisfied unless that truth shine on it, beyond which no truth has range.
>
> Therein it rests, as a wild beast in its lair, as soon as it has reached it; and it can reach it, or else every desire would be in vain. Because of this, questioning [literally, *doubt*] springs up like a shoot at the foot of truth and this is nature which urges us to the summit, from height to height.
>
> (*Canto IV*, 118-132)

These words point to the unending and, at times, anguished questions and doubts that we all have from time to time about the truth of our faith. Dante tells us that these doubts are rooted in our human nature, which is unable to comprehend fully the truth. It is therefore natural to have such doubts. They do not spring from bad will, but rather from a good desire to know: a desire planted within us by God, the Eternal Truth. This desire, far from being a denial of faith, actually deepens faith and draws us closer to its source. Although we cannot expect

to have all the answers in this life, our hope projects us
into the eternal life where God will reveal this truth to
us.

This full revelation of the truth is gradually unfold-
ing before Dante as Beatrice leads him little by little into
the truth. Her action of revelation is an act of love, and
the truth that she reveals to Dante kindles greater love in
him. She says so in these words:

> If I flame on you in the warmth of love beyond
> the measure that is seen on earth and so van-
> quish the power of your eyes, do not marvel. It
> comes from perfect vision, which, according as
> it apprehends, so does it move its foot toward
> the apprehended good.
>
> Well do I see how in your intellect already is
> shining the eternal light, which once seen al-
> ways kindles love. And if something else se-
> duce your love, it is nothing but some vestige
> of that light, badly understood, which shines in
> it.

> (*Canto* V, 1-12)

The teaching of Virgil in *Purgatory* on the nature of
love is confirmed here by Beatrice. We see again that
human philosophy coincides with divine revelation on
this cardinal truth. The human soul is naturally attracted
to whatever is apprehended as good, and the soul is free
to choose the highest good or some lesser good which
contains some "vestige" of that supreme good. Beatrice
then extols the unique grandeur of human freedom:

> The greatest gift which God in His bounty
> bestowed in creating, and the most conformed
> to His own goodness, and that which He most
> prizes, was the freedom of the will. With this

gift the creatures that have intelligence—they
all and they alone—were and are endowed.

Now, if you argue from this, the high worth of
the vow will appear to you, if it be such that
God consents when you consent. For in estab-
lishing the pact between God and man, this
treasure becomes the sacrifice.

(*Canto* V, 19-30)

Beatrice thus defines a vow as a sacrifice of that
treasure, the freedom of the will, to God. It is a most
sacred pact—a covenant of love—between God and the
human soul. It should therefore never be taken lightly.
Beatrice cautions Christians to be more serious in making such a commitment. She recommends that the Scriptures as well as "the shepherd of the Church" be guides
in this matter.

Mercury
(*Cantos* VI-VII)

Beatrice and Dante then speed, like an arrow shot
from the bow, to the second star, Mercury. Here a thousand souls gather at their arrival. Dante describes them
as fish in a clear pool that are attracted to some food
which drops into the water. Each of the souls exclaims,
"Lo, here is one who shall increase our loves!" This one
verse describes the dominant mood of Paradise: agape,
the pure love which joyfully embraces every person. Paradise is no complacent state of elitism, no "holier than
thou" club, which excludes those it declares unfit. The
blessed do not selfishly resent the arrival of another; on
the contrary, they perceive in each person a cause for

increased joy. The stranger is truly another person to be loved. Their already perfect love and joy is increased by their sharing with yet another.

One of the souls emerges from the throng and identifies himself as Justinian, the great Roman emperor and lawgiver. He states that he now feels "the primal love." He explains that this little star is populated with spirits who, like him, sought honor and fame in the world, but their love for earthly honor swerved them from the "true love" which was, as a result, less lively in them. But now they are free of earthly desires and ambitions and rejoice in the heavenly harmony whose "living justice sweetens their affection."

Justinian then narrates the history of the Roman Empire, mentioning in particular the emperors Augustus, Tiberius, and Titus, three rulers whom Dante connects with the birth and crucifixion of Christ. Dante sees God's "living justice" working in human history through these emperors. Under Augustus "heaven willed to bring the world to its own serene mood." This is a reference to the *Pax Romana* which reigned when Christ was born. It was under Tiberius that Christ was crucified. Dante interprets the crucifixion as a glorious act of Roman justice—a strange interpretation, but yet consistent with his understanding of Roman justice as the agent by which divine justice did vengeance for divine wrath, caused by man's original sin.

The Emperor Titus, who destroyed Jerusalem, was God's agent in His vengeance on the Jews for the sin of crucifying the innocent Jesus. Such an interpretation of history strikes us today as provincial and naïve. Above all, we find the bias in favor of Rome and the prejudice against the Jews totally unacceptable. This prejudice against the Jews for their part in Christ's crucifixion persisted for centuries until finally the Church at the Second Vatican Council officially condemned and deplored this unjust imputation of guilt to the entire Jewish people.

After Justinian's summary of Roman history in Canto VI, Beatrice gives in Canto VII a more profound interpretation of human history in the light of God's loving plan. By contrast with the preceding analysis of God's justice, this is truly a magnificent discourse: a summary of the main theological themes of Christian faith. Dante's composition reveals his profound knowledge of medieval theology, especially the works of St. Thomas Aquinas and St. Anselm. Although we have to reject some of Dante's narrow historical theories, the basic theological vision presented here is worth our careful attention. It is deeply rooted in the Scriptures and the best traditional theology of the Church.

The enduring truth and beauty of this theological vision lies in Dante's perception that ultimately it is God's love that gives meaning to human history. It was God's love that created man in the first place; God's love that redeemed him after his sin; God's love that will raise him at the resurrection of the body. All the paradoxes of human history—its justice and injustice, its tragedies, sufferings, and sins—are all interpreted in the light of God's love.

Dante's vision embraces the creation and all the main events of salvation history: the fall, the Incarnation, the Crucifixion, and the final resurrection. As to the creation, Dante sums up in one tercet the creation of the human soul as an act which far surpasses the creation of the plants and animals, which are composed of various elements and thus subject to corruption:

> But your life [the human soul] the Supreme
> Goodness breathes forth without intermediary,

and so enamors it of Himself that it desires
Him ever after.

(Canto VII, 142-144)

The creation of the human soul is thus a direct and
personal act of God's love; He places in that soul at creation an eternal desire and love for Himself. Therefore,
because of God's eternal love for each of us we not only
exist but we have within us an innate desire to return to
our loving Creator. He remains within us calling us back
to Himself. This is the mysterious nostalgia in every
human heart. His agape for us created our eros for Him.

The human soul not only exists and is oriented toward God, but it also bears the stamp of God's beauty and
excellence. It is created in His image. This seal or imprint
can never be removed. The human soul is created eternal,
beautiful, and free because it flows from and reflects its
Creator, Whose goodness and love "burning within Himself so sparkle that they display His eternal beauties in
His creatures." The human creature is thus endowed at
creation with all these divine gifts. Only sin disfigures
him and renders him unlike the Supreme Good. Beatrice
sheds light on the mystery of sin and its consequences:

> Because he did not endure for his own good
> a curb upon the power that wills, that man
> [Adam] who never was born, in damning him-
> self damned all his progeny; wherefore the hu-
> man race lay sick down there for many centuries
> in great error, until it pleased the Word of God
> to descend where He, by the sole act of His eter-
> nal love, united with Himself in person the
> nature which had estranged itself from its
> Maker.
>
> . . . This nature, which was thus united to its
> Maker, was, when it was created, pure and

good; but by its own self it had been banished
from Paradise because it turned aside from the
way of truth and from its proper life.

(*Canto* VII, 25-39)

The mysterious tragedy of sin, with all its miserable
consequences of physical evil and death, was not powerful enough to stop the flow of God's eternal love. God's
love proved stronger than death; His love overcame evil.
Dante understands the Incarnation, God's act of union
with humanity, as primarily an act of His love which
brings estranged, sinful humanity back into loving union
with Himself.

The Incarnation is a divine choice which baffles the
human mind. Could not God have merely forgiven man
and reconciled him to Himself by a mere act of His will,
a mere word or gesture? Why the descent into human
flesh, into the messy world of corruption, sin, injustice,
and death? Why choose this hard way? Dante concludes
that this act of descent best displays "the goodness of the
heart" of God:

> The Divine Goodness, which puts His imprint
> on the world, was pleased to proceed by all His
> ways to raise you up again. Between the last
> night and the first day there has never been nor
> will there be so exalted and so magnificent a
> procedure, either by one or by the other.
>
> For God was more bounteous in giving Himself
> to make man sufficient to uplift himself again,
> than if He solely of Himself had forgiven. All
> other ways were scant in respect to justice, if
> the Son of God had not humbled Himself to be-
> come incarnate.

(*Canto* VII, 109-120)

The Incarnation then is the most exalted and magnificent act of God's overflowing goodness. It is the culmination of all His actions, outshining the first day (Creation) and the last night (the final judgment). It is truly the climax of both human and divine history. But, paradoxically, that exalted peak is actually a descent, a humiliation. It is God's descent which makes possible man's ascent.

This pattern of descent and ascent is at the very heart of Dante's *Comedy*. Dante had to descend to Hell and later had to gird himself with the reed of humility at the bottom of Purgatory before he could begin the ascent. This follows the pattern of Christ's humiliation in His Incarnation and Crucifixion, which led to His Resurrection and Ascension to the Father.

We must now consider more closely this paradox of paradoxes: the Crucifixion. The Crucifixion of Christ is not an act isolated from the Incarnation. Dante considers them together as "the act" of God's loving descent. The Crucifixion is the final depth of that descent, that journey to the lowest pit of death, which was really a downward movement of love.

When Beatrice directs Dante's attention to the Cross, he confesses that this strange way chosen by God for our redemption simply boggles his mind. Beatrice then gives the supreme clue, which is really the only key to unlock this mystery: "Brother, this decree is buried from the eyes of everyone whose understanding is not matured (*adulto*) within love's flame." Beatrice uses the word *adulto*, which means full-grown, mature, adult. Human understanding can penetrate the mystery of the Cross only when it is full-grown in love. For only love can understand the infinite love of God displayed in His sacrifice of Himself for humanity. Only the "inner eye of love" can see the meaning of the Cross, Love's sacrifice.

Dante thus far had been trying to understand this mystery in terms of justice, but he kept running up blind alleys. The theology of his time had wrestled with this paradox, attempting to understand how God's offended justice could be satisfied by a just act of reparation which could atone for man's sin. Many theories were proposed, based on the idea that God's justice required a proportionate act of reparation on man's part. But since man could not sufficiently repair the harm done by sin, God in His mercy took the initiative of becoming man so that the act of reconciliation came from man and united man to God again. Man's sin (his injustice) was repaired by God's mercy (His justice).

Aside from such legal terminology, Dante's basic concept is derived from the Scriptures (The Old Testament and St. Paul), which perceive God's justice primarily as His mercy. God's justice is not an imitation of the human justice of proportionate retribution, the *quid pro quo* type. This kind of justice breeds revenge and further estrangement. As the psalmist sings:

> The Lord is merciful and loving, slow to anger and full of constant love. He does not keep on reprimanding; He is not angry forever. He does not punish us as we deserve, or repay us for our sins and wrongs.

> (*Psalm* 103: 8-10)

The paradox of God's justice shines forth in the Crucifixion of Christ. It is an outrage to all justice, since not only was an innocent man condemned and executed, but "the Person Who suffered, with Whom human nature was bound up," was God the Son. The "Crucifixion of God" then is the shocking reality of God's personal love displayed in the most convincing and moving way. St. Thomas Aquinas perceived this as the deepest motive of Christ's Crucifixion:

> In the first place, man knows thereby [by the Crucifixion] how much God loves him, and is thereby stirred to love Him in return. And herein lies the perfection of human salvation. Hence the Apostle (in Romans 5:8) says: "God has shown us His love for us, for when we were still sinners, Christ died for us."
>
> (*Summa Theologiae*, III, 46, art. 3)

This act of God's love shook the foundations of the world. It penetrated into the depths of the earth, causing cracks which Dante had observed in his journey through Hell. This descent of Christ into death was simultaneously the cause of man's ascent to heaven.

> From one act issued things diverse, for one same death was pleasing to God and to the Jews. Because of it the earth trembled and heaven was opened.
>
> (*Canto* VII, 45-48)

Our minds and emotions shudder at the thought that this act of cruelty, torment, and innocent suffering was "pleasing" to God, but if we sharpen the focus of our inner eye of love we may see some light in this dark event. Although Catholic theology has traditionally stressed that God is "impassible,"—incapable of suffering—it has also maintained that any act of a Divine Person is simultaneously an act of the Trinity. Thus in the suffering of the Son, the Father also suffered. The pathos of God has been a rather neglected theme in theology. *The Crucified God* by Jurgen Moltmann has focused attention in recent years on this important topic.

The mystery of God's suffering shocks us into probing the depth of His love. His suffering is paradoxically His joy. The Father is no sadist enjoying the Son's suffering; nor is the Son a masochist taking delight in suffering. The Son in His suffering continues His eternal dialogue of love for the Father, His loving submission to Him; but now in the flesh He expresses this filial loyalty "for *us* and for *our* salvation." The Father is pleased because He loves us and wills this reconciliation. He sees us now in His Son's willingness to sacrifice Himself.

The contradictory experiences of joy and suffering coincide in this act of sacrificial love, directed not only to the Father but also to us. Humanity's response of love to the Father up until the Crucifixion had been a long story of outright rebellion, indifference, or at best, lip service. In this perfect act of love the consummation of the marriage between Creator and creature radiates in all its splendor. Union and communion are at last accomplished. Jesus' last word from the Cross was: "It is consummated."

The Crucifixion is not only the supreme act of God's love, but it is also a strange encounter of God's justice and man's injustice. Dante stated that this act also pleased the Jews who committed this injustice. We today should not use the misleading term "Jews" since that general term does not express adequately the complex, historical question of Jewish *and Roman* complicity in the death of Jesus. The few individuals—Roman and Jewish—who were instrumental in Christ's death, were motivated perhaps by political interests and thus were ignorant of the full import of their actions. Besides, the Crucifixion was essentially an eternal act of God's love expressed in time and human history.

In this unique event we come face-to-face with the hidden meaning of suffering and death. The mystery of God's willingness to suffer and die is the blinding light in which the meaning of any suffering can be understood. As Beatrice teaches, only the mature flame of love gives light to this mystery. Dante through his own suffering—his exile and all the injustices he suffered—had reached this maturity of love. His personal growth through suffering had brought him to penetrate into the very meaning of suffering. He had learned that humiliation and suffering force the human creature to realize his total and radical dependence on the Creator. What appears to be an unjust, uncaring God is finally understood as a grace. What seems like a curse is understood as a grace which opens a person to see that everything—from our very existence to the air we breathe—is sheer gift.

The temporary deprivation of some gifts—prosperity, social position, security, family, and friends—purified Dante's soul and painfully sharpened his sensitivity and receptivity toward God. It was similar to Job's catharsis. Dante came to experience the desert within himself which is empty and lifeless, awaiting the life-giving waters of God's gifts. His willing acceptance of this desert—his submission and sacrifice—transformed this "injustice" to him into innocent suffering, similar to Christ's suffering. Dante teaches us that only a humble recognition of our total dependence—our nothingness before God—can prepare us to accept suffering and wait joyfully for His gifts.

Such is the meaning of the Cross: it is Christ's innocent suffering willingly given as a response of love to the Father. The disobedience of Adam (and all of us) is "overcompensated" by the willing submission of Jesus. Human pride, that sins of sins, is overcome at last only by humility. The devastating act of man's pride is wonderfully healed by the loving act of God's humility. *O Felix Culpa*, the Latin Easter liturgy proclaims. Suffering then takes on meaning: it is no longer passive endurance of some evil which cannot be avoided. It becomes by love an active giving of self to the God Who silently allows the suffering, but Who is silently responding with love, supporting with grace, strengthening with hope, "anxiously" awaiting His own time for bestowing glory and joy.

All the agonizing, human questions of guilt and innocence, justice and injustice, dissolve in the flame of Love. Love created humanity; Love descended to suffer and die with humanity; Love raised up fallen humanity to the perfect joy of Paradise, where the eternal activity of Love satisfies all desires. All the contradictions and paradoxes of life are thus seen as so many scattered pages of one book, bound by Love. Love is the unique binding force which holds it all together, which makes sense of life and bestows meaning on the meaningless, absurd sufferings of reality. Suffering is real, but Love is *more* real and more powerful. This was Dante's deepest intuition. It sums up the entire *Comedy*: God's love transforms the human tragedy into a divine comedy. The misery of evil yields to the happy ending.

Venus

(*Cantos* VIII-IX)

Dante and Beatrice now soar into the next heavenly sphere, the star of Venus. Here they encounter souls who were dominated on earth by a strong passion of love. If we compare these cantos with Canto V of *Hell* we will notice the same theme of human eros treated in both places. This same eros became for Paolo and Francesca a hell, whereas for these souls it was transformed into the agape of Paradise. The same basic orientation had opposite outcomes.

Dante encounters at first a dear friend from his youth in Florence, Charles Martel, the young king of Hungary. They had been united on earth by a deep bond of friendly love. Charles had been attracted at first by Dante's love poetry and here he recalls the opening lines of one of Dante's famous poems. He then answers questions that Dante poses about the abuse of kingly power on earth. Charles's brother was also a king, but he had misused his regal office. Charles explains that individuals (like his own brother) are often forced into roles for which they are unfit. He advises individuals to follow the particular gifts and temperament which nature has given them:

> And if the world there below would give heed to the foundation which Nature lays and followed it, it would have its people good. But you distort the pattern and force someone into religious life who was born to gird on the sword, and you make a king of one who was born to be a preacher; so that you wander far from the right path.
>
> (*Canto* VIII, 142-148)

Dante is stating here a very important psychological and spiritual truth. The scholastics of his time had insisted that "Grace builds upon Nature." Nature, which endows us with particular gifts, should always be respected and followed. It is ultimately an expression of Divine

Providence, Who by diverse ways, like an archer shooting different arrows to their proper targets, arranges and predisposes everything for a good end. Nature is God's good work of art and should be followed unless we want to invite disorder and disaster.

Without succumbing to the superstitions of astrology, Dante recognizes the influence of the stars on each individual. One's particular "sign" or temperament—an aspect of one's individuality—is most important and sacred. It should be followed and developed and not repressed or denied. The differences among individuals express the splendid variety of God's art, calling each back to Himself by diverse routes.

The interest in recent years in one's astrological sign and the general enthusiasm about "being one's own person" and "doing one's own thing" are basically wholesome attitudes as long as they take into account certain propensities that *can* lead to perversions. Let us recall Francesca in Hell. She followed her penchant for passionate love, but her eros was no more than a projection of her own ego. She was the center of her erotic drive. She had not centered her love on the Other (God) or another (human person). She is thus eternally "off-center," lost, abandoned to the aimless drive of uncentered eros. Following one's natural proclivities must always be attentive, intelligent, and responsible. She lost the "Good of the intellect." A life of "doing one's own thing" can thus be an irrational flight into a selfish, immature fulfillment of infantile fantasies. Francesca refused the maturity of love, the responsibilities to the Other and to the other. The natural gift of eros became a hell for her.

Let us now look at another woman, Cunizza, a blessed soul in the star of Venus. She too had a natural proclivity for love. Her love life had been very varied. It almost reads like a modern soap opera. She abandoned her first husband for a troubadour, then traveled widely in Italy with a knight, and later remarried three times. Her amorous affairs are so well documented that writers of the period referred to her as "a child of Venus."

In her later years, however, Cunizza became known for her compassion and outstanding social concern. She granted freedom to her father's and brother's slaves. Dante probably knew this other side of her personality. It was really that same eros which had grown and matured into agape. Eros, which can be misdirected into selfish love, can also reach its fulfillment in selfless compassion and charity. Cunizza had been generous with her favors (The troubadours and knights knew that well); but that very generous spirit—that good drive to love and to share— eventually led to her conversion and transformation. How mysterious are God's ways! His mysterious art creates beauty and order out of the chaos and ruins of human sin.

Cunizza can now reflect on her past sins with a smile of self-indulgence. She sings and rejoices as she tells Dante her story:

> I was called Cunizza and I am shining here because the light of this star overcame me. But I gladly forgive myself for the reason of my lot, and it does not grieve me—which might perhaps seem strange to your vulgar herd.

(*Canto IX*, 32-36)

She joyfully forgives herself. She no longer remembers her sins since she has drunk of the sacred waters of Lethe. Now she can forgive herself with no trace of remorse or guilt. This is the ultimate humility: acceptance of the total truth about oneself. Cunizza recognizes that her life had been dominated by inordinate eros, but she had transformed that wandering eros into responsible love. She had channeled the gift into the right direction. The memory of her past is now only a cause for joy because the power of God's forgiveness in her life overcame the pain of remorse and turned it to laughter and song.

Cunizza then introduces another soul to Dante. It is Folquet of Marseilles, a famous troubadour poet who eventually repented of his amorous affairs and became a Cistercian monk and later a bishop. He too briefly tells his story of how he used to burn with that same passion which overcame Dido. We recall that Paolo and Francesca were in the same group of sinners with Dido in the first circle of Hell. Folquet expresses his present sentiments:

> Yet here we repent not, but smile; not for the sin, which does not return to mind, but for the Power that ordained and foresaw. Here we contemplate the art which beautifies its great effect and we discern the Good which brings back the world below to the world above.

> (*Canto* IX, 103-108)

What a marvelous conception of God. He is the Power, the Art, and the Goodness which bestows greater beauty on His works, His human creatures, and skillfully draws them back to Himself. He implants in them the eros which will guide them into the beauty and goodness of agape. The creature thereby becomes beautiful and good like its Creator.

Folquet then introduces Dante to the splendid soul next to him. It is Rahab, the famous pagan harlot of Jericho. She had risked her life to help Joshua and the Israelites capture the City of Jericho in their conquest of the Holy Land. By her selfless courage and faith she had cooperated in that great enterprise and act of God for His people.

Dante mentions that she was the first soul to be taken by
Christ when He triumphantly descended into Limbo to
rescue the souls of those who had hoped in Him.

In Christian literature Rahab had become a symbol
of the Church, at one time sinful and Gentile, but by faith
forgiven and saved by Jesus. *Joshua* is really the original
Hebrew name which comes to us through the Greek translation as *Jesus*. The Gospel truth of the last becoming
first shines out in Rahab, once degraded by her prostitu-
tion and Gentile blood, but now brilliant because of her
selfless love and faith.

The words of Jesus come to mind abut the prostitutes
and tax collectors who will enter the Kingdom of God
before the self-righteous. We also recall the gentleness of
Jesus toward the woman who was considered a public
sinner. She washed His feet with her tears, kissed them
and dried them with her hair. Her repentance and grateful love evoked Jesus' response: "I tell you, then, the
great love she has shown proves that her many sins have
been forgiven. Whoever has been forgiven little shows
only a little love." (Luke 7:47)

Here on this planet of Venus we encounter women
and men whose great capacity for love led them finally to
experience the tender love of God for them. In Dante's
universe human eros is an asset: it freely, humbly, and in-
nocently admits the basic human need to be loved and to
love. Eros's sensitivity opens the human soul to receive
the divine guest knocking at the door. The self-righteous
remain closed and hardened by their own justice and
pride.

Dante's mind now turns to the present state of the
Holy Land and the Christian Church on earth. The bliss
of Heaven does not obscure Dante's concern for the earth.
He sadly reflects that the popes and cardinals are no

longer concerned about Nazareth, the town in the Holy Land where Jesus lived. They no longer read the Gospels but instead they study their own *Decretals*, the documents of Canon Law which regulated the offices and financial aspects of Church government. Dante angrily denounces the greed and ambition of these ecclesiastics who have corrupted the Vatican, the ancient cemetery where St. Peter and the other martyrs were buried. Dante predicts that the Vatican will soon be freed from this "adultery."

We notice here that Dante continues to use the language of love. The sin of the high-ranking clergy is an infidelity in love. Their marriage to Christ and His Church had been corrupted by adultery: their love for money and power. All sin is radically a distortion and perversion of love.

The Sun
(*Cantos* X-XIII)

Dante and Beatrice leave the heaven of the lovers to enter the heaven of the theologians, the sun. Dante begins this new phase of the journey with a joyous hymn of praise to the Trinity:

> Gazing upon His Son with the Love which the One and the Other eternally breathe forth, the first and ineffable Power made everything that revolves through the mind or through space with such order that he who contemplates it cannot help tasting of Him.

> Lift then your sight with me, reader, to the lofty wheels, straight to that part where the one motion strikes the other; and amorously there begin to gaze upon that Master's art Who

within Himself so loves it that His eye never
turns from it.

(*Canto* X, 1-12)

The eternal activity of the Father and the Son—their
looking upon one another—is Love itself, the Holy Spirit.
The divine act of contemplation is in essence an act of
love. Dante sees this as the model of human contemplation. The human mind is invited to contemplate this mutual contemplation of the Father and the Son and thus to
enter into that same community whose bond is love, the
Holy Spirit. The human person, the image of the Trinity,
is capable by her mind and will of these divine activities
of contemplation and love. Dante invites the reader to
join with him in this supreme foretaste of the heavenly
joy.

Dante is describing here the very nature of prayer. A
classical definition of prayer is "the lifting of the mind
and heart to God," and here Dante is inviting us readers
to do that with him. It is fitting that this moment should
occur here in the heaven of the theologians, for theology
is first of all and last of all prayer. It is a loving contemplation of God and His works. It is not a merely intellectual exercise. Of course the mind leads, but it should lead
the will and the affections into a greater experience: love.
This concept was unfortunately lost for many centuries.
Theology became an exercise in mental gymnastics, a
fruitless juggling act with abstractions, distinctions, and
polemics. Too often it degenerated into a witch-hunt for
heretics or a triumphant gloating over the pretentious
possession of all truth.

Scholastic theology, which flourished in Dante's
time and exercised such a strong influence on him, has
received a "bad press" in recent times. It has been gener-

ally misunderstood and misrepresented as a dry, abstract study of hair-splitting distinctions or an antiquated form of intellectual snobbery. Its true nature, however, was quite different. Scholastic theology breathed the air of contemplation. It was the mind in love, in love with God and with all reality. And it expressed that love in prayer. Thomas Aquinas, for example, was a confirmed intellectual but also an ardent mystic.

In the opening words of this canto Dante contemplates the Divine Persons, their community of love, and their overflowing work of art, the created universe. The order and beauty of the cosmos is a work of art which leads us to look on the artist with wonder, praise, and love. All this looking and gazing is nothing other than contemplation. Contemplative prayer is looking, understanding, wondering, praising, and—the crowning experience—loving. It is deeply personal and intimate, bringing us into loving union and community with the Divine Persons. Anyone who thinks that scholastic theology is impersonal or too intellectual and abstract has not understood the very heart of that theology: contemplation, prayer, and love.

The universe as a work of God's art is the starting point for prayer. The created world is not an enigma to figure out or a hostile reality to fear, but an expression of His art, a work of His love. God's act of creating is still happening now. We often call that His providence. Dante writes that "He so loves it (the universe) that His eye never turns from it." In contemplating the universe we come to see His loving eye, always looking at us through the cosmos, always loving us through His created gifts.

There is no room in scholastic theology for a negative attitude toward the world or toward the flesh or any material thing. The vision of the twentieth-century French theologian and scientist, Pierre Teilhard de Chardin, has much in common with the vision of Dante and the scholastic theologians of the thirteenth century. The eros of the human spirit in all ages—its unrestricted desire to know and understand the universe—leads to wonder and prayer. The truly great minds of all epochs have arrived at this same experience.

The experience of contemplation is often thought to be an esoteric privilege of a few individuals whom we call mystics, but Dante invites all of us to share in this experience, which is as natural as a butterfly's tasting the sweet nectar of a flower. This experience is believable and should be the object of our desire:

> Although I should call on genius, art, and practice, I could not explain it so that it could be imagined; but it can be believed—and may humans long to see it.

(*Canto* X, 43-45)

Prayer is a first taste of God, a foretaste of the eternal feast for our minds and hearts. The foretaste here whets our appetite for the full satisfaction hereafter. When Dante sees the great theologians in this heaven, they appear as lights standing out against the sun—light on light. They are ecstatically rejoicing in the vision of the love relationship of the Father, Son, and Spirit. Dante describes these souls on the fourth star as "the fourth family of the exalted Father Who always satisfies it, showing how He breathes and begets."

Beatrice invites Dante "to give thanks to the Sun of the angels, Who by His grace has raised you to this sun of the senses." Dante is so filled with gratitude at this point that his heart gives itself totally to God. He confesses that his love is so wholly committed to Him that it eclipses Beatrice into oblivion. But he quickly notes that this does not displease her. In fact, she smiles at Dante "with laughing eyes," rejoicing that her role is being fulfilled. She, the light of faith and revelation, leads to the transcendent experience of love. She is happy when her ancillary role is completed and that supreme experience is tasted. Beatrice, as Dante remarks, is constantly leading him "from good to better" in their flight through the spheres.

The souls begin to address Dante. The first to speak is St. Thomas Aquinas, the theologian who had the most profound impact on Dante's mind. Thomas, too often appreciated by Catholic tradition only for his intellectual gifts, is here overflowing with "true love" and "continuously growing by loving." The vision of the Trinity for Thomas is not a static or cold intellectual activity. It is dynamic and keeps inflaming the soul toward greater love. He compares himself to a man with a vial of wine who cannot refuse his wine to another man who is thirsty. He also uses the metaphor of water which naturally flows to the sea. His love of God simply overflows, and he can't help sharing it with someone like Dante who is thirsting after it. Thomas describes the other souls surrounding him as "plants which enflower this garland and amorously circle around the beautiful lady who strengthens you for heaven."

Thomas identifies these souls: his own teacher, St. Albert the Great, the famous mystical theologian Dionysius, and several others. He surprisingly mentions one of his intellectual opponents on earth, Siger of Brabant, a celebrated teacher in Paris whose theses were often vehemently contradicted by Thomas. Dante is telling us here that in Paradise the opposing schools of thought are at harmony because they have all reached the full truth which they had only partially perceived on earth. The full truth, God, is the Love which unites them into mutual love and respect. This is an important lesson for us even today. Opposing views in theology, or in any field of study, should never rupture the bond of mutual love which is so much more important than a cheap victory in an intellectual argument. Diversity in our intellectual positions can and should co-exist with a deep harmony of love and mutual respect. The full truth can never be grasped by us here on earth, but we can love and respect one another as we differ intellectually.

All the souls then spontaneously join in a song, whose sweet harmony expresses their eternal joy. This burst of music reminds Dante of the chimes which call the Church to Matins, the morning prayer which was sung and still is sung in religious communities throughout the world. Dante compares the Church to the bride of God who rises early in the morning to sing her love song to the Spouse Who loves her. Dante is describing prayer as a love song, begun by the Church on earth, but continuing into heaven. This continuity of liturgical prayer unites the Church on earth to the Church in heaven in one hymn of cosmic praise to God.

St. Francis and St. Dominic
(*Cantos* XI-XIII)

As Dante and Thomas continue their conversation, the topic of the Dominicans, the religious order to which Thomas belonged, is introduced. Thomas takes the occasion to point out that St. Dominic, its founder, together with St. Francis, the founder of the Franciscans, were two men sent by God's providence to reform the Church, which had wandered so far from her true nature and purpose. The Church, the bride of Christ, had been unfaithful to Her spouse, Christ. He "had espoused her with loud cries and his blessed blood," but His bride had abandoned Him for the love of earthly power, prestige and wealth. God's loving providence, however, whose eye is always fixed on His Church, sent two guides to bring the Church back to her original ardor.

These two guides, Dominic and Francis, are compared to the two orders of angels: the cherubim and the seraphim. In Christian symbolism the cherubim represent the light of God's truth and the seraphim represent the fire of love for God. Since Dominic's work focused on preaching the truth and combatting the errors of heresy, he is described as splendid with the cherubic light of wisdom; Francis is seraphic in his ardent love. Thomas, however, insists that to praise the one is to praise the other, since they both worked toward the same goal: the return of the Church to her loving union with Christ.

Thomas, the Dominican, will sing the praises of St. Francis in Canto XI and St. Bonaventure, the celebrated Franciscan theologian, will eulogize Dominic in Canto XII. This is another example of the harmony that binds together the souls in Paradise. Franciscans and Dominicans in Dante's time were often "at loggerheads" over theological and other issues. St. Thomas, usually considered the epitome of serene, abstract intellectualism, will now sing the highest praises of St. Francis, the man of emotional enthusiasm and fervent religious zeal. This is the "other side" of Thomas which historians have often neglected.

Thomas's enthusiastic words about Francis are, of course, an expression of Dante's own admiration for

Francis and the Franciscan movement. Dante was deeply
moved by the spirit of Francis from his early years in
Florence until his final years in Ravenna, where he was
very close to the friars. He was buried in their church in
Ravenna, clothed in the Franciscan habit, and Franciscans ever since have jealously claimed him as one of their
own: "Brother Dante."

Dante shared Francis's lively joy in God's creation,
in spite of the rather stern, pensive portraits of Dante
which have come down to us. The thirty-three cantos of
Paradise are proof enough of Dante's enthusiastic, Franciscan joy. The grim, pessimistic author of *Hell* also exposed his soul in the joyful celebration of *Paradise*, and
it is here that we see this "other side" of Dante. Joyful
optimism shines out here as it did in Francis's life and
in the life of Christ. The joyful good news—the Gospel—which Jesus proclaimed and lived was the source of
Dante's optimistic joy, as well as the wellspring of Francis's enthusiasm.

Dante narrates the life of Francis, stressing how similar Francis was to Jesus. He even uses the bold symbolism of the rising sun to describe the birth of Francis and
his coming into the world as a light which would give
new life. Such religious symbolism was usually reserved
for Christ alone, but Francis was so conformed to Christ
that Dante does not hesitate to employ such a strong
metaphor.

Dante was certainly well aware of Francis's deep
love of nature and of all God's creatures. Dante himself
shared this "creation spirituality" for which Francis is so
well known and loved. That aspect of Francis, however,
is often trivialized today by sentimental admirers of Francis and societies of animal lovers. Francis has even been
hailed in recent years as the "patron saint of ecologists

and environmentalists." That is all very appropriate and true, but Dante focuses mainly on Francis's conformity and likeness to Christ. Francis was so much like Christ that toward the end of his life he even bore the marks of Christ's suffering (the *stigmata*) on his own body. Francis lived Christian spirituality to its perfection: transformation into Christ.

This final configuration with Christ was the "ultimate seal" of the austere discipline of poverty and humility. Christ's poverty and humility were the virtues which Francis embraced with an enthusiasm and "insanity" which baffled his family as well as the Church and society of his time. Francis's literal following of the Gospel shocked his contemporaries, who had grown comfortable and complacent with their watered-down Christianity and all their compromises with the values of medieval society. The Church since the time of Constantine had become wedded to wealth and worldly power, having abandoned the poverty and humility of Christ. Christianity in the Middle Ages, for all its emphasis on pilgrimages, had really lost the spirit of a pilgrim's soul. The Church had settled down to wealth and earthly power. The Crusades, originally conceived to make pilgrimages to the land of Christ possible and safe, degenerated into a "gold-rush" for greedy European merchants, kings and churchmen. The European Christians with all the weapons at their disposal waged a "holy war" against the "infidels" in the Holy Land, and very often greedily exploited and plundered their own fellow Christians on the way to and from Palestine.

Dante narrates how Francis courageously went to Egypt to convert the Saracens. He was armed only with the peace of Christ and was consumed with "a thirst for martyrdom" rather than for gold and domination.

Although his mission was not successful in terms of conversions, he nonetheless gave witness to Christ's gospel of peace in a unique way. Francis was unafraid of being a fool for Christ; his pacifism was a voice crying in the wilderness of greed and ambition.

The voices of pacifists throughout the centuries and even into our own times—like Dorothy Day, Martin Luther King, or Daniel Berrigan—have been few and isolated, since the Church and so-called Christian nations have usually settled their differences by means of violence and war. The concept of holy war or crusade has persisted in Europe, America, and other parts of the world. Wars are still waged with the full support of Church authorities. The war in 1983 between Argentina and Great Britain, two "Christian" nations, was one such example. Some Church leaders, however, are brave enough and Christian enough to speak out against the use of violence and to proclaim by words and actions the gospel in all its purity. These pacifists are usually ridiculed for their "political naïveté" and lack of realism. Such was the world's judgment about Christ and St. Francis.

Although Francis was not successful as a missionary and peacemaker, he was successful as a lover: a lover of Christ, His poverty and humility, His Church, and all humanity and creation. Francis related to everyone and to everything in a *personal* way: poverty was not an abstract idea but the Lady whom he loved, the bride of Christ who had been left a widow when Christ and the apostles left this world. Francis espoused this widow, abandoned for more than ten centuries. Dante describes Francis's love affair with "Lady Poverty" with all the charm and style of a troubadour poet. Both Francis and Dante in their youth had been under the spell of the wave of romantic love poetry that swept through Europe in the

Middle Ages. Although they were not contemporaries, both had been influenced by that same outburst of romantic love. Both had experienced the rare, spring-like beauty and the exquisite emotions of love; both had intuited that human eros reaches its fulfillment in agape. Both Francis and Dante were poets of love, troubadours of Christ, the supreme lover and poet.

As Thomas ends his praise of Francis, a second group of souls, described as living flames of light and eternal roses forming a garland, join Thomas and his companions in a song and dance of "high great festival." The two groups are also described as two rainbows; their harmony of song, dance, and colors recall the rainbow which God placed in the sky as the sign of His covenant of peace with all humanity in Noah's time.

A light emerges from the second group. It is St. Bonaventure, the Franciscan theologian and mystic, who will now sing the praises of St. Dominic. He begins with the words, "The love which makes me beautiful draws me to speak of the other leader on whose account such fair speech is made here concerning mine." Bonaventure thus expresses the love which unites all the blessed, a love which knows no petty jealousies, party loyalties or competition between Franciscans and Dominicans.

He speaks of Dominic as an "ardent lover of the Christian faith." Just as Francis was wedded to Poverty, Dominic was espoused to Faith. His baptism was the wedding ceremony. Dominic was the "farmer" whom Christ had chosen for His orchard, the Church. He too, like Francis, loved and lived the first counsel of Jesus: "Blessed are the poor." Dominic not only lived a life of poverty, but by his preaching he was a champion and "sacred athlete" for the truth of Christ's gospel. He rooted out the "stumps of heresy" which had sprung up in the

garden of the Church. Bonaventure compares Dominic
and Francis to the two wheels which supported and guided
the chariot of the Church.

Bonaventure concludes this panegyric by pointing
out the other luminaries in his group. The last one he
mentions is the one right by his side: Joachim of Fiore,
the famous Calabrian monk and visionary who had lived
long before the time of Francis and Dominic. St. Bonaventure, as the superior general of the Franciscans, had
often strongly opposed the writings and prophecies of Joachim. Many of the "spiritual Franciscans" were devoted
followers of Joachim. The movement of Joachim was a
widespread reform movement in the medieval Church,
but high Church leaders had repeatedly condemned some
of its radical ideas. The Joachimists stressed the "spiritual" nature of the Church and considered the institutional Church "carnal" and corrupt.

Dante was an admirer of Joachim, even though some
of Joachim's doctrines had been condemned by the Church.
Dante was making a courageous statement by placing
him in Paradise. Dante was always a man of integrity,
true to his convictions. He was convinced of the need for
Church reform and shared with the Joachimists the hope
that the Holy Spirit would eventually accomplish this
work. He did not, however, share their radical theology
about the necessary demise of the institutional Church
as such, which would be replaced by a new epoch—the
Age of the Holy Spirit, also called the Eternal Gospel.

Dante's theology and spirituality were firmly rooted
in the Incarnation. Christ had eternally joined Himself to
the flesh and to His Church, which is both carnal and
spiritual. For Dante there was one Church, an extension
of the Body of Christ with the Spirit dwelling in her. This
Church with all her imperfections—her wrinkles, warts

and sins—must constantly reform herself and grow into the beautiful bride who will meet her Spouse at the last day when she will be finally perfected.

Although Dante was sympathetic to some of the Joachimists' causes, he nevertheless maintained a wholesome spirituality which did not deny the basic goodness of the flesh and the Holy Spirit's energizing and purifying power in and through both human flesh and the human, institutional Church. Dante's spirituality was not a disembodied spirituality. In the next canto he places these words in the mouth of the wise Solomon:

> When the flesh, glorious and sanctified, shall be clothed on us again, our persons will be more acceptable because they will then be all complete. Then the gratuitous light which the Supreme Good gives us will be increased . . . our vision will increase, our ardor will increase . . . and our radiance will increase.
>
> (*Canto XIV*, 43-51)

In this passage Dante states the traditional teaching of the Church on the resurrection of the body. Our human spirits are not complete persons until they are joined again to the flesh. This wholeness and completion will take place when God's Spirit glorifies our flesh on the last day. In the same way, the "carnal" Church now labors under corruption and sin—the weakness of the flesh—but she too will be glorified at the end. Christian faith upholds the goodness and eternity of the flesh, its transformation by God's power, not its annihilation or absorption into spirit. Christian hope is always for reform, not destruction.

Some Joachimists had hoped for a time when two reformers would liberate the Church from greed and corruption. The spiritual Franciscans saw Francis and his original rule of perfect poverty as a partial fulfillment of the prophecy. By the time of Bonaventure the Franciscans had long abandoned Francis's austerity for a more relaxed rule. The spiritual Franciscans were agitators for a return to the primitive rule and were very troublesome to Bonaventure.

It is interesting to note that Bonaventure now praises Joachim as one "endowed with prophetic spirit." His condemnations of Joachim on earth are now turned to praises. This is a parallel to Thomas's praise of his old enemy Siger of Brabant. Once again we see that the limitations of human knowledge and judgment are overcome now by mutual love and understanding. This love is a greater wisdom which comes from the heart and embraces persons rather than ideas.

PARADISE FROM CANTO XIV

Mars

(*Cantos* XIV-XVII)

Dante is now transported with Beatrice to the planet Mars. He describes it as a star glowing with a reddish smile. As he arrives here, he feels a new experience, a "newly given grace." It is now the mid-point of the journey through Paradise. Dante "with all his heart" makes an ardent "holocaust" of himself to God. He knows that his self-sacrifice is accepted as he is now granted a vision of the Cross of Christ.

The gleaming white light of the Cross flashes before him. It is such an overwhelming vision that his memory cannot recall it, nor can his intelligence describe it. Dante states that only the person who takes up his cross and follows Christ can understand the meaning of the cross and see Christ vividly in that experience. This vision of the Cross is the first of three visions of Christ granted Dante in Paradise. They perhaps correspond to the three dreams on the mountain of Purgatory. Those dreams were visions of what was happening in Dante's spiritual life. The visions here in Paradise are also signs of what is happening in Dante's soul. This vision of Christ's Cross enlightens Dante and moves his whole heart to complete acceptance of his own cross in life. He surrenders himself in sacrifice to his own fate of suffering, recognizing that suffering, like Christ's suffering on the Cross, is ultimately an act of love which conquers evil.

The blessed souls here are like jewels—rubies and other gems—which decorate two ribbons, the two bars of the Cross. They glow like flames of fire behind alabaster. The dominant color throughout these cantos is red, the color of blood and love. These are the souls of the courageous warriors of Christ, the martyrs. Their love glows through the blinding white of Christ's Cross. They sparkle as they move up and down and from side to side on the four equal bars of the Cross. As they meet and pass one another they sing a triumphant song of praise to Christ: "Arise and conquer." These words no doubt refer to Christ's victory over sin and death by means of the Cross, but they also refer to their own victory with Him and to Dante's victory. Dante's reaction to the hymn is a love which up until this point he had not felt. He confesses that he was never until then bound by "such sweet chains."

As the hymn falls to silence, Dante pauses to reflect on the love which is being revealed to him by these souls. They are like the strings of a lyre that are moved and then silenced by God's hand. Their love is directly inspired by "good will," just as avarice (love of material things) is inspired by "bad will." Dante thinks of the souls in Hell whose love was for things which do not last. Those souls are forever deprived of this eternal love in Paradise because their bad will freely chose other objects of love.

One of the glowing jewels addresses Dante in these words:

> Oh blood of mine! Oh grace of God abundantly poured into you! To whom was this grace ever granted: that heaven's gate should be opened twice to you?

> (*Canto* XV, 28-30)

The soul is Dante's great-great-grandfather, Cacciaguida, who greets Dante as his own "blood," a classical term for one's relatives, or "kin." Dante had mentioned already that the souls of the blessed not only long for their reunion with their own bodies but also for reunion with their loved ones and family members. This meeting is one of the most moving encounters in Paradise. It is also one of the most autobiographical passages. In many ways it is similar to Dante's meeting with Beatrice on the summit of the mountain. There Beatrice spoke to Dante about his past failures. Here in Paradise Cacciaguida speaks to Dante about his future exile and sufferings as well as his eventual salvation and heavenly glory. Although Dante obviously wrote this during his exile, the fictional date of this vision is 1300.

Cacciaguida, the spokesman for all these warriors of Christ, had been a knight and crusader who shed his blood during the Second Crusade in 1147. Dante considers him a "martyr" since he gave his life in that holy cause of liberating the Holy Land for the Christians' pilgrimages to the places where Christ lived and died. Cacciaguida's love for Christ and His Cross expressed itself in self-sacrifice. Dante obviously has in mind here the original purpose of the Crusades, not their later decadence.

Cacciaguida recalls the "good old days" of Florence when the Florentines were "peaceful, sober, and chaste." He recalls his baptism in the baptistry of St. John, where Dante also was christened. He tells Dante that his martyrdom in the Holy Land brought him directly to the peace of Paradise. (Christian martyrdom, we have already noted, was considered an act of perfect love which led immediately into glory.)

After narrating a long history of the Florentines' increasing greed, corruption, and warfare, Cacciaguida predicts the grim fate of his great-great grandson. The passage was quoted earlier in the biographical sketch. Cacciaguida foretells that Dante will be unjustly and cruelly treated by corrupt political men and that he will eventually become a party to himself. This isolation as "a party to himself" will be the result of Dante's own integrity and fidelity to the truth, but in time Dante's good reputation will be restored.

Cacciaguida counsels Dante to accept his fate and not to envy his enemies. Dante now recalls that his written visions of Hell and Purgatory will make many more enemies down on earth. We recall Dante's harsh condemnations of contemporary popes, kings, and other important figures. Dante begins to dread the return to earth. He confesses that he is "a timid friend of truth," but Cacciaguida tries to calm his fear:

Conscience darkened by its own or another's shame will certainly feel your speech to be harsh. But nonetheless make known all that you have seen and then let them scratch where the itch is. For if at first taste your voice be annoying, it shall later give vital nourishment when digested.

(*Canto* XVII, 124-132)

Dante is told that he will suffer tremendous hardships not only because of his exile but also because of his poem. But his ancestor encourages him to be true to his fate as a witness (martyr) to the truth. The truth will be bitter for those whose consciences will be disturbed by it. They will dislike it at first, but it will be for their salvation if they accept it. Dante was thus aware of his role as prophet, bearing a healing message of salvation to his society and Church. He was also a timid, reluctant prophet as many of the Hebrew prophets were; but this only adds to his credibility and amiability as an honest, humble servant of the truth.

Dante's destiny, as described by Cacciaguida, was to suffer injustice, exile, poverty, isolation, as well as antagonism from the great ones of the earth. This would be Dante's cross, his martyrdom and witness to the truth. Cacciaguida, who shed his own blood for the Cross, has exhorted his "blood" (Dante) to continue that witness. The cross of suffering on earth will lead Dante one day to share in Christ's glorious Cross in Paradise.

Suffering is not a blind, passive resignation to some cruel, impersonal law of the universe: the "fate" or "necessity" of the Greek and Roman philosophers. For the Christian, suffering is active, creative, and redemptive.

Christ spoke of His own suffering in terms of a woman's labor pains in giving birth. A woman's suffering is the necessary work which produces the unspeakable joy of bringing a new life into the world. Jesus used that example to prepare His disciples for the scandal of His own suffering and death. The scandal of the Cross was the necessary route to the glory of the Resurrection.

St. Paul in Romans 8, made this same connection between suffering and glory. He perceived that all of creation was destined for suffering, but a *meaningful* suffering: "because God willed it to be so." It is a suffering rooted in the hope "that creation itself would one day be set free from its slavery to decay and share the glorious freedom of the children of God." He observed that "all of creation groans with pain like the pain of childbirth; but not just creation alone: we who have the Spirit as the first of God's gifts also groan within ourselves as we wait for God to make us His children and set our whole being free."

Dante's own suffering in his years of exile created a great work, the *Comedy*, which gave hope, light, and life to the world. The truth which he proclaimed was a liberating truth that would set people free from their misery and enslavement to sin and transport them to joy and happiness. His work and his exile were the painful childbirth which eventually brought hope and joy to himself and to all his world.

One of the greatest obstacles in our own spiritual progress is our intolerance and fear of pain and suffering. Suffering is the stumbling block (the "scandal"), or perhaps the road block, which brings us to an impasse. It seems unrealistic and downright impossible to experience "joy in suffering," as St. Paul and other saints have written. No doubt this impasse was the "dark forest" which Dante described. He did not immediately emerge from that confused state. It took time and effort to learn and to discern the meaning of suffering.

It was only after the journey through Hell and Purgatory that Dante came to see the Cross of Christ in glory. The grace of that vision finally moved him—"his whole heart"—to embrace with love his own cross and to offer himself as a holocaust in union with the sacrifice of Christ. Only then did St. Paul's attitude become his own: "And now I rejoice in my sufferings for you. For by means of my sufferings I help complete what still remains of Christ's sufferings on behalf of His Body, the Church. I have been made a servant of the Church by God Who gave me this task to perform for your good." (Col. 1:24)

The paradox of "rejoicing in suffering" defies human logic and understanding. Suffering is such an ambiguous experience: it leads many to impatience, if not to despair. Impatience literally means "not suffering." It often takes the form of escape through complaint and self-pity. The escape route is often drugs and alcohol. The one who escapes is saying: "I will not suffer; I will not accept this fate. I want complete happiness and wholeness now!" This is the typical rebellion of the creature refusing to accept the fate of creaturehood. It is the root of all sin: wanting it all now, not waiting for God.

Another attitude to suffering is patient endurance: the inscape into God. This inscape is by way of faith, hope, and love. These gifts from God give us willingness to suffer and even—strange to say—a joy in suffering, a knowledge that the wise and loving God wills it for our greater good. Dante received and lived these gifts, which are also ours for the asking.

Jupiter

(*Cantos* XIX-XX)

In the heaven of Jupiter Dante witnesses a spectacular sight: the souls of the just lawgivers of mankind are sparkling lights which spell out the words, "Love justice, you who rule the earth." They then dance about and change places in order to form the outline of an eagle, the traditional symbol of justice and Roman law. Dante's artistic technique for "special effects" seems very modern to us, who are accustomed to such clever effects in advertisements and pageants at sports events.

The Eagle here represents not an earthly justice nor the abstract ideal of justice, but the very mystery of God's justice. It speaks to Dante in a personal way. The various souls form one voice; they are "one sound issuing from many loves." Dante compares the Eagle to a mother bird hovering over her nest and feeding her young. Dante himself is the young one, hungry and eager to know more about God's justice, the mystery which has tormented Dante's soul all his life.

One of the questions which haunted Dante was the salvation of non-Christians, those born before the time of Christ as well as those after Christ who had never heard of Him. This question was very close to Dante's heart, given his high regard for Virgil and the many other pagan writers, rulers, and philosophers. Dante had always felt a deep concern about their eternal salvation. The Eagle responds to this question first of all by telling Dante that mortals simply do not comprehend the eternal justice of God. On the one hand the Eagle states that no one enters

Paradise unless he has believed in Christ, either before "He was nailed to the tree" or afterwards.

But the Eagle immediately adds that many at the last judgment will cry, "Christ, Christ," but they will be "far less near to Him than he who knows not Christ." The good pagans at the last judgment will condemn the so-called Christians who knew Christ but gave only lip service to Him. They had not practiced love and justice. To our minds this is a contradiction. We cannot fathom how faith in Christ is absolutely necessary for salvation and at the same time how some non-believers will be saved and some believers will be condemned. The mystery of God's justice becomes even more mysterious for Dante and for us at this point.

The Eagle becomes silent and then bursts into songs whose beauty and wisdom Dante cannot describe. He simply exclaims: "O sweet love, clothed with a smile, how glowing did you seem in those flutes, which were filled only with the breath of sacred thoughts." Dante is addressing God in these words. He discerns that it is God Himself—Sweet Love—Who is speaking through the songs and words of the Eagle. Dante begins to intuit the great truth that God's justice is but the expression of His love. The contradictions and puzzles in the human mind begin to fade away as he penetrates more and more into the mystery of God's love.

The Eagle then identifies the six lights which form its eye. Two are Hebrew kings, David and Hezekiah; two are Christian emperors, Constantine and William of Sicily; and two are pagans, Riphaeus, a Trojan warrior, and Trajan, a Roman emperor. The Eagle, almost with a sense of amusement, smiles at Dante's surprise and responds: "I see that you believe these things because I tell you them, but the *how* you do not see. They are hidden, yet believed."

The Eagle then explains that these pagans actually were—to use a modern designation—"anonymous Christians." They had believed "in the feet which suffered," a reference to the feet of Christ nailed to the Cross. Riphaeus believed centuries before the Crucifixion and Trajan some time after the fact. There was a popular medieval legend that Pope Gregory the Great had prayed for the salvation of the emperor Trajan, who had been dead for centuries. As a result of Gregory's prayer Trajan returned to earth to become a Christian, and was "kindled into so great a flame of true love that at his second death he was worthy to come to this joy." Riphaeus, mentioned by Virgil in the *Aeneid* as "the one man among the Trojans most just and observant of righteousness," also received this grace of God to believe in the redemption by Christ. Dante writes that Riphaeus "set all his love below on justice, and God with grace upon grace opened his eyes to our future redemption."

Dante in these words seems to echo the teaching of his master in theology, Thomas Aquinas. Thomas had taught that pagans by following their natural reason could receive faith, even though they never became Christians in a formal, explicit way: "God reveals to them what is necessary for salvation, either by inspiration or by sending a teacher." Contrary to some popular misconceptions, the rigid medieval doctrine of "No salvation outside the Church" was not so rigid after all. Thomas had clearly taught a broader interpretation of that doctrine, which unfortunately was not generally adopted by ecclesiastical and secular authorities, who for centuries fostered hatred and persecution of non-Christians.

The question of *how* pagans enter the Kingdom of Heaven is thus not a question for human minds. God in His mysterious justice and love has His own ways. Dante alludes to God's mysterious ways in this magnificent passage:

> The Kingdom of Heaven suffers violence from fervent love and from living hope which van- quish the Divine Will: not as man overcomes man do love and hope vanquish His will. But He wills to be vanquished, and vanquished, vanquishes with His own goodness.

> (*Canto XX*, 94-99)

These are among Dante's most profound words on the hidden nature of God. All our questions about divine justice, all our theological disputes on who will be or will not be saved, all our fears about eternal salvation, should be immersed into the mystery of God's goodness, which totally transcends our puny intellects. Dante uses the metaphor of the ocean: near the shore its bottom can be seen, but out in the deep water its depth cannot be pene- trated by the naked eye. Such is the inscrutable and un- fathomable abyss of God's love.

God's impartial love showers unknown but abun- dant graces into the hearts of all His human creatures at all times and in all places. They can respond to these graces by their faith, hope, and love. Dante states that faith, hope, and love were in fact a real baptism for the pagan souls of Riphaeus and Trajan. Riphaeus had lived a thousand years before Christian baptism; and Trajan, in the second century after Christ, was not a formally bap- tized Christian. And yet they are saved. We see in this broad understanding of baptism that Dante was not rigidly locked into a magical concept of baptism, as if it were a passport to salvation. Religious formalism or superstition had no place in Dante's theology and spirituality.

The Eagle further cautions Dante against all rash judgments, since "we who see God know not as yet all the elect." Even the beatific vision of God in Paradise does not reveal all the mysteries of God, especially the exact number of the saved. How much more limited is the vision of those still on earth! The souls in the Eagle do not express regret for their ignorance because they will what God wills. Their wills are completely at one with God's will, which is only goodness and love. As we hear these words from the Eagle of God's justice, we realize the sheer futility of the ceaseless human calculations and arguments for centuries over the questions of predestination and the salvation of non-Christians.

Recently the Second Vatican Council reiterated in modern terms this broad vision of God's mysterious justice and love, but human pettiness, prejudice, and self-righteousness still persist among Christians of all denominations. This vision which Dante shares with us in this passage was no doubt an insight which came to him after years of agonizing questions. It is the fruit of years of inquiry and growth in understanding. We should probably conclude that it is one of the supreme graces he received in his last years, or perhaps in the last months of his earthly life.

Saturn

(*Canto* XXI)

Dante now enters the last of the seven planets, Saturn, where the souls who devoted themselves to contemplative prayer on earth descend on a golden ladder to meet him. The ladder was a traditional symbol of contemplation, based on Jacob's vision of the ladder between heaven and earth. It came to represent the contemplative's ascent to God and his descent in compassionate love back to the world. As one of the souls approaches, Dante says: "I perceive well the love which you are signaling to me."

This one phrase sums up the meaning and purpose of the contemplative life. It is in essence an activity of love which ascends to God, Love itself, but is not complete until it shares itself in loving condescension with the human family. Today that way of life is often misunderstood as if it were a selfish flight from the world to a cozy existence free from the worries and responsibilities of a normal life in the world. Far from being an escape from reality, it is in fact an entrance into the Supreme Reality, the Center of the universe and of ourselves. It is the total immersion into that Love which is the source of everything. There is no opposition between contemplation and activity. That is a misconception. The true contemplative does not become lost and absorbed in prayer as an end in itself. Instead the contemplative's contact with God flows into activities of love. It could not be otherwise, since contact with the flaming source of love kindles the human soul into a glowing love for others.

The history of the Christian mystics shows this pattern of ascent to God and descent to one's fellow creatures. The love which the mystics experience is a taste of God, Who is *agape*, the love which descends and shares itself fully. One of the famous contemplatives of modern times, St. Therese of Lisieux, understood this as her purpose in the Church. She realized that there were many ministries in the Church, but she understood, as St. Paul wrote, that any of them is meaningless without love.

Love is the excellent way that leads to God and embraces all the members of the Church. She expressed this intuition in a well-known passage from her spiritual diary:

> And so I understood that the Church had a Heart and that this Heart was burning with Love. I understood it was Love alone that made the Church's members act, that if Love ever became extinct, apostles would not preach the Gospel and martyrs would not shed their blood. I understood that Love comprised all vocations, that Love was everything, that it embraced all times and places . . . in a word, that it was eternal.
>
> Then in the excess of my delirious joy, I cried out: O Jesus, my Love . . . my vocation, at last I found it. . . . My vocation is Love!
>
> *(Story of a Soul*, Sept. 8, 1896)

The soul of St. Peter Damiani, a contemplative monk who used to call himself "Peter the sinner" on earth, says to Dante:

> I descended so far down the steps of the sacred ladder only to make you joyful with my speech and with the light that clothes me. For love, as much and more, is burning up there, even as the flaming manifests to you; but the high charity, which makes us prompt servants of the Will which governs the world, allots here, as you perceive.
>
> *(Canto XXI,* 64-72)

From these words we see that willing service to God and to one's fellow creatures is really motivated by the same "high charity," which condescends to share the joyful experience with others. The lack of joy in the world and this lack in our own lives can be traced to the lack of contemplation. We rarely ascend that ladder to contemplate God's love, which alone can give deep joy to our hearts. And yet the ladder is within our reach. It is the simple activity of prayer, which lifts us out of this world into God and then directs us back into the world with a new vision, a real joy, and an increased love for this world and all our sisters and brothers.

The Fixed Stars
(*Canto* XXIII)

As Dante and Beatrice ascend to the sphere of the Fixed Stars, the eighth heaven, Dante notices an eager longing in Beatrice. She is like the mother bird eagerly looking forward to the rising of the sun when she will feed her young, a task which is pleasing to her. She awaits the sunrise "with glowing love." This maternal image so well depicts the role of Beatrice as God's revelation. Revelation feeds us as a mother—as Mother Church feeds us—but it must wait for the light from above. The light is about to shine. It will be the light of Christ, Dante's second vision. His third and last vision occurs at the end of the journey.

Dante describes this vision of Christ as "the living light which glowed so brightly that my vision could not endure it." He is overwhelmed by its power. Beatrice tells him that in that light is "the Wisdom and the Power which opened the pathways between heaven and earth for which there had been such a long desire." Dante cannot even describe this burst of light. His first vision of Christ was the brilliant light of the Cross, but this second vision is the risen Christ of glory, an even more dazzling experience.

Beatrice now reveals to Dante her smile, which she had withheld for such a long time. Her beautiful smile enamors Dante, but she quickly tells him to look at the triumph of Christ, the whole company of the redeemed, which is described as a garden which flourishes under the bright rays of Christ. She points out Mary, "the rose in which the Divine Word became flesh," the lilies, who are the Apostles, and the other flowers in the heavenly meadow. Dante is aware that this is a great leap in his journey. As he gazes on Mary, the living star and greatest flame in that company, he witnesses a great coronation ceremony. The angel Gabriel, like a flaming crown, encircles Mary to the accompaniment of the sweetest melodies. Gabriel sings:

> I am the angelic love who circles the supreme
> joy that breathes from out the womb which
> was the inn of our desire. And I shall circle,
> Lady of Heaven, until you shall follow your
> Son and make the supreme sphere more divine
> by entering it.

(*Canto* XXIII, 103-108)

This is indeed a "quantum leap." Dante sees all the souls stretch their arms, like infants longing for milk, toward their mother Mary. Their "deep love for Mary" erupts into the Easter hymn of the Church, the *Regina Coeli*. The opening words are: "Queen of Heaven, rejoice, alleluia, for He whom you deserved to bear, alleluia, has risen as He said, alleluia." It is significant that this hymn to Mary focuses on the resurrection of Jesus.

The redeemed are now about to follow their mother into the ninth sphere, the *Primum Mobile*, where the most fervent desire for God will be felt before entrance to the Empyrean, the abode of God beyond space and time, the final stage of the journey. We notice that Mary, the Queen of Heaven, is not a substitute for God, the King of the universe. As Dante observes, she follows her Son, Christ, into the highest sphere. As the mother of the Church she leads her children to Christ, Who is their deepest desire and Who "made His inn in her womb."

Dante realizes, as he is about to enter the ninth heaven, that he is very close to the goal of his pilgrimage. He looks on the redeemed souls as former pilgrims who now rejoice because they have finally found the treasure which they longed for "with tears in the exile of Babylon." These words recall the song of the Jewish exiles returning from Babylon: "Those who sow in tears shall reap with songs of joy" (Psalm 126: 5). The tears of the exile are now turned to shouts of joy. The abundance of Christ's harvest makes all the deprivations and sufferings of the "sowing" seem like nothing.

Faith, Hope, and Love
(*Cantos* XXIV-XXVI)

Before Dante can enter the *Primum Mobile* he must first pass an entrance examination. This test seems to parallel Dante's entrance to Purgatory proper, when the angel held the two keys of Peter; and the three steps before the gate evoked the three acts of a good confession. (Purgatory IX, 94-132) Now Dante must confront the keeper of the keys, St. Peter himself. Peter examines him on faith; then St. James examines him on hope; and finally St. John, on love. It is significant that these three apostles were the ones closest to Christ in His earthly life. Entrance into the ninth sphere of Paradise is an entrance into a deeper intimacy with Christ, and the spiritual acts of faith, hope, and love are the necessary *rites de passage*, or initiation ceremony, for Dante the neophyte. He must consciously express in words his understanding of this transcendent experience.

The examination proceeds in the manner of the examinations at medieval universities. The strict scholastic method is followed. Dante must first define faith, then give its source and finally its content. As a definition he quotes Hebrews 11:1 in which faith is defined as "the substance of things hoped for, the evidence of things which are not seen." His explanation of the terms is very intellectual and typical of the scholastic method. When asked the source of his faith, Dante responds: "The abundant shower of the Holy Spirit, which is poured over the Old and New Testaments." The audience of blessed souls applauds with a hymn of praise to God. To the third question Dante responds:

> I believe in one God, the sole and eternal, Who, unmoved, moves all the heavens with love and with desire . . . And for this belief I have not only proofs physical and metaphysical, but it is given to me also in the truth that rains down hence through Moses, the Prophets and the Psalms, through the Gospel, and through you, who wrote when the fiery Spirit made you ardent.
>
> And I believe in three Eternal Persons, and these I believe to be one essence, so one and so threefold as to agree at once with *are* and *is*.

> (*Canto* XXIV, 130-141)

By his answer Dante shows the influence of Thomistic philosophy and theology which freely used Aristotle's concept of the "unmoved mover" as a term for God. It seems that Dante's concept of faith is overly intellectual, couched solely in philosophical terms. That is partly true, but we should note that his God is the God Who "moves all with *love*." Dante also clearly attributes his faith to the gift of the Holy Spirit, Who poured these truths into the Scriptures. Faith then is not primarily the result of human philosophy and scholastic syllogisms.

Nevertheless, Dante's idea of faith still seems rather lifeless, dry, and impersonal. It lacks the dimension of complete trust in a personal God and total surrender of self to God. These dimensions, however, are seen in Dante's concept of hope and love. It is in fact impossible to separate faith, hope, and love into three entirely different acts. They all converge into the one act by which a person commits himself totally to the three Divine Persons.

St. James now approaches to examine Dante on hope. He addresses Dante in these words:

> By His grace Our Emperor wills that before your death you meet with His saints in His most secret hall so that you may see the truth of this Court and may thereby strengthen in yourself and in others the hope that on earth enamors both you and them of it.

> (*Canto* XXV, 40-47)

We observe in James's words how hope and love are inseparable. Hope "enamors" those on earth of the heavenly court. James then asks Dante the appropriate questions; but before Dante can answer, Beatrice intervenes to praise Dante as an extraordinary man of hope:

> The Militant Church has no son with more hope, as it is written in the Sun which shines through our whole realm. That is why it was granted to him to come from Egypt to Jerusalem in order to see before his military service is over.

(Canto **XXV**, 51-57)

Hope was indeed a characteristic virtue of Dante. What else could have sustained him through the twenty years of exile and his many sufferings? Beatrice appropriately alludes to the Exodus theme, comparing Dante's exile on earth to the slavery of the Jews in Egypt and his arrival in Paradise to their attainment of Jerusalem. The metaphor of the journey or pilgrimage is thus intimately related to the virtue of hope. Besides, St. James is a fitting symbol of hope since in the Middle Ages the shrine in Compostela, Spain, where his body was buried, was the most frequented place of pilgrimage after Jerusalem and Rome. St. James through his bloody martyrdom on earth gave perfect witness to his hope for the promises which God keeps in eternity for His warriors after their "military service" on earth.

The virtue of hope seems somehow connected with the gift of artistic imagination. Dante's art was certainly inspired by his Christian hope. His masterpiece, the *Comedy*, was composed during his tragic exile, a time of fervent hope. We might also think of Cervantes, who composed his masterpiece, *Don Quixote*, while he suffered in prison. Christian hope is a wellspring of imagination: it creates images of the unseen promises of glory and sustains the weary pilgrim on his way. Some theologians have called hope the distinctively Christian virtue.

The French poet Charles Peguy aptly described hope as the little schoolgirl who marches unnoticed between her strapping grown-up sisters: faith and charity. No one bothers much about her, yet she is the one who keeps us alive and saves us from the despair of this world. Such, I think, was Dante's hope. It was his source of survival and protection against the despair that lurked in the darkness of his exile. Dante's hope not only prevented his despair, but it expanded his poetic imagination to visualize the unseen delights which God holds in store for His beloved ones.

When questioned by St. James on the nature of hope, Dante answers that it is "a firm expectation of future glory, the product of divine grace and precedent merit." He attributes the source of his hope to the divinely inspired Scriptures, and also states that the content of that hope can be found in the same Scriptures.

Then all of a sudden a flash of light joins the other two splendors, Peter and James. All three wheel around together in a burning love. Beatrice identifies the third light as St. John, "the one who lay upon the breast of our Pelican, the one chosen from the Cross for the great office." The "pelican" was a familiar metaphor for Jesus in the Middle Ages, since a popular legend held that the pelican brings her young back to life with her own blood. The pelican symbol was associated with Christ on the Cross and in the Eucharist, feeding His Church with His blood. Medieval art and liturgy often represented Jesus through this powerful image of maternal love. The "great office" entrusted to John was the care of Mary given to him by Christ from the Cross. John, the beloved disciple, who rested his head on Jesus' chest at the last supper, stood by Mary at the foot of Jesus' Cross.

St. John's light is so dazzling here that Beatrice must turn her gaze from it. Dante is even struck blind by it. The symbolism is traditional: love is a blinding force. John, who represents love, radiates a light which is too much to bear. He now addresses Dante; but, unlike Peter and James, he does not ask him to define love. Instead he says:

> Begin, then, and declare where your soul is cen-
> tered; and be assured that your sight in you is
> confounded, not destroyed. For the lady who
> guides you through the divine region has in her
> look the power which the hand of Ananias had.

(*Canto* **XXVI**, 7-12)

Love cannot be defined in intellectual terms, as was the case with faith and hope. Love is a matter of the will and the heart. That is why John tells Dante to state where "his soul is focused, or centered." I translated the Italian verb *appuntare* here as "centered," since the verb connotes an aiming at some target. John is asking Dante the object of his love, not a definition of love. Dante's answer clearly shows that God is the supreme object or center of his soul:

> The Good which makes this court happy is the
> *Alpha* and *Omega* of all the Scripture which
> Love reads to me, either low or loud.

(*Canto* **XXVI**, 16-18)

God is the Good which completely satisfies the heavenly kingdom. He is the beginning and end (the Alpha and Omega) of all their desires. His love has expressed itself in the great book of Scripture, the universe, which contains so many words of God's love. All these words, the creatures of the universe, are like so many objects of love; but God alone is worthy of complete love. He is the Creator, the supreme Lover (the Alpha), but also the most worthy object of love (the Omega).

John continues his examination of Dante, asking him for the motives of his love: "You must tell me who directed your bow to such a target." Dante, the inveterate intellectual, responds with philosophical arguments drawn from Aristotle and Thomas. He also invokes the authority of the Scriptures by quoting Moses. John accepts these good responses, but is not yet satisfied. He questions Dante further: "But tell me also if you feel other cords draw you toward Him, so that you declare with how many teeth this love grips you."

John demands a response from the heart of Dante, not just from his head. The metaphors of the "bite" and the "teeth" of love powerfully stress how love touches and pierces the heart. John wants a total response which comes not only from some intellectual notion, but rather from the feelings and emotions of Dante. This reminds us of John Henry Newman's famous distinction between a "notional" assent to religious truth and a "real" assent. The real assent is a personal commitment to God with all one's being, especially with the will and emotions—the heart. Dante finally gets the message and responds:

> All those things whose bite can make the heart turn to God concur in my love: the existence of the world and my own being, the death that He suffered that I might live, and all that each believer hopes for, as I do, with the living assurance of which I spoke—all these have drawn me from the sea of perverse love and placed me on the shore of right love.

The leaves by which the whole garden of the
Eternal Gardener is enleaved I love in measure
of the good given to them by Him.

(*Canto* XXVI, 55-66)

Dante's heart has been moved—literally, bitten—by
many incentives to love God. He lists the principal acts
of God's love: the creation of the world, his own creation,
His death on the Cross, and finally the hope given him
to reach Paradise. This accumulation of loving acts has
"worked together" to draw his heart away from perverse
love to true love. Dante repeats here his initial metaphor
of the sea in the first canto of *Hell*. He had been lost in
the sea of false loves, but has been saved from that ship-
wreck. He has found the right port because he has followed the Augustinian voyage to God. He learned from St.
Augustine to "set his love in order," which meant to love
all things in their proper measure: God first and all creatures in Him. Dante calls God the supreme "Gardener"
whose creation is the garden of the world. All the leaves
(the creatures) are to be loved for their goodness, but they
are only relatively good. The absolute Good is God alone
Who shares His goodness with His creatures.

After this beautiful summary of the motives for loving God, the whole court of heaven together with Beatrice sing "Holy, Holy, Holy," the continuous hymn of
praise to the Triune God. Beatrice then heals Dante's
blindness, as John had foretold. She has the healing power
of Ananias, the Christian who healed St. Paul after he
had been blinded by his vision of Christ on the road to
Damascus. Dante now is able to see better than before.
To see everything with the inner eye of love is perfect
vision.

Love's Rapture
(*Canto* XXVII)

As all of Paradise sings "Glory to the Father, the Son and Holy Spirit," Dante is completely intoxicated by the sweet song. He describes this experience as an ecstasy of joy, love, and peace:

> What I saw seemed to me the smile of the universe, so that my rapture entered both hearing and sight. Oh joy! Oh unspeakable gladness! Oh life completed by love and peace! Oh richness secure without longing!
>
> (*Canto* XXVII, 4-9)

The experience of rapture lifts Dante out of himself with joy. Dante the pilgrim has entered the "laughter of the universe" and joined in the eternal joy of Paradise. The experience cannot be expressed in words. He uses the only human words that come near the experience: joy, gladness, love, peace, intoxication.

At this point St. Peter again speaks. Peter has turned a brilliant red to express his wrath at the corruption of the Church and the papacy on earth. He declares that his position on earth is really vacant, that his burial place in Rome has become a sewer of blood and filth. He is alluding, of course, to the corrupt popes in Dante's time. He declares that the Church, "the spouse of Christ was not nurtured on my blood and that of Linus and Cletus (Peter's first successors as bishops of Rome) so that she might be employed for gain of gold." He deplores the abuse of his keys as a "banner for warfare on the baptized." His present successors are likened to rapacious wolves clothed in

the shepherd's garb. He tells Dante to carry this message
to earth. All of Paradise then turns red as it shares Peter's
shame and wrath at the sad condition of the Church on
earth.

This sudden change in mood from ecstatic joy to
wrath and shame is indicative of how Dante the pilgrim,
transported in spirit to Paradise, is always aware that he
is still on earth. He never loses sight of the unity of the
Church in glory (The Church Triumphant) and the Church
in pilgrimage (The Church Militant). The redeemed in
Paradise do not forget the Church on earth. This "Communion of Saints" bridges the gap between time and eternity, heaven and earth. The redeemed "saints" in heaven
express their love for the "saints" on earth in justified
anger and shame. The bride of Christ on earth has become a greedy warmonger in the person of the pope, Peter's
successor. Dante must communicate this hard truth to
the Church on earth.

Beatrice comments further on the earth. She refers to
it as a "threshing floor," an image she had used before to
indicate the place where humans fiercely compete with
one another as they greedily fight and wage war for power
and money. She now directs Dante's eyes to the earth so
that he will appreciate how far they have come and how
lofty is the sphere which they are now entering.

When Dante turns his gaze back to Beatrice, he senses
that his mind is "in love" and he burns even more amorously. Beatrice smiles on him. Her smile reveals to Dante
God's own joy shining through her face. She then explains to Dante the place to which they have arrived. It
is the *Primum Mobile*, the ninth sphere of heaven, which
moves the most swiftly. This intensity of movement por-
trays the intensity of love which moves the nine choirs
of angels which inhabit this sphere. The angels revolve

around a central point: God's love. God's love is the origin of all movement, and so this sphere is the place where all movement, and hence all time, begins. Beatrice explains this to Dante:

> The nature of the universe which holds the center still and moves all the rest around it, begins here as from its starting point. And this heaven has no other *where* than the Divine Mind, wherein is kindled the Love that revolves it and the Power which it rains down. Light and Love enclose it in a circle, as it does the others, and this encircling He alone who circles it understands.

(*Canto* XXVII, 106-114)

God's love, then, is the origin of all movement: time, place, and all things. Beatrice then contrasts God's love with man's sin, his misuse of God's creations of time and matter. Man perverts time by growing wicked, and abuses material things by greed:

> Oh greed! You so plunge mortals in your depths that no one has power to lift his eyes from your waves. The will blossoms well in men, but the continual rain turns the good fruit into "abortions." Faith and innocence are found only in children; then they flee before the cheeks are covered. . . . A child, while he still lisps, loves his mother and listens to her; but when his speech is developed, he longs to see her buried!

(*Canto* XXVII, 121-135)

These words describe the original goodness of human nature, created as an innocent child who loves his mother, God. As he grows older, his innocence turns into greed for material things, which spoil him just as too much rain ruins and "aborts" the good fruit on the trees. The story of human wickedness is told in these simple terms. Dante is also telling his own story here. His early, childlike love for Beatrice had been corrupted in time by the allurements of worldly pleasures. But now he is experiencing again his original love for Beatrice, his beloved one, his mother, the image of God's maternal love for him. He now sees more clearly how all of God's gifts— time, persons, things—can be a path back to Him or a path that leads away and corrupts the human heart.

God's Eternal Love
(*Cantos* XXVIII-XXIX)

After Beatrice has enlightened Dante with this profound truth, he refers to her speech as "the truth revealed by her who imparadises my mind." Dante continues to gaze on her eyes, "from which love had made a noose to capture me." Beatrice, as guide and revealer, draws Dante closer to the source of all truth and all love. By the beauty of her love and truth Dante is caught, but this cord does not trap him into misery: it transforms his soul into Paradise.

Dante now beholds the point of light around which the nine concentric circles of angels revolve. Beatrice tells him that this brilliant point is God:

> From that point depends heaven and all nature.
> Look on that circle which is most conjoined to
> it, and know that its motion is so swift because
> of the burning love whereby it is pierced.

> (*Canto* XXVIII, 41-45)

Our English translations cannot reproduce the original rhyme scheme here. The "point" (*punto* in Italian) has the same spelling as the verb "pierced" (*punto*, the past participle of the verb *pungere*, to pierce, sting). God is the unmoved point which causes all movement. His love moves all things with a sting, a desire, to return to Him, the source. T. S. Eliot, an ardent admirer of Dante, was no doubt influenced by this insight when he wrote in his *Four Quartets* that "at the still point, there the dance is." He described the still point as love and the movement as desire: "Desire itself is movement not in itself desirable; love is itself unmoving, only the cause and end of movement." God, the still point, moves His creation back to Himself. He is Love; we are loved. But the two come together: the *punto* (the point) and the *punto* (the pierced).

As Dante gazes on the point and the movement, his own desire to attain this end increases. He is full of wonder in this "angelic temple which has only love and light for its confines." Beatrice tells Dante that the first circle, the one closest the point, is "the circle that loves the most and knows the most." They are the Seraphim, but all nine circles, the nine choirs of angels, are held together by that same love:

> From choir to choir I heard Hosanna sung to
> that fixed point which holds and shall hold
> them to the *where*, in which they have always
> been.

(*Canto XXVIII, 94-96*)

Dante describes this place and this activity as an "eternal spring." The angels perpetually "unwinter" their Hosanna. Once again we encounter a word that defies translation. Dante employs here a verb used by the troubadour poets to express the singing of the birds in spring. The birds "unwinter," that is, sing, their gladness and joy at the arrival of spring.

This experience of sheer delight which erupts in perpetual song and dance in praise of God is the eternal activity of the angels. Their delight flows from their love, which flows from their vision. Dante carefully distinguishes these interrelated activities which correspond to the created faculties of intellect, will, and emotions. The angels first see the truth (God), which satisfies their intellect; and then love follows on that vision. Love then breaks out into delight and joy.

This experience of the angels is also the goal for which we human creatures are destined. Although this experience cannot be fully tasted in this life, it can be tasted to a great degree through prayer. When our minds and hearts are lifted to God in prayer, we enter that "still point," the "where" which is our true home and place. We are drawn to that point and we are forever lost and "out in the cold" until we find it. When we do find it, we enter the eternal spring where we "unwinter" and sing and dance our Hosanna joyfully. And that is prayer: finding our center, knowing and loving it and rejoicing it it. The impersonal words "it" and "center" and "point" are merely inadequate terms to express the Person whose "personality" is so warm and loving that no word—not even "person"—can express that loving reality. We discover our own "personhood" only when we find and enjoy that center.

As Dante and Beatrice contemplate the point, Dante is overcome; Beatrice simply smiles and is silent. She then turns to Dante and breaks her silent contemplation:

> I tell, not ask, what you wish to hear, for I have
> seen it there where every *where* and every

when is centered. Not for gain of good for Himself, which cannot be, but so that His splendor might in resplendence say: 'I subsist.' In His eternity beyond time, beyond every other bound, as it pleased Him, the Eternal Love opened into new loves.

(*Canto* XXIX, 10-18)

What a marvelous insight this is into the ultimate reason for creation. God by creating does not look for any gain for Himself. He freely shares Himself, just as a flower opens itself and forms new petals. Creatures are "splendors" of God, rays of light which flow from the Light. Thus the creature can say: "I subsist" (The Latin word here, *subsisto*, means "I stand under"). The existence of creatures is a derived existence, but a real and splendid reflection of God. Creatures are "loves" which emanate from the one Love. Creation is an act of Eternal Love which produces similar realities: created loves which exist in time and space and find their centers in Him.

Beatrice says that some of these created splendors fell from their high place. The fall was "the accursed pride of him whom you have seen constrained by all the weights of the universe." She is referring to Satan, who was once called Lucifer (the Light-Bearer). Those angels who followed him refused to recognize their being as derived being. They could not say, "I subsist." Beatrice is touching here the very essence of all sin—the creature's pride, his unwillingness to be under any power greater than himself. Sin is the radical refusal to recognize oneself as created. The opposite of sin is not servile debasement or groveling on the ground, but a boastful delight in saying "I subsist": I exist under God, created by His love, created free to love Him in return. Being created is cause for standing, singing, dancing, and loving! By accepting our creaturehood with gratitude and love we join in the cosmic dance and song of joy.

The Empyrean
(*Cantos* XXX-XXXIII)

Dante and Beatrice now enter the last heaven, the Empyrean, the heaven of pure light beyond time and space. Beatrice hints briefly at what this experience will be: "Light intellectual full of love, love of true good full of joy, joy that transcends every sweetness." It will be a total experience for Dante: it will satisfy his intellect, his will, and his emotions. His intellect will see God, the highest good, which his heart has longed for. The vision will fill him to capacity and overflow in joy.

As Dante enters, a blinding light greets him. Beatrice explains that this light is the salutation which Love gives to the newcomer in this realm. Dante the newcomer is blinded by the light and becomes like an extinguished candle that is prepared for a new light. A river of light then appears to him: it flows between two banks of blossoms, which are like rubies set in gold. The marvelous splendor of this sight and the fragrances of this springtime spectacle inebriate Dante's senses; but Beatrice quickly informs him that these beauties are only "the shadowy prefaces of their truth." Dante is being gradually introduced by Beatrice to a greater light and a more beautiful garden. His anticipation and desire grow like an infant's desire for the milk of his mother. The metaphor of an infant returns here at the end of the journey to show that Dante is now entering a new life. The end is really the beginning. The end of time is the beginning of eternity.

Dante now gazes on the heavenly kingdom, which is flooded by the light of glory. It has the form of a pure white rose of countless petals. It breathes forth an odor of praise to the Sun, which is creating perpetual spring here. The white petals of the rose are the white robes of the thousands of blessed souls assembled in this heavenly amphitheater. They are all arranged in perfect symmetry like rows of seats in a circular stadium. They celebrate the eternal marriage feast with Christ, Who "made them His bride with His own blood."

The angels are compared to a swarm of bees which continuously flies back and forth between the yellow center of the rose and the center of light, God, where their love abides forever. Dante here inverts the meta-phor of the bees: here the bees bear nectar *from* their hive (God) *to* the flower. They communicate to the flower the peace and love which they have acquired at their source, God. Their flying about does not obscure the vision or the splendor, since God's light penetrates throughout this kingdom where all the souls joyfully direct their "look and love on one mark."

To describe this spectacular sight Dante imagines the astonishment of the barbarians when they first be-held the splendors of Rome. Dante too is "stupefied" as he realizes that he has come "to the divine from the human, from time to the eternal, from Florence to a peo-ple just and sane." He compares himself to a pilgrim who is refreshed at last when he reaches the temple to which he had journeyed.

In his wonder he turns to Beatrice to ask her about the sights that he cannot understand, but she is no longer at his side. Instead there is an old man clothed in glory like the other souls. The old man, like a gentle father, informs him that Beatrice has taken her place on the throne allotted her. Dante then addresses this beautiful prayer to her:

> O lady, in whom my hope is strong, and who for my salvation did endure to leave in Hell your footprints, of all the things which I have seen I recognize the grace and might to be from your power and your excellence. You have drawn me from slavery by all those paths, by all those means by which you had the power so to do. Preserve in me your great munificence so that my soul, which you have made whole, may be loosed from the body, pleasing to you.

(*Canto* **XXXI**, 79-90)

These words summarize the role that Beatrice played in Dante's conversion. Beatrice, as the grace of Christ personified, was the power that lifted Dante from the bondage of sin to a new freedom and wholeness which brought him to this joy of Paradise. She had descended into Hell, just as Christ had descended there, to rescue the fallen and lost soul of Dante. Dante has now acquired the freedom, wholeness, and happiness which were the goal of his journey from Hell to Paradise. Beatrice smiles on Dante, but then turns again to God. Dante is not saddened or distressed because she turns away from him. He knows now that they are united at last in their one loving contemplation of God.

The holy elder, Dante's new guide, then speaks to him. He is St. Bernard, a great medieval mystic, reformer, and adviser to kings and popes. He tells Dante that he can complete his journey only after looking on the Queen of Heaven and asking her the final grace of the beatific vision. Dante sees so much love radiate from the face of

Bernard that he realizes that this "living charity" must be the fruit of contemplation, which is a taste of the peace of Paradise. Bernard had written a treatise entitled *On Contemplation*, a work quoted by Dante in his letter to Can Grande. Dante now sees with his own eyes that Bernard's contemplation of God on earth was in fact a foretaste of the love and peace which is now fully experienced.

The radiant love on Bernard's face astonishes Dante. His amazement is like the joyful wonder of pilgrims who see the image of Christ's face imprinted on the veil of Veronica, a famous relic preserved in Rome in Dante's time and shown to pilgrims on certain feast days. Once again the pilgrim theme appears as Dante reaches the goal of his pilgrimage.

At this point we may wonder why St. Bernard replaces Beatrice as Dante's guide. Many reasons have been given. Bernard, in the allegory, stands for the "light of glory," a light superior to the "light of faith," represented by Beatrice. This higher light brings the soul into that loving union with God, a foretaste of which is given in the earthly contemplation of God. Since Bernard was well known for his contemplation and mystical experience, he represents here that third light, given after the light of faith (Beatrice) and the light of human reason (Virgil). Reason leads to faith, and faith leads to perfect vision and loving union—the mystical experience. The three lights, or guides, were all necessary for the completion of the soul's journey into God. This interpretation is a theological approach to Bernard's role in Dante's journey.

On a psychological level, Bernard is the "wise old man," who is the image of the self which appears after the soul has integrated his masculine, conscious aspect (his *animus*, represented by Virgil) with his feminine, unconscious side (his *anima*, represented by Beatrice).

Bernard is the wise man within Dante, Dante's authentic self, the integrated person whose mind, will, and emotions are finally at peace because they have reached their ultimate goal.

Bernard, famous also for his ardent devotion to Mary, directs Dante to her: "Look now on the face which most resembles Christ, for only its brightness can prepare you to see Christ." Some Christians have balked at this typically medieval devotion to Mary, as if it were a hindrance to a direct relationship to Christ. Catholic tradition, however, has always maintained this strong attachment to Mary. Mary, of course, is human and not divine; but God chose to become human in her. She was the chosen channel of His Incarnation. The Church sees our humanity raised in her to become a receptacle of God Himself. She is truly an image of the Church herself: the human creature gloriously saved and elevated to union with God. Since God came to us through the human channel of Mary, we return to Him through her glorious and graced humanity.

Bernard now addresses his magnificent prayer to Mary for the final grace, the vision of the Primal Love:

> Virgin Mother, daughter of your Son, humble and exalted more than any creature, fixed goal of the eternal plan, you are the one who did so ennoble human nature that its Creator did not disdain to become its creature.
>
> In your womb was rekindled the Love under whose warmth this flower has unfolded in eternal peace. Here you are for us the noonday torch of charity, and below among mortals you are the living fount of hope.
>
> Lady, you are so great and so powerful, that whoever would have grace and has not recourse

to you, his desire seeks to fly without wings.
Your loving kindness not only helps him who
asks, but often freely anticipates the asking.

(*Canto* **XXXIII**, 1-18)

Mary is described in terms of God's love. She is the
receptacle of God's love. In her womb was rekindled
God's love, which had been obscured by humanity's sin
in the garden. Now in her, the new garden, the white rose
of Paradise has blossomed again under the rays of God's
love. The sin of *Eva*, the first woman, has been reversed
by the *Ave*—the Latin word for "hail," addressed to Mary
when Christ became flesh in her. The tragedy of sin has
become the divine comedy in her. Every Christian soul
who gratefully receives God's love becomes like Mary:
humble and exalted at the same time. Dante sees his own
destiny in her, as well as the destiny of every Christian.
The great work of his life, his *Comedy*, is truly divine
since it has received the life-giving breath of God's love.

Dante now comes to the long-awaited vision of God,
the beatific vision. He describes the experience as a penetration into a beam of light, but is unable to say anything
more about it. His memory fails him, just as snow melts
and disappears when the sun penetrates it. He describes
his experience of the Eternal Light in these words:

In its depth I saw gathered together, bound by
love in one single volume all that is dispersed
in leaves throughout the universe: substance
and accidents and their relations, as though
fused together in such a way that what I tell is
but a simple light. The universal form of this
knot I believe that I saw, because in telling this
I feel my joy increase.

(*Canto* **XXXIII**, 85-93)

Dante sees everything—the whole universe—as so many pages of one book, bound by God's love. The mystery—the mysteries—of all things and their relationships to one another are now seen in their unity. All has meaning: it now all makes sense because God's love holds it all together. The final words of T. S. Eliot's *Four Quartets*, his farewell to poetry, express this same intuition:

> And all shall be well and
> All manner of thing shall be well
> When the tongues of flame are in-folded
> Into the crowned knot of fire
> And the fire and the rose are one.

The fire—God's love and light, which fill the Empyrean, the fiery place—is one with the rose, His beautiful creation. Creative love and the created universe are one. The restless pilgrim heart of Dante is at last at one with God and His multiplicity of creatures. This experience of unity in multiplicity—the one and the many becoming one—is the experience of love, peace, and joy, which Dante is attempting to communicate to us. He confesses how inadequate are his words to express this inexpressible experience.

The supreme Light appears to him as three circles which are interconnected:

> Within the deep and shining subsistence of the lofty Light appeared to me three circles of three colors and one magnitude. The one seemed reflected by the other, as rainbow by rainbow, and the third seemed fire breathed forth equally from the one and the other.

> (*Canto* XXXIII, 115-120)

Dante is describing here through geometrical figures and colors the Divine Persons of the Trinity, equal yet different. The Son is the reflection of the Father; the Spirit is the fire of love which unites them. He then perceives in the Son "our image." In other words, he sees our humanity in Christ. This is Dante's third and final vision of Christ. This is the mystery of the Incarnation: our humanity, our flesh, eternally united to God in the person of Christ. The end of Dante's journey is seeing our humanity—himself, ourselves—in God. The pilgrim has reached his goal: union with God.

Dante cannot understand how this image of humanity is "conformed" to the circle of divinity. But it is. The baffling mystery of God united forever with humanity! Dante does not understand "how." He cannot say anything but:

> My own wings were not sufficient for that, except that my mind was struck by a flash in which its wish came to it. Here my powers failed their lofty fantasy; but already my desire and will were being turned, like a wheel that is evenly moved, by the Love whch moves the sun and other stars.

> (*Canto XXXIII*, 139-145)

These are the final words of the *Comedy*. The final flash of light produces in Dante not so much an intellectual experience as a complete movement—a conversion—of his whole being. All his desires—his appetites and yearnings—are moved together with his will and his mind. His whole being is now in harmony with the total reality. That reality is God, Who is Love.

The pilgrim, whose eros led him through many loves, has now found *the* Love—Agape—which was drawing him all the time. Dante the pilgrim has found his peace in finding his true home, God. We should notice that the perspective of these final words of Dante is from earth. Dante is looking up at the sun and the other stars. He identifies with us, who are still pilgrims on earth. He looks up, a fellow pilgrim with us, and sees the Love which moves everything and moves us to loving union with that Love, Who is God. If we let ourselves be drawn into this movement, we too can experience Dante's joy and peace. We too can feel our whole being "turning with" the Love Who moves the sun and the other stars.

Bibliography

General Works:

Fergusson, Francis, *Dante*, Macmillan, 1966

Fox, Ruth, *Dante Lights the Way*, Bruce, 1958

Luke, Helen, *Dark Wood to White Rose*, Dove Publications, 1975

Papini, Giovanni, *Dante Vivo* (in English), Macmillan, 1935

Sayers, Dorothy, *Introductory Papers on Dante*, Harpers, 1954

————, *The Divine Comedy* (Translation and commentary in 3 volumes) Penguin Books, 1962

Singleton, Charles, *The Divine Comedy* (Italian text, translation and commentary in 6 volumes), Princeton University Press, 1970

Toynbee, Paget, *Dante Dictionary* (Revised by Charles Singleton) Clarendon Press, 1968

Particular Works Used In This Book:

Dante Alighieri—A Biographical Sketch:

Chubb, Thomas, *Dante and His World*, Little, Brown, 1966

Dinsmore, Charles, *Aids to the Study of Dante*, Houghton, Mifflin, 1903

The New Life:

Haughton, Rosemary, *The Passionate God*, Paulist, 1981

Singleton, Charles, *An Essay on the Vita Nuova*, Johns Hopkins University Press, 1980

Williams, Charles, *The Figure of Beatrice*, London, 1943

The Banquet:

Gilson, Etienne, *Dante and Philosophy*, Harper and Row, 1963

Rossetti, William, *Dante and His Convito*, London, 1910

The Divine Comedy—An Introduction:

Singleton, Charles, *Dante Studies I* (Commedia: Elements of Structure), Harvard, 1954

Thompson, David, *Dante's Epic Journeys*, Johns Hopkins University Press, 1974

Hell:

Carroll, John, *Exiles of Eternity*, Kennikat Press, 1971

Ciardi, John, *The Inferno*, New American Library, 1954

Purgatory:

Berrigan, Daniel, *The Discipline of the Mountain*, Seabury, 1979

Carroll, John, *Prisoners of Hope*, Kennikat, 1971
Fergusson, Francis, *Dante's Drama of the Mind*, Princeton, 1953
Singleton, Charles, *Dante Studies II* (Journey to Beatrice), Harvard, 1958

Paradise:

Carroll, John, *In Patria*, Kennikat, 1971
Gardner, Edmund, *Dante and the Mystics*, E. P. Dutton, 1913
Moltmann, Jurgen, *The Crucified God*, Harper and Row, 1974
Nygren, Anders, *Agape and Eros*, London, 1957
Reeves, Marjorie, *Joachim of Fiore*, Harper and Row, 1976